Daniel O'Connell

Daniel O'Connell

Nationalism
Without Violence

an essay by
RAYMOND MOLEY

NEW YORK
FORDHAM UNIVERSITY PRESS
1974

Contents

Illustrations

to reach an American audience, it may well serve to remind the Irish, of both the North and the South, to pause
in their present unhappiness to consider what O'Connell
said about constitutional change.

The great Irish agitation, of which O'Connell was the
undisputed leader for forty years, had its roots in the great
surge for national identity which produced the American
Revolution. The Irish and the American colonists had a
common enemy, the government of George III. Also, from
the earliest times it has been something more than the
fact of geography which has made the Irish such compati-
ble neighbors of the Americans. Throughout the generations, Irishmen, in their poverty and unhappiness, have
established new homes and a good life on these shores.

Intellectual likenesses have characterized the more
thoughtful natives of both countries. There is an amazing
parallel between O'Connell and Jefferson. The Irish
leader, in his student days in London and Dublin, was
reading the same books which had been so influential with
Jefferson earlier. Their political and philosophical conclusions were almost identical. Both were children of the
French Enlightenment and English liberalism. Both, influenced by the anti-clerical literature of the times, embraced Deism—O'Connell for a very few years, Jefferson
permanently. O'Connell records among the books which
he read, a volume by John Adams.

O'Connell earned and held in the Western world high
rank among the individuals who promoted religious liberty and separation of Church and State, cardinal principles in the American tradition. Since the first half of
his public life was devoted to the restoration of Catholic
rights, he realized that he could not rationally insist upon
rights for his fellow communicants which he would deny
to others. His concept of true religion was of something
lived wholly apart from interference or support by civil
authority. As we shall see, he carried his zeal for re-

Preface

THE COMPULSION I FEEL in committing these months toward the end of a long life to this essay on Daniel O'Connell comes from something more than a wish to pay a tribute to a statesman I have admired since, as a small boy, I first heard of him. It is because in my mature years I formed the conviction that he has something relevant to say to Americans here and now.

O'Connell, as we bring him into focus, after generations of bitter criticism, misrepresentation, and neglect, becomes a very modern man. The principles which he held with such consistency and expounded with such consummate eloquence are, by modern standards, enlightened, even prescient. They are wholly pertinent questions which are of deep concern to all of us.

The reader of history will perceive that the span of O'Connell's life, 1775–1847, witnessed profound changes in political arrangements, in power structures, and in national boundaries in the Western world. One of the more important of these developments has been the growth of nationalism, not only here but throughout the world. As this national consciousness affected Ireland, it cannot be interpreted, even understood, except as it was awakened by O'Connell. He entered public life as an opponent of the Act of Union of 1800, a measure which was to infect British relations with Ireland for a century and a quarter.

The chapters which follow stress those aspects of O'Connell's career which should be of concern to every American, whether or not his ancestry is Irish, or whether or not he subscribes to the religious faith of O'Connell. Moreover, while this book is mostly intended relevant not only to Ireland at the present time but to all democracies, and especially to all subject peoples struggling for their independence. A nation must develop self-discipline, respect for law, and a sense of politics if it is to achieve stable democracy. He sees O'Connell as having taught his people these lessons.

Though he is not a professional historian and though he insists that his work is not a comprehensive academic study, Moley has written a distinguished book. Of all the popular biographies of O'Connell it is, in my opinion, the most politically perceptive and, in many important respects, the most able.

MAURICE R. O'CONNELL

Fordham University

Foreword

RAYMOND MOLEY is one of the more distinguished Americans of his generation. As an adviser to President Franklin D. Roosevelt and a member of his first administration Moley was one of the architects of the New Deal. For over thirty years he was an influential commentator on the public scene as the Editor of *Newsweek*. He dealt with politics at the academic level when Professor of Public Law at Columbia University.

Moley is unique among biographers of O'Connell in having known politics from the inside and at many levels. And the most interesting parts of his book are those in which he has brought that knowledge and understanding to bear on his subject. His explanation of why O'Connell claimed he could gain Repeal of the Union in 1843—that puzzle for all his biographers—is original and credible.

Moley is deeply concerned about the decline in O'Connell's reputation which set in toward the end of the nineteenth century and continued until almost our own day. This was caused in the first instance by the hostile writings of the Young Irelanders with whom he had quarreled in his last years. But the more general reason for that decline arose from his devotion to moral force and his hatred of violence as a political weapon. To a twentieth century which has (until fairly recently) seen violence as normally essential to the winning of their freedom for subject peoples, O'Connell's principles and methods seemed effete.

Moley regards O'Connell's teachings and example as

ligious liberty to the support of the Jews in their struggle
to lift the disabilities imposed by English law.

The two objectives which dominated the career of
O'Connell were, first, the freeing of the Irish Catholics
from the prohibitions and discriminations imposed by the
English government, and, second, the winning of Irish
self-government—not independence—through the repeal
of the Union. In pursuing these objectives (he was the
recognized national leader for nearly half a century), he
insisted, with passionate emphasis, upon peaceful and constitutional means, to the *total* exclusion of the threat or
the reality of violence. The proof of his success in impos-
ing this restraint is the historical record, for from 1798 to
1848 there was no country-wide revolt against the government.* This is the more remarkable because for centuries violence had been an important characteristic of
life in Ireland. "Rather than shed one drop of Irish
blood," O'Connell was quoted as saying, "I would welcome the return of all the horrors of the Penal Laws."

We Americans have not always observed a similar restraint. Our independence was won by a six-year revolution and, after living for three-quarters of a century according to a written Constitution, we fought a bloody
civil war to determine whether we were one or several
commonwealths. And as we have learned no later than
the past two decades, resort to violence still mars our domestic tranquillity.

Once more the news from Ulster reminds us of the still-
unresolved conflict between force and violence and peaceful agitation as a means of change. It was on this issue that
O'Connell cast the die for peace, compromise, and constitutional means. We shall see how it divided his fol-

---

* This is not to say that there was no violence in Ireland in those years. There
was plenty of homicide, arson, and destruction of crops and livestock by persons
acting individually or as members of loosely organized bands such as the Whiteboys and Ribbonmen, mostly against landlords, their agents, police, and suspected
neighbors.

lowers and embittered his old age. And since his opponents survived him, violence had the last word. Many
years later, violence seemed to prove itself in 1916–1921.
But now the drift is toward non-violence. For the continued depredations in the North have so shocked Irish
opinion that the wisdom of O'Connell's teaching is beginning to dawn in the minds of both sides of the struggle.
What he said on the subject comes to have new pertinence,
not only in Ireland but over here where we have seen so
much exaltation of violence in the past decade.

The immense influx of Irish immigration into the
United States has been a significant contribution to our
political life. The amazing aptitude for politics of the
descendants of these immigrants is an inheritance from
what the people of Ireland learned in the churning political waters during the ascendancy of O'Connell, for, along
with his agitation, he became the great teacher of the
Irish. He taught his generation the meaning of constitutional government, the lifeblood of which is political action. He created a nation in which political instinct has
been a means of survival. One of his biographers said of
him: "He left his successors nothing to do but to follow
him. They added precision to his definition, but the definition is not altered."

It is not strange that the Irish who came here have
taught us so much about modern practical politics.

I find among my Irish-American friends an appalling
lack of knowledge about O'Connell. Some merely identify
him as one of the unhappy leaders of the past. Others who
have visited Ireland in recent years have scarcely asked
themselves why O'Connell Street in Dublin was so named,
and why, in other cities of the country, there are so many
O'Connell Streets and so many monuments in his honor.
I shall in this book recite some of the reasons for this
neglect and some of the evidences that now, in another
century, the true O'Connell is coming to be recognized in
Irish history.

O'Connell taught the Irish people far more than the political way of survival. Those Americans who are so proud of their Irish blood and their traditions sorely need to be reminded that O'Connell, more than any other member of his race, created that pride long ago in a people who were, before he came, miserable, hopeless serfs. It was O'Connell who gave them a sense of nationality. With all the extravagance, which is an Irish trait, he inspired them with a hope of a future on earth when their religion taught them only the hope of a life beyond their miserable graves and the fundamental Christian virtues. He taught them the rudiments of civil government. And his concept of self-government with allegiance to a crown which they shared with the British anticipated by many years the Commonwealth of Nations.

I have too much respect for the historian's craft to claim that what I present in this book is in any sense a biography of O'Connell. Neither the time nor the facilities have been available for such an undertaking. What I have written is an essay centering on some of O'Connell's activities, the principles he maintained, the methods he used—mainly political—and the immense role he played in the evolution of modern Ireland. These, I believe, are relevant to the interests of Americans in this day and age. For the most part, my reliance has been upon secondary sources. I shall mention some of these presently.

In hunting amid the very considerable O'Connell literature, in ascertaining the validity of the many accounts of what was involved, and in appraising the man himself, I have been immeasurably helped by the generosity of my friend, Professor Maurice R. O'Connell of Fordham University, a direct descendant of the Liberator, and the editor of a series of volumes of his letters. Professor O'Connell read and reread two drafts of this manuscript and made innumerable corrections of fact and suggestions of great value in matters of emphasis and judgment. He also kindly contributed the Foreword.

I am also indebted to the patience and competence of Denison Kitchel of Arizona who read two of my drafts and offered most helpful suggestions.

I am also indebted to Lucy Grassl, who has assisted me throughout the two years of labor in writing this book. She was responsible for typing two versions of the manuscript, and checking with painstaking accuracy the innumerable facts and other material which went into its composition. Her advice was also most useful in many matters of taste and relevance. She also prepared the Index.

A NOTE ABOUT SOURCES

Since this book is intended for popular rather than academic and scientific reading, I have not added a formal bibliography. Where it has seemed necessary to verify some of my facts or references, I have given sources through the text, usually in footnotes. In doing so I have avoided the temptation, to which so many authors of books on history or biography succumb, of inordinate padding of bibliographies with innumerable references which have had no part in providing the material in the book. Indeed in some instances the multiplication of references raises doubts whether the short lifetime of the author was long enough to provide time for their consultation.

Since I confess to my major reliance upon secondary sources, it seems useful in this instance to mention only a few of the sources upon which I have placed most reliance.

Among the historical works I have most often consulted, I should mention Professor J. C. Beckett's two volumes. The first is his *Short History of Ireland* (London: Hutchinson, 1966) which is beyond comparison as a sound, accurate, and simple reference. Also, for the period with which this book is concerned, his *The Making of Modern Ireland, 1603–1923* (London: Faber and

Faber, 1966) is most important for completeness and impartiality in the treatment of events and personalities.

I have also found useful *A History of Ireland* by Professor Edmund Curtis, first published in London in 1936
with several new editions and reprintings (London:
Methuen, 1950). It is less readable than Beckett.

When I had completed the first draft of this book, there
appeared Robert Kee's *The Green Flag,* which is a more
detailed political history from Wolfe Tone and 1798 to
the events of the 1920s. The average reader should not
be repelled by the sheer size of this volume. He will find
the narrative of absorbing interest. And so far as I am
able to judge, the scholarship is entirely reliable. It was
originally published in London by Weidenfeld and
Nicholson in 1972; an American edition appeared in the
same year from the Delacorte Press, New York.

An exceedingly useful and attractive series of historical
essays is *The Course of Irish History,* edited by T. W.
Moody and F. X. Martin (New York: Weybright and
Talley, 1967). These essays cover the range of Irish history from prehistoric time to the twentieth century.

The first and at the time most helpful of the biographies
which I read was Denis Gwynn's *Daniel O'Connell, The
Liberator* (London: Hutchinson, 1929). It ranks high as
a source but is weak on the years of O'Connell's career
after his election to Parliament. More recently published
works, such as Kee's *The Green Flag,* are much more detailed and consequently useful. The first version of
Gwynn's biography appeared on the centenary of Emancipation, 1929, and the second on the centenary of O'Connell's death, 1947. In 1949 Gwynn published *Young Ireland and 1848* (Cork: Cork University Press, 1949).
This is a thoroughly documented account of the Young
Ireland movement from the founding of *The Nation* in
1841 to the aftermath of the 1848 revolt. Gwynn was
greatly assisted in this undertaking by the newly opened
and edited Smith O'Brien papers in the National Library

in Dublin. A paperback edition of the biography was recently published by the Cork University Press.

In the centenary year of Emancipation, 1929, there also appeared a biography by Michael MacDonagh, *Daniel O'Connell and the Story of the Catholic Emancipation* (London: Burns and Oates, 1929). MacDonagh was a parliamentary reporter who in his book not only showed considerable understanding of politics but enlivened his text with colorful anecdotes. This book was published earlier, in 1903.

The second volume of William E. H. Lecky's *Leaders of Public Opinion in Ireland* is a biography of O'Connell. This first appeared in 1861 (London: Longmans), sufficiently soon after O'Connell's death to precede most of the critical works of the Young Irelanders. I agree with most historians' opinion that this book ranks very high in its detailed account of the Liberator's career and of the social and economic problems he confronted. The book was reissued in 1908, revised and enlarged. Considering the furor which by that time had been created by the Young Irelanders and the influence of other critics of O'Connell, Lecky's view is remarkably sympathetic and free of bias.

To enjoy sheer brilliance of writing and at times remarkable sympathy and insight, the reader interested in O'Connell and his period should read Sean O'Faolain's *King of the Beggars*. As a work of art it is grievously marred by the author's prejudice and his acceptance of the calumnies of the Young Irelanders' written works. The book was published by the Viking Press in New York in 1938 and also in London the same year. It is now available in paperback (Dublin: Cahill, 1970).

In 1948 there was published a biographical work under the title *Daniel O'Connell: Nine Centenary Essays*. It was edited by Michael Tierney, President of University College, Dublin. In certain chapters in this book I have

leaned heavily upon some of these essays (Dublin:
Browne and Nolan, 1948).

In the long period of O'Connell's neglect there were
scholars loyal to his memory, two of whom published
biographies. One was a short work published on the centenary of O'Connell's birth. It is by John O'Rourke
(Dublin, 1875).

For devoted scholarship performed under most adverse circumstances, high praise is due to the writer of
two two-volume works, *The Liberator, His Life and
Times* (Dublin, 1872; also entitled *Life of Daniel O'Connell, the Liberator* [New York, 1872]) and *The Speeches
and Public Letters of the Liberator* (Dublin, 1875). The
author of the former and editor of the latter was (Miss)
Mary Frances Cusack. She was born in Kenmare of Anglican parents but embraced the Catholic religion and became a nun. Before her work on O'Connell, she wrote histories of Ireland, of County Kerry, and of County Cork.
She was compelled to do the research on her O'Connell
books while in the convent and thus was compelled to
obtain all of her material by interlibrary loans. Later she
went to Rome and obtained permission from Pope Leo
XIII to found a new religious order in the United States
to care for Irish immigrant girls, the Sisters of St. Joseph
of Newark. The remarkable Mary Cusack then turned
back to the Anglican faith.

Her life of O'Connell is marred by her adulation of
the man. One wishes she would give the reader some lee-
way in making his own appraisals. The O'Connell volumes, beautifully and expensively bound in the Irish editions, appear to have been financed by public subscription,
many of them from Protestant firms and individuals.

The two volumes by Mary (Mrs. Morgan John)
O'Connell are much more than a biography of O'Connell's uncle, the Colonel. They are a gold mine of information about the immense O'Connell clan and life in

Kerry in the eighteenth century. The full title of the two-volume work is *The Last Colonel of the Irish Brigade: Count O'Connell and Old Irish Life at Home and Abroad, 1745–1833* (London, 1892).

In my early chapters on O'Connell's education I relied heavily upon Arthur Houston, *Daniel O'Connell, His Early Life and Journal, 1795–1802* (London: Pitman, 1906).

Angus MacIntyre's book *The Liberator: Daniel O'Connell and the Irish Party, 1830–1847,* I found most informative on the period covered especially because of his most meticulous treatment of O'Connell's efforts to create a responsible party organization in Ireland (London: Hamilton; New York: Macmillan, 1965).

Lawrence J. McCaffery's small volume *Daniel O'Connell and the Repeal Year* is, as the title indicates, limited to the short period before the Famine when the Repeal movement was at its height. It is based upon primary sources and is scholarly and fully documented (Lexington: University of Kentucky Press, 1965).

The Famine is extensively treated in the essays included in the book *The Great Famine: Studies in Irish History, 1845–1852* edited by Professors R. Dudley Edwards and T. Desmond Williams of University College, Dublin (New York: New York University Press, 1957). There is also *The Great Hunger* by Cecil Woodham-Smith (New York: Harper & Row, 1962).

From time to time in this essay I have referred to and quoted from the monumental collection of O'Connell's letters, a great many of which were exchanged with his wife Mary. The preparation of the definitive edition was entrusted to Professor Maurice R. O'Connell by the Irish Manuscripts Commission. The plan is to publish these in eight volumes, the first of which are now available with others soon to come. They are extensively annotated by the editor and will, when completed, be a most important

Preface

txxi

primary source of information for future scholars (published by the Irish University Press, Shannon).

Whoever writes about O'Connell must be heavily indebted to two contemporary publications. The first is *Personal Recollections of the Late Daniel O'Connell, M.P.*, by William J. O'Neill Daunt, in two volumes (London, 1848). The other is *Correspondence of Daniel O'Connell, the Liberator*, edited by W. J. FitzPatrick (London, 1888) ; this is also in two volumes.

The literature criticizing O'Connell produced by the New Irelanders after the so-called revolt in 1848 is quite considerable. I found considerable repetition among the books. I have listed what I have considered the most important in Chapter 20, with dates of their publication. To the ones listed there, which were written by Charles Gavan Duffy, John Mitchel, and Michael Doheny, should be added *Thomas Davis and Young Ireland,* good for its considerable bibliography (Dublin: Stationers Office, 1945) ; also Denis Gwynn's *O'Connell, Davis and the College Bill* (Dublin, 1953). An attractive collection of Thomas Davis' essays and poems was edited by D. J. O'Donoghue (Dundalk: Dundalgan, 1914).

Daniel O'Connell

INTRODUCTION

An Old Widow's Tales

IT WAS DURING THE LONG WINTER'S EVENINGS at home in Ohio that I first heard about Daniel O'Connell. I was about ten years old and my instructor was my Irish-born grandmother who, after the death of her husband some years before, lived with us for many years. Her stories went back to the atrocities of Cromwell, the long night of the Penal Laws, the Wolfe Tone rebellion, the hated Act of Union. But most of all, to the coming of the great Daniel O'Connell who awakened his people, made them proud, and won their civil rights from the great Duke of Wellington, Prime Minister of England.

My grandmother was born Mary Ann Kane. Her father, Joseph Kane, was a citizen of Dublin, and a graduate of Trinity College, which was a distinction well exploited by the Moley family. When I examined the records at the College, I found that he had matriculated in 1821 and graduated in 1825. His father, Nicholas Kane, was listed as a "gentleman," which, it was explained, merely meant that he was able to pay his son's tuition. Joseph Kane became a civil engineer and apparently did well. As was inevitable in prosperous Irish families, he sought certain cultural accomplishments for his children and to that end he employed a French tailor of his acquaintance to teach Mary Ann the French language.

Romance was awakened with the intransitive verb and a marriage followed. Her husband, my grandfather, was Hypolite Molé, who was born near Versailles. As a youngster he dropped out of school and joined a traveling

circus. A fall from a horse resulted in a broken leg, and
during his convalescence he learned the tailoring trade.
After his recovery, his ambition carried him to Dublin
where, with a partner, he established a shop on Wicklow
Street. The record shows that in a year or two he dissolved the partnership and moved to a more fashionable
address, 16 Nassau Street, which borders on Trinity College. After 1847 his name disappears from the city direc-
tory, apparently because he and his small family had
migrated to America. His eldest son, Hypolite, Jr., was
a year or two older than my father, Felix James, who was
born in 1846.

According to my grandmother's stories, Daniel O'Connell, in the 1840s, became a customer of Hypolite's, and as
a result of this contact the growing Molé family lived in
part of a house on Sackville (now O'Connell) Street,
which belonged to O'Connell. (I have been unable to
verify this part of the account.) The grim reason for leaving Ireland in 1847 was the Great Famine, then in its
third year. Their trip was on one of the "coffin ships" of
that dreadful period; it was a wretched voyage and several passengers died en route. They landed in New York
and, after a brief stop, moved on to Cleveland. After a
few years in Cleveland, they sold some property they had
accumulated there and moved to Olmsted Falls, about a
dozen miles west on the main line of what was then the
Lake Shore Railroad. There Hypolite invested what he
had brought, in several properties and new buildings, and
set himself up in a tailoring establishment and store. He
became quite a prominent citizen of the growing village.
He had received some military training as a boy in France
and assembled a troupe of young men in preparation for
the war that seemed inevitable. This was called the La-
fayette Guard and he was commissioned Second Lieutenant by Governor Salmon P. Chase. I have the original
commission. When the Civil War came, it had heavy impact upon the village and the Moley family. Hypolite

Junior responded to the President's call for volunteers and was ultimately lost in the service.* My father enlisted but his father rescued him because of his tender age.

After the war Grandfather Hypolite established my father in a "gent's" furnishing store in Berea, three miles from Cleveland. There his children were born, including this writer in 1886, the year which saw the death of Hypolite. In 1893 hard times compelled our family to move to Olmsted Falls where we occupied one of the combined homes and stores built by Hypolite. My grandmother moved in with us and lived as one of the family until her death. Her income from her various properties left by her thrifty husband was sufficient for her needs, with something left over. Since she was interested in my education, this enabled me, when the need arose, to draw upon her for loans. She was a devout Catholic and her reading of the Boston *Pilot* and the Cleveland *Catholic Universe* occupied many hours of her days. But what interested me were the times when she dipped into the prodigious wallet of her memory and told me what she had seen and learned in Ireland half a century before. There were walks with her father when she was a young girl, and how one day they met the aging Tom Moore in the park. Her store of historical knowledge consisted mostly of stories of English misrule. The Great Famine, she claimed, was caused by the export to England by the landlords of all the food raised in Ireland, except potatoes, which were stricken during the Famine.

But mostly there were tales of the great O'Connell. Hypolite and his wife knew him only as he visited the shop for fittings when, as was his habit, he carried on

* The military exploits of young Hypolite were rather unusual. In the first months of the war he was captured, paroled, and sent back to Cleveland. He violated his parole and enlisted in the navy under the name of his grandfather, Joseph Kane. Serving on a gunboat at the siege of Vicksburg, he was struck in the head by a piece of shell, which seemed to derange his mind. Hospitalized in an asylum in Cleveland, he soon escaped and presumably returned to the army. His family never heard of him again.

friendly discourse with all sorts and conditions of his countrymen. She remembered the openhearted generosity of the man, which, I have since learned, kept him in a perpetual state of debt. She did not claim that O'Connell unburdened himself of his political views, for the tailor was not an educated man. But she remembered that, before her marriage, O'Connell often visited with her father, whose education was attested by his degree from Trinity College. She remembered O'Connell in the year when he was Lord Mayor, passing through the streets in the gorgeous regalia of his office. In those final years of O'Connell's life, after the news of the great Monster Meetings reached Dublin, the city was seething with political excitement. My grandmother knew nothing of the growing conflict between O'Connell and the Young Irelanders. This was not to surface until later. The public, of which the young wife of the tailor was such a vigorous part, knew the beloved Dan as their guide and leader and hope of the future. Fifty years had not withered those ties of affection and respect.

A boy of ten does not rationalize his attitudes toward political leaders. He forms strong prejudices, emotional attachments: great love or vehement dislike. The impressions I gained from my grandmother's stories created in me a powerful indictment of England and English governments. And her words about the Liberator supplied me with the first great hero of my life. I am quick to admit that what I have learned from books and professors, and many visits to England, greatly modified my early prejudices. I have learned that I should not inflict upon all English government all the sins of the cruel and benighted Tory establishment of the eighteenth and early nineteenth centuries. But I hope the reader of this book will realize that the basic indictment I have drawn of the English governments of those years still holds, and, in stressing that view, I am in such distinguished company as Gladstone, Macaulay, and Churchill.

Seventy-five years have passed since stories about O'Connell first captured my mind and imagination. The impression of O'Connell as a great romantic figure remained in all the years since. It may have been the excitement of that political year of 1896 and it may have been the influence of my father which aroused my interest in politics. But surely what I learned about O'Connell had something to do with it. When I was a senior at a Methodist college, the subject of my required "oration" was Daniel O'Connell and the Catholic Emancipation of Ireland.

While the business of my life crowded O'Connell aside, the idea of writing about him always occupied a back burner of my concern. A few years ago a visit to London and Dublin afforded the opportunity to begin gathering the material about him and his times from the bookstores and official records. Meanwhile my experience in and my observation of political life here in the United States have provided the wisdom and judgment so essential to an understanding of O'Connell, the statesman and the leader. When retirement provided time for ruminating and writing, I turned to the composition of this essay. It has, I trust, added critical judgment to the hero-worship of my youth.

1

English Dishonor and Irish Decay

Go into the length and breadth of the world, ransack the literature of all countries, find if you can a single voice, a single book
in which the conduct of England towards Ireland is anywhere
treated except with profound and bitter condemnation.

WILLIAM EWART GLADSTONE, 1886

TO UNDERSTAND WHAT DANIEL O'CONNELL FACED when
he entered public life at the time of the Union in 1800
requires some recall of what happened in Ireland and to
Ireland in the eighteenth century, the most wretched, perhaps, in all Irish history. For our purpose that story
should begin with the Treaty of Limerick, executed by
the Jacobite leaders with King William in 1691. This
followed by two years the defeat of the deposed James by
William's army at the River Boyne. This treaty, which
was singularly favorable to Irish Catholics, was almost
immediately repudiated by the solidly Protestant Irish
Parliament with the consent of the English King and
Council under the terms of Poynings' Law, which required the prior consent of London to an enactment by
the Irish Parliament. For William could only propose;
his masters at Westminster disposed.

In Ireland the Protestant ascendancy after the defeat
of James became so complete that the Irish Parliament
proceeded to the enactment of a long series of laws which
were designed to keep the Catholic majority in a state of

permanent subjection, with no voice in the government,
and without the right of acquiring land or of ensuring
education for their children. These restrictions and prohibitions, inspired by a quite genuine fear of Catholic
domination, came to be called the Penal Laws.* It should
be understood that there were other restrictions on Catholics passed before 1688 and later. There were also so many
restatements, additions, and amendments that no purpose
would be served here by attempting a detailed description
of what were generally called the Penal Laws. Although
a secondary purpose of these laws was to strike down and
gradually destroy the Catholic religion, they signally
failed. For that secondary purpose they were never systematically applied. Maureen Wall says this:

> Although many bishops and hundreds of the regular clergy had
> left the country after the banishment act was passed in 1697, and
> had been forbidden to return under penalty of suffering death for
> high treason, about a thousand diocesan priests had been permitted
> to remain; and gradually, during the first two or three decades of
> the century, despite the savage laws on the statute books, the Catho-
> lic Church was reorganized and reformed; and before the middle
> of the century the hierarchy had been restored to its full strength
> for the first time since the reformation. . . . Priests went about
> their duties with little fear of molestation by the authorities, so
> long as they inculcated, or tried to inculcate, in their flocks respect
> for their rulers. . . . Despite the Penal Laws, most of the cities
> and towns outside Ulster had their Catholic chapels, and new ones
> were being erected from early in the century.

---

* There are so many distortions and inaccuracies in descriptions of the Penal
Laws in the many histories and records of the period, and so much divergence
between the written statutes and the practice of enforcement, that after an
examination of the available literature I have decided on the advice of current
scholars to lean heavily upon the writings of the best of the modern authorities,
Maureen Wall. She was, until her very recent death (1972), College Lecturer
in Modern Irish History, University College, Dublin. Her excellent short essay
on the Penal Laws is contained in *The Course of Irish History*, edited by T. W.
Moody and F. X. Martin. She was also the author of a brochure of 72 pages
under the title of *The Penal Laws, 1691–1760, Church and State, from the
Treaty of Limerick to the Ascension of George III*. This monograph is largely
devoted to ecclesiastical matters. It is published by Dungalgan Press (Dundalk,
1961) for the Irish Historical Association.

It is noteworthy that of all the laws passed in the period of William and Anne, which are commonly but inaccurately called the Penal Laws, the ones which were aimed at exterminating the Catholic Church by eliminating the clergy did far less to impoverish and degrade the people than those with an economic objective. The Church emerged rather stronger from its ordeal. Since the education of children had traditionally been an important function of the Catholic Church, and since teaching of religion was a considerable part of the curriculum, the prohibitions of Protestant ascendancy fell heavily upon education. Indeed the restrictions laid upon schools and teaching seemed heavier and of longer duration than those which limited the practice of religion among adults. Lecky, the celebrated Protestant historian, said of the provisions of the Penal Laws pertaining to education: "The legislation on the subject of Catholic education may be briefly described, for it amounted simply to universal, unqualified and unlimited proscription."

In another chapter, in describing the education available to Daniel O'Connell between the ages of four and fourteen, I shall describe the form of education which was contrived to provide for children despite the restrictions of the law and their enforcement. Mostly the education of the younger Catholic children was provided by what were called "hedge" schoolmasters in improvised "hedge" schools. Such schools continued despite the introduction of other means of education in the late-eighteenth century until the Catholic Emancipation of 1829.

The historian Curtis comments that from 1714 to 1760 Ireland had little or no political history. The Protestant ascendancy was so complete in religion, law, Parliament, and local government as to be suffocating. But on the edges of the realm, such as on the remote coast of Kerry, the incompetence of the central government was so great as to permit considerable trade with France, such as was carried on by the hardy O'Connell clan. Also there were

the "wild geese," the boys from Kerry and nearby areas
who fled by sea to France. It is estimated that between
1690 and 1760 no fewer than 400,000 of these joined the
French army.

It would be a mistake to attribute to the Penal Laws
the unspeakable conditions under which most of the population lived in the eighteenth century. For these enact-
ments in the main concentrated upon denying to the Irish
three rights generally recognized in modern states: the
right to hold office and participate in the civil life of the
state; the right of religion to serve without hindrance the
spiritual needs of the people; and the right to an education. But people can maintain a reasonable physical well-
being without these three rights. What reduced the population, both the peasants and the townspeople, to the level
of wretchedness were the limitations upon the capacity to
eke out a decent living. The restrictions of an economic
nature were imposed in part by London and in part by
the Irish Parliament. Most important among the economic restrictions were the provisions of law which re-
stricted the ownership and use of the land. Protestant
supremacy could not endure any considerable ownership
of land by Catholics since political power was based on
the ownership of land. Hence, Catholics were forbidden
to buy land or to take leases for more than thirty-one
years. They were compelled to bequeathe their property
equally among their sons. The purpose of this enactment
was to break up large estates. However, if the eldest son
became a Protestant he could inherit the entire property.

As a result of the Williamite confiscations Catholics by
the beginning of the eighteenth century owned only 15
per cent of the arable land. Because of the operation of
these laws and of the fact that several Catholic landowners
for one reason or another went over to the Established
Church, the proportion of land owned by Catholics in
1778 (the year of the first Catholic Relief Act) was probably not more than 5 per cent. But, regardless of who

owned the land, the condition of the small tenant farmers became more and more deplorable as the agricultural population expanded in the second half of the eighteenth century. The pressure of the increasing population on the land left these peasants scarcely the means of a bare existence. The rents were frequently collected by the callous and corrupt agents of the landlord. There was also unbelievable bitterness because of the tithe, an exaction from all regardless of religion, for the support of the (Anglican) Protestant clergy. This was collected by proctors who tended to be arbitrary in estimating the proportion of the crops constituting the tithe and to be hardhearted in its collection. In the towns Catholics were sometimes forbidden to ply any trade unless they paid a tax called quarterage. But the population of the towns and cities, regardless of their religion, had problems of another sort. The great and influential manufacturing classes in Britain were determined to protect their interests by the suppression of competition from Ireland. Thus there was a virtual prohibition on the export of woolen goods from Ireland. Furthermore, the British Navigation Laws placed serious restrictions on Irish foreign trade. These economic measures were a crushing blow to all classes and religious denominations, not just to the Catholics. The result was a considerable emigration of Protestants, and particularly of the Presbyterians in the north of Ireland, to the New World where they supported the American Revolution and enlisted readily in Washington's armies. Since the Thirteen Colonies were unlikely to welcome Catholic immigrants, Irishmen of that religion tended to emigrate to France where, as already mentioned, they joined the army in large numbers.

Trades other than wool felt the ban. Brewing aroused English jealousy, and an act was passed which prohibited the importation of hops from any country other than England. The monopoly thus created raised the price of this essential element in brewing so that some of the brewing industry died out, throwing the workers out of employment. Guinness, founded in 1759, remained. The glass industry was struck down in 1746, and restrictions were imposed upon other small trades such as gunpowder, sailcloth, and ironware. In the rural regions the deplorable conditions were made worse by the practice among landlords of turning large areas of productive land into grazing, narrowing the available land upon which the peasants existed. Thousands of the wretches thus evicted crowded into areas already crowded. Finally, the plight of the population was rendered doubly acute by the forces of nature operating in the people themselves. As Mrs. Wall says: the fall in the standard of living was "due largely to the rising population which brought with it keen competition for farms and pushed up the already high rents."

One must pause to reflect, in noting the severity of the two governments, that the conditions in Ireland were due not only to the inhumanity of the rulers but also to their stupidity. The root cause of wonder is that in those years those entrusted with government were so blind to the real interests of the country for which they were responsible. By their calculated oppression they were creating at their very doorstep a peril to their own security. Compared with the potential rivals and enemies on the Continent, England was really a small country, isolated and dependent only upon the sea to assure its safety. It was more than foolish to create an implacable enemy at its rear, a country which was capable of producing enough food and fiber to supply the margin of England's need and more for export, and, with war ever present and the desperate shortage of manpower, men to man its ships and fill the ranks of its armies.

Throughout the eighteenth century the Irish Catholics had no effective defenders within their own ranks. The Penal Laws by excluding Catholics from office, and the trade restrictions by preventing the development of strong industrial leadership, left no one of that religion to speak for the Catholic majority. But chance had it that from the ranks of the Protestants there came two men of genius whose sympathy and understanding assisted the Catholic cause. One was a churchman and literary figure in the first half of the century, Jonathan Swift. The other, a statesman and patriot who came to prominence later, was Henry Grattan. Both were Irish-born. Swift was born of English parents in Dublin in 1667. He was educated in Kilkenny School and Trinity College. After a somewhat troubled career in England, he became Dean of St. Patrick's (Anglican) Cathedral in Dublin, where he spent the rest of his life. The stupid misgovernment of Ireland moved him to devote his literary talents to its defense. The prodigious output of his pen comprised serious economic arguments, satire, humor, and burlesque. He was greatest in his satirical works such as *Gulliver's Travels* and the *Tale of a Tub*. Toward the end of his controversial writing, he became discouraged with the rate of his progress and composed what is probably the most bitter, mordant piece in the English language. He called it *A Modest Proposal*. By way of attacking the political system it suggested that the way to cure hunger and to reduce the population would be to use the surplus babies as food. There is nothing in his chosen forms of literary expression in the English language to compare with Swift. The simplicity of his style and the color of his material gave him great influence among all classes. No inconsiderable part of the improvement of conditions after his death in 1747 was due to his influence upon literate opinion, which in the main was Protestant opinion.

After 1775 the supporters of an embryonic nationalism in Ireland hailed the revolt of American colonies as the promise of hope for Ireland. For the war of the Americans was Ireland's war and the colonists, by defying the English Parliament, were striking at Ireland's oppressor. Finally when victory came at Yorktown and Lord North's government fell, the hopes of Ireland reached new bounds. Henry Grattan, who had entered the Irish Parliament in 1775, hailed the concessions of the English Whigs, who had succeeded to the government after the fall of North, and declared that Ireland had become a nation. The English Parliament specifically renounced its claim to legislate for Ireland, and Poynings' Law was drastically modified. Grattan's influence became so great that the Irish Parliament came to be known as Grattan's Parliament. These years saw the removal of many of the social, religious, civil, and economic disabilities which had been imposed upon the country.

In 1792 a Catholic committee, which had been formed thirty years before and which had managed to keep itself together in the years since, found strong leadership in one of its members, John Keogh. The more daring members of this committee, led by Keogh and assisted by Wolfe Tone, proceeded to draw up a petition directed to the King, thus by-passing the Irish Parliament. The King graciously received the petition. Thus encouraged by this royal reception, they secured from the Irish Parliament substantial concessions of a political nature for the Catholics. In 1793 the franchise was granted to the forty-shilling freeholders. Catholics were permitted to serve on juries, hold the office of justice of the peace, and send their sons to Trinity College. Certain of the professions were opened to Catholics which permitted the young Daniel O'Connell to enter his chosen profession five years later.

Despite the many concessions to the Catholics and the rising prosperity over the country, unsettled conditions prevailed in Ireland during the last decade of the eighteenth century. The threat of war between England and France fostered Irish sympathies one way or the other. Young Irishmen, liberated and encouraged by the effect of the French Revolution, were stirring once more the demand for more independence for their homeland. One of these was Theobald Wolfe Tone, a young Protestant barrister. After he published tracts supporting Irish claims, he joined in 1791 with Napper Tandy, a restless and eccentric radical, in founding the United Irishmen.* The purposes of this society were at first quite moderate, but as their efforts were frustrated, their plans, abetted by Tone's radicalism, turned violently militant. When the government in 1795 moved to break up the society, Tone was permitted to migrate to the United States. A short stay there brought him into contact with the French Minister and from then on his main concern was French assistance to a revolt in Ireland. He succeeded in persuading the French government to launch two invasion forces but they failed in their purpose. Tone, who had been commissioned an officer in the French military, was captured, tried, and, after being sentenced to hang, committed suicide. This was in 1798 when an armed revolt by the United Irishmen was summarily crushed.

Thereupon Pitt, beset by threats from the Continent and by a restless Ireland, decided upon a measure which he had long entertained: the abolition of the Irish Parliament and provision for representation from Ireland in the Parliament at Westminster. This act, the Union, was carried through the Irish Parliament by a process of gross corruption. The Parliament thus voted its own extinction. Gladstone was to say many years later that "no blacker or fouler transaction in the history of man was the making of the Union."

It was at this moment that Daniel O'Connell, newly admitted to the Irish bar, first appeared in public, an opponent of the Union.

---

* The name Napper Tandy has had a certain immortality because of two factors, neither deserved by his deeds. His name is used in the famous Irish song *The Wearin' of the Green*, and a famous case in international law dealing with him is still studied in courses in American colleges and law schools.

2

The Brawny O'Connells
of Kerry

IT WAS AN AFTERNOON IN AUGUST 1970, during our first
visit to Kerry. We were sitting on a rude bench beside the
highway which, by American standards, is far too narrow
for safe driving. This highway swings around the tip of a
peninsula created by Dingle Bay to the North and the
wide mouth of the Kenmare River to the South. This area
is the extreme southwestern tip of Ireland—the "heel" of
Kerry, it is called. The sign on the post office down the
road tells the tourist that this is the village of Caherdaniel.
A still narrower road leaves the highway where we are
seated and winds down nearly two miles to the house surrounded by trees called Derrynane, and beyond that to a
land-locked harbor. On the edge of this bay is the ruin
of an old abbey. As we sat there, we noted the cars that
passed, mostly tourists enjoying a drive through "The
Ring of Kerry," which originates at Killarney and en-
compasses the peninsula, a distance of about one hundred
miles.

It was not difficult that day to envision this area two
centuries ago when Morgan O'Connell brought his four-
year-old Dan to Derrynane and gave him over to his older
brother Maurice, who was the master of the Derrynane
property and of the thriving business which he directed.
Those two centuries have laid a light hand on that land-
scape. Some of the structures might have been there before Daniel was born and a few more modern houses and

barns are scattered about. But all else is as it was. The
Kerry mountains rise steeply inland from the highway:
rockbound, with patches of green; clambering goats and
sheep find a bare subsistence. Over these hills scamper the
hares which provided rare hunting for O'Connell and his
friends when he retired for a holiday during his busy
years. Along the highway and on the endless designs of
stone fences which mark the mountain slopes grow the
beautiful fuchsia, so common all over southwestern Ireland. The rugged beauty of that seacoast strikes the visitor
today and the Liberator himself described it in his letters
as incomparably impressive. But the O'Connell clan,
which lived there when Dan was a boy, found no beauty
in those hills which provided such scanty fare for their
flocks. It was, as Sean O'Faolain says, "a hard place for
hard men."

Although the O'Connells did well, and suffered little
want, the peasants they knew lived in the depths of
wretchedness far into the nineteenth century. Mud walls
enclosed their living quarters, few of them enjoyed the
luxury of shoes, and for the most part their food consisted of potatoes. They lived in the dark, damp shelters
by night with their sheep and goats. Again O'Faolain:
"The rain-swept, hungry peninsula jutting out into the
Atlantic, can never be thought lovely as long as we know
that it was even in its brightest days, as hard as the welts
on the hands of the men and women, as lonely as the cock
crow." Daniel O'Connell, great-great-grandfather of the
Liberator, leased the land at Derrynane late in the seventeenth century from the Earl of Cork, and his son, John,
began the construction of the house which little Dan knew
as a boy. The grandfather of the Liberator (John's son),
called "big" Daniel, married Mary O'Donoghue who
presented him with twenty-two children. The couple
came to be known as Donal Mor and Maire-ni-Dhuiv
which translated is "Mary of the Dark Folk." Twelve of

these children survived their childhood, four boys and eight girls.

Donal Mor and his accomplished wife maintained a thriving business at Derrynane. The harbor offered a fine place for the going and coming of small ships in trade with French ports. This commerce consisted in shipping the products of Kerry to France, and there the ships were loaded with products of French manufacture, which the thrifty O'Connells sold to the Protestant landlords of Kerry. The exports were sheep, beef, mutton, cattle hides, and wool. Returning, the ships brought wine, rum, brandy, lace, books, textiles, and tea. This import trade was not troubled by customs duties, for smuggling was a considerable way of life, not only on the coast of Kerry but quite generally in other parts of Ireland as well as England and Scotland. It was especially safe for the O'Connells because of the remote location of the base at Derrynane.

While Donal Mor lived, his wife actively participated in his business, as did his two sons, Maurice and Morgan. Upon the death of the father, Maurice became the master of Derrynane. He came to be known as "Hunting Cap" because of the velvet headgear he preferred to the beaver hats of the more affluent, which were subject to a tax. Maire-ni-Dhuiv survived her husband for twenty-five years. In addition to her remarkable labors as a mother, Maire-ni-Dhuiv was something of a poet. Surviving verses in the native Gaelic throw light on the life at Derrynane. A dirge which she composed marks the departure from the shore of a contingent of young men who boarded the ships bound for the military service of France. Among these young men and boys who sought service in France was Daniel Charles, the youngest surviving son of Donal Mor and Maire-ni-Dhuiv. Destined to share with the Liberator in bringing honor to the O'Connells, he was sixteen in 1761 when he left Derrynane for service in France. From the beginning of his life on the Continent,* the letters of Daniel Charles, later the Colonel, written to his brother, Hunting Cap, were lively, informative, and highly personal. His financial support, for his service pay was small, came from Hunting Cap. The letters repeatedly remind the thrifty brother of how the expenses of keeping up appearances and winning friends required considerable outlays of cash. Apparently with some grumbling Hunting Cap provided what was needed for his brother, who rose in a few years to a commanding position in the service of the King. In 1783 he was created a Count by Louis XVI, and in the final years before the Revolution he seems to have had the run of the palace. At the Revolution, he fled to Koblenz in 1792 and, after a short period in the emigré army, he went to England where he was active in organizing an Irish regiment for service against revolutionary France. He lived until 1833; his age was 88.

Hunting Cap, as his business grew, gave employment to the peasants in the area around Derrynane and, according to the evidence, was a hard-fisted employer. He gave them only enough wages to keep body and soul together but offered a place to worship at Derrynane. For a time, as he needed more land, he employed a very practical method of acquiring it. As a Catholic he was unable to acquire it himself, and so he employed a cousin, Hugh Falvey, a lawyer who had turned Protestant, to buy and hold land for Hunting Cap's use. The house turned its back to the sea and looked to a walled courtyard surrounded on two sides with trees. The needs of the in-

---

* The career of Daniel Charles, Colonel O'Connell, has been told in a remarkable biography, *The Last Colonel of the Irish Brigade,* by a highly literate woman, the wife of Morgan John O'Connell, a nephew of the Liberator. It was written in the last decades of the nineteenth century and was published by Kegan Paul in London in 1892. The author, who signs herself Mary O'Connell, had the good fortune to find at Derrynane a great quantity of letters preserved by Hunting Cap, in an elaborate secretaire "with brass handles and many drawers." From these and other contemporary sources, she created a most comprehensive account of the O'Connells and of life in Kerry.

habitants had required additions to be built from time to time. It had dark parlors with deep wainscoted window seats. The main part (now demolished) was two stories high and had gables and dormer windows on the roof. Offices occupied the wing, and kitchens and servants' quarters were at the back. A bridle path passed by outside the walled enclosure and beyond was a garden sheltered from the Atlantic storms by trees. The cellars were stored with food and wine, for Hunting Cap had many visitors, mostly his customers, the Protestant landlords, who must have been well entertained. A chapel is now attached to the structure. It was built by the Liberator in 1844. About a hundred yards from the house amid the trees the Liberator built a two-storied stone tower, the second floor of which was high enough to overlook the trees, with a view of the ocean. This was where the mature statesman was wont to retire for study or rumination and rest, protected from intrusion by the many visitors who, in his later years, invested the house.

Hunting Cap's business, other than his half-illicit trade with France, was considerable. The main source of Hunting Cap's considerable income was rents from his estate. He was also a lender of money to the Protestant landlords and to the more prosperous Catholic farmers. The Protestant landlords were also Hunting Cap's main customers for the products he imported from France. These landed gentlemen were eager purchasers of the wine and textiles, and they winked at the methods by which their wants were provided. They made up the grand juries which were the real government of Kerry. So far as there was a law, they were the law. In 1793 Hunting Cap became a magistrate and a deputy-governor for County Kerry (both being unpaid positions). This was before the Union, which he heartily supported.

Daniel, the subject of this essay, was born on August 6, 1775, on Morgan O'Connell's farm called Carhen. The stone house, where the Morgan O'Connells lived and

which served as a general store providing the family with
their subsistence, is about a mile east of Caherciveen. Its
ruins are still visible from the Ring Highway. Morgan's
wife, Daniel's mother, was Catherine O'Mullane, a
daughter of John O'Mullane ("Chief of the Name") of
County Cork. According to Gaelic custom, Daniel was
farmed out for nursing care to a peasant family in the
Iveragh Mountains. There he remained during the first
four years of his life, and as he emerged from infancy he
came to regard the peasant couple as his real parents.
When O'Connell was about four, he was returned to Morgan's home. While there Morgan asked him whether he
had had any meat to eat at the peasant's home. According
to the story, he answered "One day my 'father' stole one
of Morgan O'Connell's sheep and we had meat to eat for
a week." Morgan, who had missed the sheep, was greatly
amused. Shortly after this, Hunting Cap exercised a prior
offer of adoption and little Dan was taken to Derrynane.
The boy was to remain there for ten years; then he was
taken to County Cork for schooling under a Father Har-
rington. Later, with his brother Maurice, he was sent to
the Continent for further education.

For nearly ten years while he lived with his uncle at
Derrynane, his education was either acquired from the
books that he read or by what was known as "hedge
schoolmasters." Education had persisted in many forms
in the long history of Ireland, but the persistence of this
mode of educating children was one of the most remarkable features of the long night of the eighteenth century
in Ireland. Above all, it shows the insatiable instinct of
even the most illiterate peasants for the schooling of their
children. Early in the eighteenth century, as the Penal
Laws substantially prohibited all Catholic means of education, the hedge schools took root in Ireland. These
schools were more prominent in Munster and especially
in mountainous Kerry. The schoolmasters or teachers operated not only outside the law, but in direct violation of

the law. Any householder was subject to severe penalties
if he harbored one of these schoolmasters—who consequently lived and taught his pupils, when the weather permitted, out of doors. He would select a remote spot on
the sunny side of a ledge or hill, use rocks for desks and
seats, with the pupils scattered on the ground before him.
In winter the schoolmaster moved from place to place,
sheltered always by peasants in their miserable huts. In
bad weather he would usually acquire an abandoned
cabin, more often without windows and heated by sods of
peat brought by the pupils. Much of the instruction was
in Gaelic, but the English language, Latin, and occasionally Greek were taught. Reading, writing, and "cyphering" were also included. In Kerry, where young Daniel
enjoyed the advantage of this form of education for several years, classical languages were very important. A
traveler who toured Kerry at about the time Daniel was
receiving this instruction noted that he saw in a little hut
a schoolmaster sitting with four small boys who were
reading Homer.

Young Dan's preparation for life included far more
than his education in the hedge schools. He loved to read.
One of the books, Captain Cook's *Voyages 'Round the
World,* he mentioned later in his life as especially fasci-
nating. While much of what he heard in the busy atmos-
phere of Derrynane was in the native tongue, his reading
and his contacts with Hunting Cap sharpened his English.
His subsequent use of Latin expressions in the courts and
in speeches suggests that he must have been equipped with
certain of the classics, perhaps from his schoolmasters.
The place was humming with the language of trade and
his quick mind acquired familiarity with figures and cal-
culations. Another influence in those early years was the
letters from the Colonel who was rising in the service of
France. This uncle's constant correspondence with his
relatives in Kerry was full of the exciting events in pre-
revolutionary France. He learned from that source and

from his elders in Derrynane of the adventures of the many young Kerrymen who had migrated to France. In those years in the service of the Bourbons, the Colonel seems to have been moderately affluent, and with his letters he often sent small gifts of cash to various relatives. Thus it is easy to see why, at the age of fifteen, Daniel was so anxious to continue his education on the Continent.

In 1790, Daniel and his brother Maurice, a year younger, felt that they had about exhausted the opportunities for schooling in Ireland. Hunting Cap, who was also concerned about his nephews' education, corresponded with the Colonel about sending the boys to a school in France of the latter's choosing. Since the shadow of trouble was already hovering over France, the Colonel advised Hunting Cap to "lay aside all thought of sending our young nephews over." But since the boys had already been apprised of the plans of Hunting Cap, they were insistent and Hunting Cap decided to take the risk. There was a short delay during which the boys attended a school near Cork, but toward the end of the year 1790 they left Cork by sea and reached Ostend after a calm journey. From there they traveled to Liège, but found that Daniel was over-age and could not be accepted. The boys had received from the Colonel certain letters to the school authorities at Louvain, so the boys went there to await further orders from Hunting Cap and the Colonel. They were well treated in Louvain. They were not eligible to enter the university but Irish Franciscans and Dominicans who maintained centers there arranged for university lodgings and permission to attend lectures.

After six weeks, on orders from Hunting Cap, they proceeded to Saint-Omer and money was supplied by a French agent of Uncle Maurice. "St. Omers" had been a Jesuit school until the Jesuits were expelled by the government, after which classes were maintained by members of the English secular clergy. The O'Connell boys were installed in January 1791. After some time Hunting

Cap, concerned about getting his money's worth, wrote asking the principal, a Dr. Stapleton, how the boys were doing. The answer was that Maurice was not deficient in ability but was "fond of amusement." Daniel, marked from the beginning, elicited the good teacher's enthusiasm: "He is destined to make a remarkable figure in society." Hunting Cap's letters and business papers, carefully noted and filed in his secretaire, show examples of the letters the boys wrote during their stay in France. These letters give an interesting picture of the type of education the nephews received and some indication of the news which filtered through from Paris about the exciting happenings there, for matters were approaching a pass which was to change the course of history. In the light of Daniel's subsequent public career, it is most interesting that heavy emphasis was observed at St. Omers on language training and public speaking.* Classical oratory was stressed with readings from Cicero, Demosthenes, and Homer, all in the original. French orators were also studied in their language. Thus Daniel found good use of the languages he learned from the hedge schoolmasters. Emphasis on languages and oratory was supplemented by enforced collective activities during the day. Daniel needed this because as a youth at Derrynane he had been something of a loner. One exercise which was required was the writing of compositions which were declaimed before the student body.

While Daniel seemed to be quite happy with this schooling, the Colonel, a soldier and activist, was not satisfied with St. Omers. In June 1792 he took steps to have the boys transferred to the more austere and mature college at Douay. However, just as the boys were preparing to move in July, conditions in Paris became so unpleasant

---

* This is described in one of the essays, in a centenary series, written by Thomas Wall of University College, Dublin. Michael Tierney, President of University College, is general editor of the book, *Daniel O'Connell: Nine Centenary Essays* (Dublin: Browne & Nolan, 1948).

and dangerous that the Colonel found it necessary to seek asylum ultimately in England. There he immediately plunged into counter-revolutionary activities. Pursuant to plans made by the Colonel in June the boys went to Douay in August. There, it was hoped by the Colonel, there would be less concentration on languages and more on philosophy and "cyphering." At about this time Daniel announced his intention of becoming a lawyer. A few years earlier the Penal Laws would have barred this career to him as a Catholic, but the relaxing of some of the prohibitions in 1793 had thrown the profession open to Catholic students. It was a most unfortunate time to have entered Douay because the revolutionary tide was gaining strength and such an institution as the college at Douay was likely to be the victim of violent attack.

There were, in addition, requirements for money at Douay greater than at St. Omers. The boys were required to furnish their own rooms and to pay for several services which were provided by the school at Saint-Omer. There were agitated letters addressed to Derrynane for financial aid. But more serious matters than lack of money approached, for the fury of the Revolution was moving out from Paris to the country around Douay. Later in the autumn the two O'Connells and some other students from the school were on a walking tour when a mob assailed them with shouts of "jeunes jésuites" and "capucines." The boys were able to escape by running all the way back to the safety of their lodgings. After that there was a considerable exodus of students who were able to obtain permission from home to leave.

Daniel had an illness in early January and the task of writing to Hunting Cap was taken over by Maurice. A letter dated January 4, 1793, told of the perils confronting Douay. He said that the rapid increase in the number of students leaving for home meant that he and Daniel might at any time be forced to follow them with or without permission from Derrynane. In that case, he said, they would get the necessary money from the college authorities or Mr. Kirwan and go to England. (Mr. Kirwan was a London merchant through whom Charles Casey of Cork, Hunting Cap's butter agent, transmitted money for the payment of the O'Connells' education at St. Omers and Douay. Through Casey, Hunting Cap had been apprised of the conditions in France and the probability that the boys at Douay would find it necessary to escape to England.) Before a reply to Maurice's letter could have reached them, the boys on January 21st left Douay on their own initiative. That was the day Louis XVI mounted the guillotine. Despite threats and insults from the people along the way, the boys were able to reach Calais and the packet boat to England. When they were safely on the ship, they took the tricolors from their hats and flung them into the sea. These adornments were necessary in France but now they were anxious to bid farewell to their revolutionary tormentors. Thus the educational experiment in France was concluded. They had spent six weeks in Louvain, nineteen months at Saint-Omer, and five months at Douay. In their flight they had left all of their belongings at Douay, carrying only passage money in their pockets. The Colonel, already in London, was once more called upon to assist the boys, this time in arranging for their stay in London and the pursuit of their training for life.

It had cost about £100 to meet the needs of the boys at Douay, most of which was spent for furniture, clothing, and personal items. Since all of this had been left behind, equipment was a first consideration in London where costs were exceedingly high because of war conditions. Daniel made an urgent call upon Hunting Cap for funds which were not long in coming. Daniel also wrote about his plans:

> I now have two objects to pursue. The one, the attainment of knowledge; the other, the acquisition of all those qualities which

constitute the polite gentleman. I am convinced that the former, besides the immediate pleasure which it yields, is calculated to raise me to honours, rank and fortune: and I know that the latter serves as a general passport or first recommendation. And as for the motives of ambition which you suggest, I assure you no man can possess more of it than I do.

[O'Connell 18; I 20–1.]*

No doubt this emphasis on manners was a reflection of the admonitions of the Colonel whose polish had been acquired at the Bourbon Court. The Colonel, in his earlier letters to Hunting Cap soliciting funds, constantly emphasized the necessity of social graces in winning promotion in the military services in which he served. In London the Colonel, despite his own vicissitudes, lent his knowledge, influence, and money for adjusting the boys to a new life. For a short time they were assigned to a school conducted by a Mr. Fagan. After that, Maurice, despite the suggestion of Hunting Cap's that he study law with Daniel, preferred some form of military service and this was promoted by the Colonel. He was given a commission and departed for the West Indies. After two years in the pestilential climate encountered there, he died of a fever. Daniel needed no urging to pursue the study of law, and he entered as a member student at Lincoln's Inn in January 1794.

Hunting Cap, who had heard references of the Colonel's to the need of money to keep up appearances for many years, from time to time complained in his letters about his nephew's "extravagance." But Daniel's way of cozening his uncle was usually successful and he had the means for living a remarkably comfortable life. At about the same time that he entered Lincoln's Inn, he also registered for entering the Irish bar as a student at King's Inn

* References to and quotations from O'Connell's letters are taken from *The Correspondence of Daniel O'Connell,* edited in eight volumes by Maurice R. O'Connell (Shannon: Irish University Press for the Irish Manuscripts Commission, 1972———) ; reprinted by permission of the Irish Manuscripts Commission.

in Dublin. This was in anticipation of his later removal
to Ireland. In London Daniel lived for a time in the
lodgings of a Mrs. Reacey but the diversions which prevailed near the center of law study caused him to move
later to Chiswick where he found lodgings with a Mrs.
Rigby, where he had more time to pursue his reading.
However, he found his landlady to be a rabid democrat,
a Deist in religion, and, because of her love of strong
drink, a disorderly housekeeper. Despite inconveniences,
he had sufficient privacy to pursue his reading and he
remained there until his removal to Dublin.

3

A Child of
the Enlightenment

DURING THE YOUNG DANIEL'S STUDENT DAYS in London
and Dublin, Hunting Cap was rising in his world of
Kerry. Since he had amassed a considerable fortune, his
interest in smuggling declined and he began to view with
increasing concern his status in the county.* He became
one of its chief magistrates, which gave him considerable
influence in public affairs. He also became more testy
with advancing age, and this kept Daniel's talent for writing conciliatory letters in constant practice. In 1795 Daniel made a short visit to Derrynane. He greatly enjoyed
himself, meeting old acquaintances and hunting in the
mountains. We have an indication of the young man's
diversions in a letter from Hunting Cap to Daniel's
mother:

> Your son left this house ten days ago and took with him my
> favorite horse. Had it not been for that, I might have dispensed
> with his company. He is, I am told, employed in visiting the seats
> of hares at Keelrelig, the earths of foxes at Tarmons, the caves of
> otters at Bolus, and the celebration of Miss Burke's wedding at
> Direen—useful avocations for a nominal student of the law! The
> many indications he has given of a liberal mind in the expenditure
> of money has left a vacuum in my purse, as well as an impression on
> my mind, not easily eradicated.

* An additional reason for the decline of his interest in smuggling was greater
strictness and efficiency in enforcing the customs laws.

One must accept such complaints from the old autocrat
with some reservations. They are not unusual among
elderly people who become aware of the generation gap.
And this is especially notable among the Irish whose complaints are always expressed with an overtone of humor.
In this comment about his nephew, there is clearly implied plenty of an adoptive parent's pride and affection.
In addition, Hunting Cap, like his nephew, was prone to
exaggeration. The real differences between those two
strong characters were to come later. The comment about
Daniel's being a "nominal" law student was quite unfair.
For from the moment the young man arrived in London,
and especially after he was entered in Lincoln's Inn, he
was pursuing his reading with great energy. It is true
that his reading ranged over a wide area, but there was
enough strictly limited to law to qualify him for his profession. Preparation for the bar in those days was largely
a matter of self-direction. There was nothing suggesting
formal training. The student read where he could, in a
law office or elsewhere, until he presented himself for admission to practice. In London Daniel did his reading in
his lodgings. Later in Dublin he spent many hours in the
Public Library where he paid two guineas for membership.

We get a good idea of what he was reading from what
he called his Journal.† The first entry was in December
1795, and the notations, each of which was designated by
the date of its entry, were kept until January 1799. Then
there followed a considerable neglect of the Journal, but
in 1802 three entries were made. The latter are not very
important and, since he was in active practice by that time,

---

† In 1906 there was published a book written by Arthur Houston who lists
himself as "One of his Majesty's Counsel" in Dublin. It includes a sketch of
O'Connell's life up to his admission to the Irish bar and the texts of the Journal
with elaborate notations by Houston. It also includes the texts of several of
O'Connell's letters and a great deal of collateral information. The title of the
book is *Daniel O'Connell: His Early Life and Journal, 1795–1802* (London: Pitman, 1906).

he apparently decided that maintaining his "fee book" was a sufficient record of his activities. Despite his expressed resolve when he started the Journal, the entries are most irregularly kept. Apparently when he approached the end of a year and the beginning of another, he thought that it was time to make a record of what he was thinking and what he was reading. There is very little account of what he was actually doing in the world outside. There are entries for several days in December 1795. Then there is an entry dated February 1796. There are no further entries until December 1796 when several are shown. The entries then following are for the months of January, February, and March of 1797. Then except for a brief note in May, there are no more for that year except in December. There are entries in January 1798, but, probably because of the great excitement that year occasioned by the Wolfe Tone rebellion and O'Connell's flight from Dublin, the Journal seems to be forgotten.

It is quite probable that the text of the Journal which survived was far from all that the author originally wrote, for many pages in the book which he used were torn out, perhaps to provide pages for letter-writing or because O'Connell thought the entries were not worth preserving. Or perhaps he felt that they were too personal, although some of the comments which remain certainly reveal a great deal of his personal reflections upon the student's life and habits. There appear repeatedly those reactions which are so common in the introspection of sensitive individuals in their formative years—rigorous self-examination and self-criticism. Some of these matters of self-reproach were references to his habit of sleeping late into the morning, occasional excesses in eating and drinking, and neglect in keeping up the entries in the Journal.

Personal experience and the testimony of others have convinced me that most intelligent people indulge in more, and more painful, reflections about the mystery of death and the hereafter before they are twenty-one than they

do later in life. Certainly this was true of the student
O'Connell. He wrote this on December 31, 1795:

> With this day the year closes. How fleet it has been in its prog-
> ress, how rapid in its course! It seemed to commence but yesterday
> and, behold, it already is no more. A few more such years and the
> scene will close on me. I, who now write, who now think, who
> now move with strength and velocity, shall be stretched, pale, mo-
> tionless, inanimate. My mind can now grasp in its comprehension
> the millions of "admantine spheres rolling unshaken through the
> void immense." It can descend from this elevation gradually or
> with one bold stride to the minute insect that escapes the eye of
> the microscope. What is to become of this comprehensive mind?
> The body placed in a solitary corner, a prey to worms and vermin,
> will soon restore to the elements the portions of each which it has
> absorbed, I should rather say of which it is composed. But the mind,
> the mind! Through what variety of untried being is that to roam?
> What changes is it to suffer? Does it perish as a dependent of the
> corporal system? Such are the questions, to the solution of which
> the light of reason cannot direct the inquirer. Reason faintly glim-
> mers on futurity, or perhaps, did not prejudice vitiate our senses,
> we should perceive that reason affords no light to enable us to dis-
> cover whether the mind is immortal or not. Of things not arrived
> we can only guess. Our best surmises are founded on an analogy.
> Now, what analogy can there be between any part of corporal exist-
> ence and the state of mind when separated from the body, supposing
> separation actually takes place? The subject may afford matter for
> further speculation.

These speculations upon death and dissolution seem to
have been prompted by his reading of Tom Paine's *Age
of Reason*. Such comments have raised serious questions
about O'Connell's religious convictions. There seems to
be a preponderant belief among O'Connell's biographers
that, through Paine and his own cogitations, he entertained a strong belief in Deism.* Certainly that was a

---

* O'Connell's Deism seems to have dated from 1796. His newly published correspondence shows that he was still a rationalist in 1803. He had returned to
his Catholic faith by 1809.

trend in the rationalist climate of the closing years of the eighteenth century. Thomas Jefferson, like Paine, was a pronounced Deist. This seemed to be part of the revolt against authority and organized religion. O'Connell's second comment after reading Paine was this:

> I this day finished the second part of *The Age of Reason*. This part has given me more satisfaction than the former. It has put the foundation of the religious question of the Christians in a point of view in which a judgment is easily formed on its solidity. I now have no doubts on this head. I may certainly be mistaken, but I am not wilfully mistaken, if the expression has any meaning. My mistakes I refer to that Being who is wise by excellence. To the God of nature do I turn my heart; to the meditation of His works I turn my thoughts. In Him do I find my soul saturated. He will not, justice tells me, punish for a darkness, if such it be, that cannot be removed. He will not punish for the unbiassed [sic] conviction of the soul. To affirm the contrary would, in my apprehension, be to calumniate.

We have no clear indication in anything O'Connell wrote or said of the exact year in which he returned to the Catholic faith. We do know however from a letter written by his wife that he was again a Catholic by 1809. No doubt he would have worked just as hard for Emancipation if he had never been a Catholic. The passionate stand he took for religious liberty may well have arisen from a conviction which had nothing to do with his personal religion. He probably concluded that *any* religion which taught the importance of a moral life should be accepted as essential to a sound social order and should be free from state interference.

Such religious speculations as O'Connell's have constituted a phase in the lives of many people and offer nothing new and original. It is the political convictions that he shaped in those years of study and reflection which are of major interest to the student of his career. He lived as a young man and student in a period of tremendous political ferment. This was reflected in a tide of polemical literature, much of which was published before the Revolution in France. After the Revolution, fundamental questions of liberty and order were raised by English writers. Much of this centered in the opponents and proponents of Burke's great *Reflections on the Revolution in France.* Any great social or political upheaval will produce a host of writers, each of whom will fashion his special utopian kite. This happened in the ante-bellum slavery controversy in the United States, and to a certain degree in the great depression of the early 1930s. During O'Connell's years in London, the political writers who seemed to capture O'Connell's major interest were Paine, William Godwin, and Mary Woolstonecraft. He also systematically devoured Gibbon's *Decline and Fall.* It is most curious that, although both Paine and Godwin directed much of their argument against Burke's *Reflections,* there is no mention of Burke's great treatise in the parts of the Journal which survive, and his fellow countryman is mentioned only once in a passing reference. This was despite Burke's strong support of Irish rights throughout his parliamentary career. However, O'Connell's political views at that time and later were quite contrary to those of Burke, notably with regard to the French Revolution. There was a very distant relationship. O'Connell's aunt was married to a first cousin of Burke's.*

Americans will note that O'Connell read and commented upon John Adams' *History of Republics,* a work which was written during the American's stay in England in the 1780s. The first volume of this ambitious work was published at a time when it had considerable attention: during the American Constitutional Convention of 1787. As is shown in the list of O'Connell's readings which fol-

---

* Another omission is any comment upon Rousseau. However, in Houston's list of the books O'Connell mentions among his reading is Rousseau's *Confessions.*

lows this chapter, he did not neglect his law studies. He says that he enjoyed Blackstone but was bored by Coke's commentary on Littleton. O'Connell's flirtation with the radical ideas of Godwin and Paine seems to have cooled later when the more conservative ideas of Bolingbroke captured his attention. Here the young reader's attention seemed to be centered upon Bolingbroke's account of political methods and events rather than ideology. For diversion he turned to Boswell, whom he disliked as a person, but found the account of Samuel Johnson's Toryism worthy of comment.

A considerable amount of evidence appears in his comments of his interest in style and rhetoric. Here we see his preoccupation with his ambition to become an advocate and orator. O'Connell's speaking and writing in later years, aside from the bombast which he fell back upon in addressing unlettered audiences, could be highly sophisticated. No orator of his time had a greater command of the color and variety of the English language. In his comments upon the plays he attended, there are acute comments upon the way in which actors spoke their lines. Two of the actors he admired were Charles Kemble and his sister, Mrs. Siddons. This interest in public speaking also had its outlet in debating exercises with student groups to which he belonged. In London there was the Coger's Hall group and in Dublin there was the Historical Society.

No doubt O'Connell would share our regret that the Journal was so irregularly kept, for during the long periods when he neglected to make any entries, he must have read and formed opinions upon many books like those named in the following list. It is evident from what he did write that few statesmen in history without the advantage of formal instruction so industriously prepared themselves for public life.

A Classified List, compiled by Houston, of the works mentioned by O'Connell in his Journal

BIOGRAPHY

Boswell's *Life of Johnson*

Condorcet's *Life of Turgot*

Johnson's *Life of Cowley*

Milton's *Life*

Plutarch's *Lives*

Rousseau's *Confessions*

FICTION

Caleb Williams

Hugh Trevor

The Ring

The Man of Feeling

HISTORY

Adams' *History of Republics*

Barthelemy's *Travels of Anacharsis*

Gibbon's *Decline and Fall of the Roman Empire*

Mirabeau's *Cour de Berlin*

Whitaker's *History of Manchester*

LAW

Blackstone's *Commentaries on the Laws of England*

Boote's *Historical Account of a Suit at Law*

Coke's *Commentary on Littleton's Treatise on Land Tenures*

Cruise *On Fines*

Cummin *On Fee Tail*

NATURAL SCIENCE

Buffon's *Natural History*

Dutens' *Les origines des découvertes attribués aux modernes*

Hall's *Encyclopedia*, "Aerology" article

Mémoires de l'Académie des Sciences, article on observations made on the planet Jupiter and its satellites by Cassini

POETRY

Akenside's *Pleasures of Imagination*

Cowley's *Poems*

Johnson's *London* and *Vanity of Human Wishes*

Macpherson's *Ossian*

Milton's *Paradise Lost*

Pindar's *Poems*

Shakespeare

Voltaire's *Tragedies*

POLITICAL AND SOCIAL SCIENCE

Adam Smith's *Wealth of Nations*
Bolingbroke's *Answer to the "London Journal"*
Bolingbroke's *Vindication*
Colquhoun's *Police of London*
Godwin's *Political Justice*
Hume's *Essays*
The Jockey Club
Manual of Liberty
O'Brien's pamphlet against the Ministry entitled *Utrum Horum*
The Rolliad
Voltaire's works
Woolstonecraft's *Vindication of the Rights of Women*

THEOLOGY

The Bible   Paine's *Age of Reason*
Blair's *Sermons*   *Recueil Nécessaire*
                    Zapata's *Questions*

MISCELLANEOUS

Bayle's *Dictionary*
Collins' *Account of New South Wales*
Encyclopaedia Britannica, "Gladiator" article
Encyclopédie, "Gladiateur" article
Gibbon's *Miscellaneous Works*
Grose's *Antiquities of Ireland*
Plan of a Dictionary by Dr. Johnson
Transactions of the Royal Irish Academy
A play, the name of which is not given

4

The Cockpit of the Courts

AMONG THE DISABILITIES inflicted upon Catholic lawyers
was their exclusion from what was called the Inner Bar.
Those favored lawyers who were entitled to be called
King's Counsel were an exclusive professional group who
directed all of the more important cases, importance being
reckoned mostly in terms of money or property. This distinction within the profession was based on many things.
In O'Connell's case it was religion which excluded him
until after the Emancipation Act of 1829. After that, for
some time, it was spite within the government, a bias
which, it was said, the senile George IV shared. The injustice of O'Connell's exclusion in most of the years of his
activity in the courts was underlined by the eminence and
distinction which was generally accorded him as a member of the bar. It is not without interest that a considerable
part of his rising income came from fees he received from
members of the Inner Bar who sought his help in their
difficult cases.

His prowess as a barrister, which soon became a source
of interest all over the reaches in Ireland where his practice extended, brought him a great deal of business and
considerable income. He was known as the poor man's
lawyer, and, though the fees from those cases were small,
they made up for this by their number. O'Connell says in
some of his letters that he would have made an additional
thousand pounds a year as a member of the Inner Bar and
he would have been spared some of the immense labor of
circuit riding. But his countrywide reputation, so essen-

tial to his later political career, was considerably en-
hanced by his regular appearances in those centers of
population to which he traveled regularly. The bulk of
his cases were the run-of-the-mill actions which in the big
law offices now are handled by junior partners: murders
and assaults—numerous in those days—thievery in all
legal categories, fraud and other small business matters.

His practice in Dublin's Four Courts was considerable,
but circuit riding carried him over the highways of south-
ern and western Ireland. His letters show him to have
spent considerable time attending the assizes in Tralee,
Limerick, Cork, and Ennis. Toward the end of his student
days when the clouds of Wolfe Tone's 1798 revolt gathered, the threat of French intervention brought about the
formation of a Lawyers' Corps of Artillery, and O'Connell joined. A French fleet entered Bantry Bay and the
authorities in Dublin and London took action to deal with
the crisis. With this threat, many Catholic as well as
Protestant Irish rallied to the defense of the realm. Thus
for a short period he was enrolled as a defender of the
government. There may have been an element of prudence
in this because he realized that as a Catholic he would be
closely watched. He had been warned that Dublin Castle
had him listed as a suspicious person because of some of
his remarks which had been reported by the ever-busy
informers used by the police. Meanwhile, he had completed the preliminary requirements essential to his admission to the bar. These consisted mostly of attending
dinners in Dublin where he mingled with judges and
other officers who were supposed to appraise lawyer-ap-
plicants. He easily met this test and in April 1798 he took
the oath and was permitted to practice.

O'Connell's contact with the United Irishmen in their
tragic uprising in the 1790s must have been slight. It must
be remembered that, when Theobold Wolfe Tone participated in organizing the United Irishmen in 1791, O'Connell was a schoolboy in France. O'Connell was living in

London, reading and enjoying himself and preparing for the bar, at the time of the abortive 1796 invasion, and he makes an adverse comment in his Journal. Later, in 1798, when Tone, an officer in the French army, accompanied a landing party, was captured, tried, and took his own life, O'Connell joined the lawyers' artillery corps whose purpose was to resist a French invasion. That summer of 1798, apparently suspecting some action against him in the mop-up after the rebellion, he absented himself from Dublin. Perhaps in a casual way he sympathized with the objectives of the revolt, but certainly by his conduct then and his convictions later, he opposed the violent methods. And it is certain that the futility of the uprising and the useless shedding of blood greatly influenced him in his life-long opposition to violence in any form.* At any rate, once admitted to the bar and in proud possession of his first brief, he decided that Dublin was no place for him at that moment of crisis. With a few companions he boarded a potato boat for Cork, and from there he found his way to Derrynane. He was confined for a few days with a cold after he reached his uncle's house and so may have missed most of the tragic news of the revolt's failure, including the suicide of the condemned Tone. By the time he was fully recovered he found Dublin full of the news of the decision of the Pitt government to impose Union upon Ireland and abolish the Parliament in Dublin. There have been assertions in some writing favorable to Pitt that his hand was forced in this step by King George

---

* It may be too extreme to say that Catholics as well as Protestants were always opposed to a French invasion. Propertied Catholics and probably most of the clergy bitterly distrusted the French under the regime which had prevailed since the coming of the Revolution. They knew what would be the fate of the Church if ever the French dominated Ireland. Educated Catholics knew that, under the Revolutionary governments which had ruled France since 1792, more than a thousand priests had suffered the death penalty. Also it was obvious that England would have fought to the last man and the last shilling to oppose French domination in Ireland, for English control of Ireland was essential to her security. It is likely that, even if the French were to take over Ireland, they would trade it to the British for India or some other desirable territory.

III. But it is now fairly certain that as a young Prime Minister he had entertained the idea of Union as early as 1784 and that, by the time of the revolt, most members of the government favored it. To achieve it, however, was a dirty business. The shock felt by the young and idealistic lawyer by the stench of wholesale corruption which accompanied the suicide of the Irish Parliament was a memory that O'Connell carried to his grave.

The young man's dependence upon Hunting Cap's remittances in his student days became more galling as the old trader became more grudging and fussy. This decided the nephew not only to become self-dependent as soon as possible but to declare his freedom from the demands for political conformity which began to come from Derrynane. For Hunting Cap, as he rose in prominence and respectability and attained rank as a magistrate, became a pillar of Unionism.

At a meeting of Catholics in Dublin in January 1800 at the Royal Exchange, Daniel made his first major speech as a public figure. This speech, which revealed the authentic stamp of careful preparation, was well received and widely reported in the press. So also were the resolutions which he prepared and presented, and which were enthusiastically adopted. But Hunting Cap was furious and, in a long letter of advice, he told Daniel that he most earnestly recommended "that you keep clear of all further interference." One of the high points in the speech conveyed the idea that "it was a foul calumny to say that the Catholics of Ireland had agreed to the enactment of the Union. . . . Indeed if the alternative were offered of Union or the reenactment of the Penal Laws with all their pristine horrors, I would prefer without hesitation the latter." Indeed this speech was so complete an indictment of the Union and so accurate a prediction of its consequences that in all the years of subsequent opposition, O'Connell never varied from this early expression of dissent. He concluded with this admonition to the

Catholics: "I know that the Catholics still remember that they have a country and will never accept any advantage as a sect that will destroy them as a people." This was meant to warn his Catholic friends that they should not believe the alleged promise of Pitt that the price of accepting Union would be Catholic Emancipation. Whether Pitt made such a promise or not, it was not fulfilled.

Shortly after that expression of disapproval from Hunting Cap, there came another shadow over Daniel's avuncular relations. The uncle suggested that Daniel should marry a Miss Healy of Cork, whose prospective inheritance was excellent but whose attractiveness did not appeal to the young man. But a young woman in Tralee named Mary O'Connell (a distant cousin), the daughter of a deceased physician, sparked a lifelong love affair. A secret marriage was arranged at the home of a relative, with a parish priest officiating. Six months later Daniel told his uncle, and six months after that the first child arrived. Seeking to cozen the old man, he had the baby christened Maurice, but Hunting Cap was not to be appeased by the christening of a namesake. He resolved to reduce greatly what he had intended earlier to bestow upon his adopted nephew.* The affectionate old Colonel would have been more effective in his appeal for a revision of the will except that he had displeased brother Maurice by marrying a French widow who had the misfortune to have an estate in Santo Domingo. The Negro revolt there, under the leadership of the famous Toussaint L'Ouverture, resulted in the confiscation of her property. But the Colonel's plea for Daniel survives in a letter to Hunting Cap.

The happiness of the couple was not immediately marred by the possible loss of an inheritance, since the income from the growing law practice sufficed—for the moment. But the incredible mess which the future Liber-

---

* See pages 93, 115–16 for the account of what Daniel actually inherited.

ator made of his financial affairs, a source of agonizing
letters between the partners, continued at least until
Hunting Cap's death because they still counted a great
deal on the expected inheritance. When Daniel O'Connell entered upon his career in the courts, harsh reality
played havoc with the dreams of his student days. Back
there, alone with his books, a bright idealism pervaded
his purposes, plans, and ambitions. He was a true son of
the Enlightenment, and the concept of that movement
tempted adherents to expect too much of the idea of the
perfectability of man. Their faith led them to expect too
much too soon. Once man's chains were removed, some of
the writers said, human behavior would be not only mor-
ally sound but infinitely wise. But the dream never calculated enough on the persistence of original sin. It could
scarcely be expected that the law courts, in which so much
of O'Connell's days would be spent for the next quarter
of a century, would fail to be stained by the state of the
public service which characterized the past century. A
special influence which affected the courts was the effect
of the unspeakable corruption that accompanied the enactment of the Union. Some who served in the Irish Parliament bought their robes with their votes for the Union.
Other products of that auction of national honor were in
most of the minor posts in the courts. It had been what
O'Faolain calls a "shambles of exploitation." I am told
by more restrained historians that O'Faolain exaggerates,
but what he says bears quotation:

> It was one of the basest periods of the Irish bar . . . for the
> bench was filled with inefficient men who, as often as not, bought
> their way to preferment. O'Neill Daunt listed nine judges who had
> risen to the bench by double dealing. . . . The result was a court
> that was always unpredictable and not far removed from a beer
> garden.

But bad as some of the judges were, it seems from contemporary accounts and some of O'Connell's reminis-

cences and letters recently published, that there were also
some good ones. O'Connell expressed some contempt for
certain individual judges but mostly he accepted things
as they were without permitting himself to lapse into
cynicism. He was not so tender, however, with most of
the crown prosecutors. One of the most distinguished
judges, at the age of 98, told O'Connell that he "always
agreed with the last speaker." Another was a brutal buf-
foon, Toler, who was made Lord Norbury; he, according
to O'Faolain, "would always mix his weird instructions
with jokes from a penny joke-book. He would become
more hortatory as he warmed to a case, standing up and
putting aside his robe, maybe flinging off his wig, pouring
out the most outlandish jumble of disconnected material,
anecdotes of his early life, snatches from Milton or Shakespeare, sarcasm at the defense, urging opposing counsel
to a battle royal of sophistries . . . at which the jury
would stare gob-eyed."

In such courts, over which there presided such judges,
gritty young counselors learned to treat the bench openly
with the contempt they felt in their minds. As O'Connell
gained confidence with success, his domination of witnesses and juries extended to the people on the bench. In
one instance, after a clash over procedure, the judge
shouted that when he was at the bar he had not behaved
that way. "No," replied O'Connell, "when you were at
the bar I never took you as a model. And now that you are
on the bench . . ." In another case, the judge suddenly
admitted evidence which he had barred the day before.
O'Connell replied, "Had your lordship known as much
law yesterday as you know today, you would have spared
me a vast amount of time and trouble, and my client a
considerable amount of injury." What is most remarkable
is that, as he progressed at the bar, he was able to retain
his essentially refined nature though his methods hardened
to meet the conditions forced upon him. He learned early
what a veteran American political leader told a young

candidate for office: "In politics," he said, "you need the patience of Christ and the cynicism of the devil." In O'Connell's cases, especially on circuit, he was generally dealing with the characteristic peasant mind, suspicious, disingenuous, evasive. Since the Gaelic was often used with witnesses who knew no English, that language itself served to confuse meaning and to permit of a variety of interpretations. In a will case, an obviously mendacious witness contended that the deceased's mark had been signed to the document before he died. But as the questioning went on, O'Connell noted that the response was always "Bhi beatha ann" which means "there was life in him." Finally O'Connell shouted "Do you deny, by the God who is your judge, that there was a live fly in the man's mouth when you put his hand to the will?" Terrified, the witness confessed. O'Connell's renown as an examiner was the talk of the circuit. He would spend an hour or more burrowing into the mind of the witness. The slightest contradiction opened new avenues for approach. Knowing the Irish mind, he would break the monotony by a joke or a compliment, but he never lost the trail until the witness scarcely knew whether he was a friend or an enemy. It is not strange that some of this Irish characteristic of ambivalence should characterize his own course, for when the larger end was clearly in view, his methods were not always straightforward.*

The gifts which nature had bestowed upon him were a legend long before his death, even before he could be called a Liberator—a magnificent presence, a face beneath those curly locks which never lost its charm. Tall, powerfully built, and with the poise of an actor, he had a sharp memory and a mind like a finely articulated mechanism. The law was an admirable tool for such an

* Professor Maurice O'Connell writes of O'Connell: "He could be eel-like and casuistical in politics. If you engaged him in a controversy, you would have to be very careful indeed to follow *precisely* what he said and not what he *appeared* to be saying."

intellect, always subject to new interpretations and sus-
ceptible to the imaginative management of a master. The
courtroom was a stage and he never lost his sense of a
drama in which he held the center of attention, and, as
one commentator has said, he got "fun out of it." His
sense of humor made the drab and grimy commerce of
justice a source of enjoyment. Nature was never more
prodigal in equipping a barrister and statesman with the
physical endowments so essential to success. No small
credit for his remarkable success goes to these natural
gifts. Contemporary descriptions of the man confirm
what we see today in the portraits and statues erected in
his memory. He was called tall—one account places his
height at slightly below six feet. His shoulders were broad
and his chest was massive. His posture was erect and commanding. He had the dark curly hair and blue eyes which
we see so often in Kerry. His shining eyes and delicate
features suggest nothing more appropriate than the cliché
"feminine sweetness." According to a contemporary, those
eyes were "kindly and honest-looking."

No doubt his frequent visits to the theater during his
student days in London taught him a great deal about the
art of acting. Had he turned from the law and politics to
the stage, he might with his natural gifts, his intelligence,
and sense of the dramatic, have rivaled the Kembles.
Every contemporary in commenting on O'Connell's natural gifts mentions his voice. In his obituary on Peel, Disraeli described him as having had "the finest organ in the
House, always excepting the thrilling tones of O'Connell." Arthur Houston, editor of O'Connell's Journal and
himself a member of the bar, has this to say of his subject's voice and how he used it:

> To these natural gifts was added that priceless one, a marvellous
> voice, powerful—leonine, as Sir Charles Gavan Duffy calls it—
> sonorous, melodious, penetrating, capable of expressing every shade
> of human feeling. But a voice is nothing without a command of
> words, and words are nothing where ideas are lacking. O'Connell

had an abundance of both. Poetic fancy and homely wit, delicate humor and deep pathos, subtle flattery and bitter sarcasm, gentle persuasion and fierce denunciation, each, as the occasion required, flowed in an inexhaustible stream to charm or to dismay. Nor was it the masses alone that fell under the spell of his eloquence. Judges and juries bowed to his influence, and this wonder at his eloquence was affirmed later by those who heard him in the House of Commons.

But O'Connell was not a man to rely upon his personality and talents for extemporaneous exposition to serve as a substitute for hard work. He labored long hours and with great concentration on the complex law in which his briefs entangled him. We have a contemporary glimpse of O'Connell at his daily labors at home preparing his cases contained in one of the chapters of Richard Lalor Sheil's *Sketches of the Irish Bar.* The piece was written by William Henry Curran, son of the famous John Philpot Curran, and it serves to remind us of O'Connell's industry and also to illustrate an Irishman's way with words.

If any of you, my English readers, should chance on your return on a winter's morning from one of the small and early parties in that metropolis . . . to pass along the south side of Merrion Square, you will not fail to observe that, among those splendid mansions there is one tenanted by a person whose habits differ materially from those of his fashionable neighbors. The half-opened parlor shutter, and the light within, announce that someone dwells there whose time is too precious to regulate his rising with the sun's. Should your curiosity tempt you to ascend the steps, and under cover of the dark, reconnoitre the interior, you will see a tall, able-bodied man standing at a desk, immersed in a solitary occupation. Upon the wall in front of him, there hangs a crucifix. From this and from the calm attitude of the person within, and from a certain monastic rotundity about his neck and shoulders, your first impressions will be that he must be some dignitary of the Church absorbed in his devotions.

But no sooner can the eye take in the other furnishings of the apartment—the bookcases clogged with tomes in plain calfskin binding, the blue covered octavos that lie about on the tables and on the floor, the reams of manuscript in oblong folds and begirt with crimson tape—than it becomes evident that the party meditating amidst such objects must be thinking far more of the law than of the prophets.

But should you happen in the course of the same day to stroll down to the Four Courts, you will not be a little surprised to find the object of your pity miraculously transferred from the severe recluse of the morning to one of the most bustling, important and joyous personages in that busy scene. . . . You perceive at once that you have lighted upon a great popular advocate; and if you take the trouble to follow his movements for a couple of hours through the several courts, you will not fail to discover the qualities that have made him so . . . his acuteness, his fluency of thought and language, his unconquerable good humor and, above all, his versatility.

Somewhat less eloquent, but more precise, was the counselor's daughter's account of the daily routine of her father. He rose at four, said a prayer, and worked on his briefs until the family summoned him to breakfast at eight-thirty. After an hour chatting with such children as were about and a long walk to the Four Courts (two miles), he worked at his professional duties from eleven to three. On the way home, a visit to the Catholic Association's headquarters and home for dinner at four when he relaxed with the family until six-thirty, then back to his briefs until ten when he made it a rule to retire. He had little time for such social amenities as dining out unless it was a dinner which mixed refreshment with political speeches and resolutions and debate.

Some of the flavor of the counselor's circuit-riding experiences is provided by the story of one of his most famous cases. It was in October 1829, when the mountains above Derrynane were already feeling the bitter wind and cold of approaching winter. Earlier that year the Emancipation had been won at Westminster and O'Connell had been re-elected at Ennis. When Hunting Cap died in 1825, Daniel had taken possession of Derrynane. He

retired there every autumn for a much-needed rest. In
1829, after his great exertions in gaining Emancipation,
he went on holiday to Derrynane as usual but, this time,
his sojourn was dramatically disturbed. The intruder was
one William Burke who had ridden frantically from
Cork with the plea that O'Connell must come if twenty
men were to be saved from the gallows. The case concerned the murder of an unpopular magistrate, who was
also a landlord, in the country around Doneraile, County
Cork. In consequence a score of farmers and workmen
were charged with conspiracy to murder.

At the trial of the first batch of prisoners the Solicitor-
General obtained a conviction by using improper methods
and with the aid of perjured witnesses. The convicted men
were sentenced to death. A like fate awaited the remaining
defendants, and it was clear that only O'Connell could
save them. He made the first stage of the journey on horse-
back since there was no road for the first twenty miles of
the way from Derrynane to Cork. After that he was able
to travel in a carriage in which he studied the briefs. He
continued at a furious pace through the night, and arrived
in Cork in the morning to find the court already in session.
With no rest or refreshment but a sandwich and a bowl
of milk, which he consumed in court while the state prose-
cutor was summing up, O'Connell plunged into the proceedings. By means of a brilliant cross-examination he
succeeded in exposing the witnesses as perjurors, and obtained an acquittal for all his clients. The government
then commuted the death sentences passed on the first
batch of prisoners. The renown that greeted O'Connell's
winning of this case added to the reputation he had earned
as the leading member of the Irish bar. On popular opinion the effect was intense, the story passing into folklore
(one version had it that when the carriage pulled up in
front of the courthouse the horses fell dead!). But the
government still denied him admission to the Inner Bar.

This was a bitter humiliation since several younger and less able Catholic barristers had been admitted since the enactment of Emancipation. This case substantially ended O'Connell's career at the bar. Thereafter he was an accredited Irish member in the House of Commons. The Irish nation became his jealous client. The tales of his triumphs at the bar survived in anecdotes for more than a century, time enough for the growth of a legend in which no doubt the imagination of the authors embellished the facts. Indeed, O'Connell's prowess was so great and so well advertised that no doubt many an exploit by some less distinguished barrister was attributed to him.

I have included enough about his court life to illustrate his great skill. I have also spared the reader from further anecdotes for, as I have read this mass of material, I have had confirmed once more an impression I have entertained for a long time: wit and humor, unlike wine, lose their flavor with time. What must have provoked peals of laughter at the time, fails to provoke the reader's smile. Much of Mark Twain I now find dull and boring. And Will Rogers' witticisms, funny half a century ago, are dated and meaningless to this generation.

Ten years after his admission to the bar, O'Connell was well known as one of the foremost practitioners in the Four Courts in Dublin and on the circuit. By 1814 he was clearly regarded as the most sought-after counselor in Ireland. This very considerably added to his income for, as mentioned earlier, members of the Inner Bar with complex and difficult cases retained him to guide their course through the labyrinth of law. In the account of his income, as he carefully entered the payments in his fee book, there is no distinction between the small fees paid in the cases in which he was the counsel of record, and the matters referred to him by members of the Inner Bar; but as his renown grew so did his income. The total collected for some of the years are shown by O'Faolain:

1798	2 guineas
1799	27
1800	205
1801	346
1803	465
1804	715
1805	840
1809	2,736
1812	3,028
1814	3,808

In 1809 he purchased a fine home on Merrion Square among the mansions of the more opulent gentry of Dublin. His growing family needed room and his position at the bar and in political life, he believed, demanded this mark of distinction.

Well before this, however, he had assumed leadership in the agitation for Emancipation and this required him to impose upon his massive constitution the burdens of both occupations; but his fame at the bar had no small part in promoting and extending his acknowledged political leadership.

5

O'Connell and Religious Liberty

THERE SURVIVED IN DANIEL O'CONNELL, from the meditations and speculations of his student days, two convictions which dominated his mind and directed his actions throughout his life. One was religious liberty, a term which implied the independence of organized religion from interference or domination by the secular state. The other was that in seeking political change, sole reliance should rest upon legal, constitutional, and peaceful means. The first of these involved a condition. The second concerns method.

Religious liberty seemed to him a condition essential to individual and collective happiness. As a student of the classics O'Connell would surely have interpreted happiness in the Aristotelian sense of the word.

O'Connell placed stress upon the moral stricture against the use of violence, but he also insisted, as a practical matter in the Anglo-Irish relationship, that force and violence would be futile and self-defeating.

It was the tenacity, consistency, and sincerity with which O'Connell held to these convictions, without deviation, that mark him as something apart from a political leader seeking profit for himself or his clan or group or, in modern terms, his minority. In almost everything he said on the subject of religious liberty he emphasized that, unless all religious groups were free from state interference, no religion and no religious group could be safe.

He has been criticized because, although he said that the State should not interfere with Church matters, he did not say that priests should not enter the realm of politics. In his movement for Emancipation he drew his priests into the very heart of the agitation. He would probably have replied that the issue for which he mobilized the priests was a matter in which the Church was vitally concerned. It was indeed the very cause of religious liberty, the right of Catholics to equality in political affairs.

O'Connell was born into a Europe in which the concept of religious liberty was known but nowhere accepted except among rationalists and in some minor Christian sects. Professor Maurice O'Connell maintains that in Europe O'Connell was the first prominent political leader among Catholics and, perhaps, the first in any major Christian denomination to espouse this freedom and its corollary, separation of Church and State. He inspired and was followed by Montalembert and other liberal Catholics in France. In all Europe, secular authority had for centuries projected itself into religious affairs. In Britain and Ireland there was the Church of England of which the crown was head and master. That O'Connell's views were of a very radical nature at that time is shown by the position taken by Rome long after O'Connell started his agitation, even after his death. Three popes in encyclicals condemned the *principle* although not necessarily the *practice* of religious liberty: Gregory XVI in 1832, Pius IX in 1864, and Leo XIII in 1885. It was not until the Second Vatican Council in 1965 that the principle was fully accepted and clearly stated. This declaration said that every man has the right to worship God publicly according to the dictates of his own conscience, to propagate his religious beliefs, and to be free from discrimination on account of those beliefs.

As I have indicated earlier, the young O'Connell as a student fell under the influence of the rationalists whose books he was reading at the time. His religious cogitations

in the mid-1790s led him to accept Deism, a position
which he held for perhaps ten years. In 1803 he wrote a
letter to his wife, saying "If I were a religionist, I should
spend every moment in praying for you; and this miserable philosophy which I have taken up and been proud of
in the room of religion, affords me now no consolation
in my misery." Between that date and 1809, there seemed
to have been a great change. This is shown by a letter written to him by his wife in that year in which she said, "I
can't tell you what real happiness it gives me to have you,
this some time back, say your prayers and attend Mass so
regularly, not to say anything of your observance of the
days of abstinence." It seems idle to speculate on the
authenticity of this conversion, which in fact was a return
to the faith of his parents and of the people who meant
most to him. In those early years of his agitation, it must
have seemed important that he should share the convictions and emotions of the masses he tried so hard to serve
since their religion was so dominant in their lives. But
the attachment he developed to all religious observances,
long after he had won the love and devotion of those
people, leads us to believe that in facing the mystery of
life and death, he found it easier to believe than to doubt.
However, it seems clear that his interest in the ideas of
the rationalists in the eighteenth century contributed
greatly to his life-long dedication to religious liberty. For
it was the rationalists whose books he read as a student
who mixed their devastating criticism of the forms of
religion with attacks upon the governments which supported and protected those religious bodies.

In 1804 when he became active in the struggle for Catholic Emancipation, he clearly saw that the liberty which
he demanded for the Catholics of Ireland could hardly
be claimed if at the same time he failed to admit equal
freedom from State coercion in the non-Catholic countries. At a Catholic meeting in Dublin in 1807, he said that
he would place the Catholic claims "on the new score of

justice—of that justice which would emancipate the Protestants in Spain and Portugal, and the Christian in Constantinople."

Speaking in Dublin in 1813, he said:

> The emancipation I look for is one which would establish the
> rights of conscience upon a general principle—which would serve
> to liberate the Catholic in Ireland but would be equally useful to
> the Protestant in Spain—which would destroy the Inquisition and
> the Protestant Orange lodges together.

In this speech he referred to the State's interference either
in support of or in restriction of any religious body. This
interference, he said, was "profane"; it carried "temporal
terrors or the corrupt influence of temporal rewards."

At Tralee in 1818, he summed up his position:

> My political creed is short and simple. It consists in believing
> that all men are entitled as of right and justice to religious and
> civil liberty. I deserve no credit for being the advocate of religious
> liberty as my wants alone require such advocacy; but I have taken
> care to require it only on that principle which would emancipate
> the Catholics in Ireland, would protect the Protestants in France
> and Italy, and destroy the Inquisition, together with inquisitors, in
> Spain. Religion is debased and degraded by human interference; and
> surely the worship of the Deity cannot but be contaminated by the
> admixture of worldly ambition or human force.

After the passage of the test act which repealed discrimination against Protestant dissenters and the Catholic
Emancipation, the Jews alone remained under the government ban. In 1829 O'Connell offered his support to
them and advised their political leader, Isaac Lyon Gold-
smid:

> I entirely agree with you on the principle of freedom of con-
> science, and no man can admit that sacred principle without ex-
> tending it to the Jew as to the Christian. To my mind it is an
> eternal and universal truth that we are responsible to God alone
> for our religious belief and that human laws are impious when

they attempt to control the exercise of those acts of individual or general devotion which such belief requires. I think not lightly of the awful responsibility of rejecting *true belief* but that responsibility is entirely between man and his creator, and any fellow being who usurps dominion over belief is to my mind a blasphemer against the Deity as he certainly is a tyrant over his fellow creatures.

Although the very nature of the crusade he was leading carried him very close to matters of theology, he was exceedingly careful not to embroil himself with religious leaders. Since he was a layman and a politician, he realized that consistency required him to accept the judgment of clerical authorities in matters of faith and morals. This reticence was more than the prudence of a very practical politician; it was a plain consequence of his belief in the separation of Church and State. As a Catholic he was confronted with revolution in France and a bit later in Italy. In France the government of the Bourbon Charles X was overthrown in 1830 and was succeeded by Louis-Philippe. To a degree this new government was anti-clerical and anti-Catholic, but O'Connell hailed the new regime because it had ended the Bourbon dynasty and seemed bent on separating Church from State.

In Italy revolutionary movements were aimed at ending the temporal power of the Vatican. O'Connell hailed these efforts although his stand caused considerable dismay in papal circles. But he could hardly be consistent with his position on the separation of Church and State if he made an exception of this exercise of civil authority by the Pope. On another occasion and in a different context, he said that he was a Catholic but not a papist. In 1836 O'Connell, along with Michael J. Quin and the Rev. Nicholas (later Cardinal) Wiseman, founded *The Dublin Review,* a quarterly. The purpose was to provide a forum for Catholic writers on general topics and religious polemics. Quin, the first editor, withdrew after two issues and as a replacement O'Connell suggested William Howitt, a Quaker. That Rome never condemned O'Connell is not hard to understand. The Church in those years had its hands full without quarreling with as good a friend as O'Connell had proved to be. Certainly he was not likely to be criticized by the Irish clergy which had traditionally observed a certain independence from Rome. Moreover, he always expressed his opinions in political rather than theological terms.*

O'Connell was, according to Lecky, a steady and most vehement opponent of Negro slavery, and he showed his hatred of it when to do so seemed very contrary to his interests. In the House of Commons he strongly attacked the grant of twenty million pounds as compensation to the slave owners in the West Indies when their slaves were freed. Later in the 1840s during the Repeal movement a considerable amount of the money for the Association came from the United States, quite a lot from Southerners. Consequently, there were loud outcries from sympathizers in the United States and some from within the Repeal movement in Ireland, because of O'Connell's numerous statements against slavery. Unmoved by these complaints, he insisted that when the Association accepted donations from slave owners and groups in slave states, it should make known its opposition to slavery. Consequently most of the donations from those sources ceased, to the annoyance of some of the Young Irelanders who held that O'Connell should not commit the Association to any position on slavery. In response to pleas that he was driving away money needed for his Repeal cause, he replied: "I would rather have one Irish landed pro-

* It was characteristic of O'Connell's practical relations that he observed no distinctions on account of religion. His family attorney in his later years, who had the difficult job of settling the estate and so far as possible caring for the debts, was Pierce Mahony, a Protestant. Mahony had been parliamentary agent in London for the Catholic Association during the final year before Emancipation. Also, O'Connell's land agent from 1822 to 1846 was a Protestant, John Primrose, Jr. It was usual in nineteenth-century Ireland to employ only co-religionists for such offices of trust.

prietor of weight than all of the slave-breeders." Lecky
says that O'Connell assailed the hypocrisy of the American government which legalized slavery while "in the
very forefront of the Constitution" it is declared that "all
men were born equal and free." Either Lecky or O'Connell got the Constitution and the Declaration of Independence confused and misquoted the latter. The sincerity
of O'Connell in opposing slavery, however, was genuine.

6

O'Connell, the Enemy of Violence

THE AMERICAN WHO HAS READ in his newspaper over the years about crimes of violence and other outrages in Northern Ireland needs to be reminded that this unhappy news is simply a flaring into physical action of a continuing controversy which has racked Ireland for two centuries. It is not because the Irish are inherently more bloodthirsty than other people. It is simply because there has never in all those years been agreement between two concepts of the most effective way to secure for the island and its people a satisfactory form of government. The two traditions which are in conflict are, on the one hand, moral and rational persuasion, and, on the other, resort to physical force. Only a hopelessly deluded Irishman would suggest that in an armed revolutionary conflict, such as prevailed in the American Revolution, Irish forces could compel the submission of the British. The rationale, if we allow it that name, of the physical-force school is to mount sufficient physical disorder for a time long enough to lead the governing authority to treat for peaceful relief from the annoyance caused by the outbreaks. It is believed that a sharp deviation from what is normal—murder, assault, an act of arson—will attract attention; will be a sort of shock treatment. Attention having been attracted, there come questions as to cause, and the normal desire for peace will win over enough support to bring about the desired result. On a smaller scale, the suffragettes in

England won the right to vote by committing such auda-
cious violations of orderly behavior over so long a period
that finally there was won enough sympathy from the neutral majority and enough desire on the part of the authorities to be rid of an annoyance, and the desired concession
was made.

The advocates of violence in Ireland have always
claimed enough historical justification to create plausibil-
ity for their case, generally through plenty of twisting of
historical facts. And the outcome of the violence which
the Irish revolutionists visited upon the establishment in
the five years before the recognition of the Free State has
seemed to win the argument for the advocates of violence.
But in this essay we are considering happenings and conditions a century before the Free State was born, and the
part played by one man who, by his own personal influence, kept his countrymen from organized violence for
half a century. No conviction, except perhaps his dedication to religious freedom, so occupied his mind and conscience from 1796 to his last words to his countrymen before he left on the last journey.

His first recorded expression on the subject of violence
was in 1796 when he was a law student in London. A
month before, a French fleet had threatened an invasion
near Bantry Bay. The young O'Connell wrote in his diary,
"The altar of liberty totters when it is cemented only with
blood. . . . The Irish are not sufficiently enlightened to
bear the sun of freedom. Freedom would soon dwindle
into licentiousness, they would rob, they would murder."
Two years later he saw, in all its wasted blood and effort,
the rising of 1798, with Wolfe Tone and his United Irishmen. In all his references to that event, he was strong in
disapproval. The next year, 1799, he recounts a conversa-
tion in which he commented upon the innocent blood that
had been shed. "Good God! what a brute man becomes
when ignorant and oppressed. O Liberty, what horrors
are committed in thy name." In 1846 when he was strug-

gling against the hostile talk of the Young Ireland group, he said in answering something that John Mitchel uttered:

> He talks of '98; several good men were engaged in that contest of '98; but alas! their struggle was one of blood, and it was defeated in blood! The means then adopted were the very means of weakening Ireland and enabling England to carry the Union.

In a speech a few years after '98 in Dublin, he referred to the rising "as having been actuated by pure, but erroneous, love for Ireland." The so-called insurrection of Robert Emmet, by the caprice of history, romanticism, and ignorance, has lifted the chief actor from his proper rating as a damn' fool to the dimensions of a national hero. His performance on July 23, 1803, was hardly more than a street brawl. From that he escaped safely to the mountains but, because of a romantic attachment to a girl, he returned to Dublin a month later, was captured, tried, convicted, and hanged in September. O'Connell in a letter written from Cork to his wife Mary, late in August, said:

> Young Emmett [sic] is, they say, certainly arrested in Dublin. If he has been concerned in the late insurrection of which I fancy there is no doubt—he merits and will suffer the severest punishment. For my part I think pity would be almost thrown away upon the contriver of the affair of the 23rd of July. A man who could coolly prepare so much bloodshed, so many murders—and such horrors of every kind has ceased to be the object of compassion.
> [O'Connell 97; I 99.]

This statement of O'Connell's offers another of his objections to ill-conceived uprisings. They not only are foolish sacrifices of the lives of the perpetrators, but they always involve the loss of lives of police, who are doing their duty, of innocent people who are drawn into the conspiracy, and of innocent bystanders.

In what follows I have omitted the tiresome quotations of the many statements made by O'Connell throughout his

long career deploring violence and the incitement to violence, until in telling of the trouble with the Young Ireland group in 1846, such quotations become necessary. I
have instead, without taking unjustified liberties with the
working of O'Connell's mind, ventured to express some of
the justification of his opposition to the use of physical
force and violence. Suffice it to say that his policy at all
times was, in words attributed to him, "Rather than shed
one drop of Irish blood, I would welcome the return of
the Penal Laws." It was a formidable task to which
O'Connell addressed himself in convincing the Irish people of the futility and evil of a resort to violence, for he
was quite aware of the instincts of the ignorant, oppressed,
and highly volatile Irish masses. For these people, from
peasant to chief, violence had been a way of life for centuries. To them the blood of the enemy was the price of
liberty, even survival. They had little foresight or capacity for calculation. They had learned nothing to warn
them of the odds against success in any revolt. I was a
teacher in Cleveland when the news came of the Easter
revolt in 1916. A colleague addressed me that morning
with the quotation: "They went forth to battle but they
always fell." *

It is so true. Perhaps the misery in their lives together
with the rich rewards beyond the grave, promised by their
religion, have something to do with the unconcern they
feel about death. On the other side the English were quite
aware of this Irish weakness. The English realized that
they would never lack provocation when they decided to
unleash the forces of repression.

Several considerations moved O'Connell as he shaped
his policy of non-violence. Of first priority was the moral
law. As a Christian, despite his early Deism, he could

---

* For a long time the origin of this quotation eluded me. One suggestion was
that it came from Yeats; also, several others who seem to have plagiarized it.
Finally I discovered that it came from Ossian who, according to the Journal,
was a great favorite of the young O'Connell.

permit no equivocation about the prohibition against the rule of an eye for an eye. The shedding of another's blood was a crime before God. But in talking to his people his great practical sense and realism dominated his arguments. To those doubters who cited the American Revolution as an example, he was at pains to remind them of geography. He said that methods must be considered in the context of Anglo-Irish relations. The odds against the success of any Irish revolt were overwhelming. The English outnumbered the Irish many times. The wars with France had built up English military forces in size and efficiency. These forces were matched by a strong civil administration which assured powerful police action.

O'Connell realized that there were in England millions of impoverished and unhappy people. If by peaceful appeals he could win from them some sympathy for the Irish cause, the attitude of Parliament might be affected. Consequently he gave time and energy in many speeches to workers in the industrial centers of England. He knew also many Englishmen of influence and substance. By adhering strictly to the constitutional methods which they held so dear, he might win support with them. Moreover, O'Connell's rejection of violence was based upon sharp foresight. He realized that, even if by some miracle of Irish strength and English diversion, a victory by force could be won, there would remain the problems already facing the two nations. There was the fact not only of geography but of interdependence. Nature had decreed that the Irish and the English (along with the Scots and Welsh) should be a community with a common language (O'Connell had little interest in the revival of Gaelic) and reciprocal interests. After an armed conflict, he realized, it would be many years before peaceful relations could be established.

As O'Connell confronted the English government with his demands for concessions to Ireland, he had the logic of history on his side. For on that neighboring island, constitutional institutions had taken root over the centuries, and they were designed to provide the means of change without the violence which had prevailed in more primitive years. It was the English who had created a parliament as a means of restraint upon royal power, and later on, in the era of the Georges, cabinet control had appeared and, over generations, a system of courts to settle disputes without violence. When O'Connell appealed to the government in London in terms of the very institutions under which that government itself exercised authority, he touched, however unavailing, the process of non-violent change of which it was most proud. For when the Stuarts were ousted in 1688, they themselves had called the revolution "bloodless." Their philosophers have been at great pains to claim that the change of sovereigns had been entirely constitutional. He asked them only to respect their own rules. The essence of his argument was that while the Irish were, by the fact of geography, a part of a large community, they were as minority members rightfully to be accorded the same privileges and powers possessed by English citizens. Also, because they were a somewhat different race, they had certain rights of self-government.

It was O'Connell's plea that the age of violent change had passed with the creation of constitutional institutions. And he redeemed this claim by restraining his own people. Finally, on the side of non-violence there was O'Connell's appraisal of his own people. He was well aware of the enormous task which would face Irish leadership if by a sudden change in English policy there should be broken the fetters which had been welded over the centuries. There would be lacking in Ireland the very rudiments of a capacity for self-government. Most of his people were illiterate. They knew nothing of the meaning of constitutional government. Thus, he must, as his agitation proceeded, assume the enormous task of education. For centuries there had been little sense of nationality. Ireland was a congeries of clans and families. The Irish must be taught the meaning of constitutional order, of representative government, and the practical exercise of the franchise. The only government they had ever known was a negative instrument of repression and force. Moreover, as he turned from the masses to the more fortunate Irishmen with whom he worked in committees and other organizations, those who had titles and owned property (many of them Protestants), he found that while they sincerely sought justice they revealed serious deficiencies in talent.

Thus the task to which he set his hand when he entered public life was a slow and painful business of education, constant contacts with all sorts and conditions in Irish life, and, above all, endless speaking. Also, after he won confidence and with it supreme control over his people, he must impose upon all the rule of non-violence. In this, to be sure, he had the invaluable help of the priests and bishops. They helped immeasurably in reminding their parishioners of the Christian doctrine of non-violence. "For all that take the sword shall perish with the sword." In the last great effort of his life, the series of Monster Meetings in 1843, the vast crowds who greeted him and the enthusiasm with which they responded to his words seemed to impress upon him, more than ever, the necessity to avoid violence. For he fondly believed that this show of Irish opinion might, after all, bring the English government to the point of repeal. When, at the close of this campaign, he and the sponsors of Repeal decided to stage a vast demonstration at Clontarf, O'Connell met his greatest test, for the Peel government prepared to meet this with overwhelming military force. O'Connell, fearing that this might end in a sanguinary débâcle, called the meeting off.

Later when he was convicted and condemned to prison

in 1844, he composed a proclamation and provided for its distribution in Dublin. This bulletin is on display at Derrynane today. It said in part:

> I tell you solemnly that your Enemies, and the Enemies of Ireland are desirous that there should be a breaking out of Tumult, Riot or other outrage. Be you therefore perfectly peaceable. Attack nobody, Offend nobody, injure no person . . . obey my advice. No Riot, no tumult, no Blow, no Violence.

Finally, on this subject of moral and rational versus violent change, it must be believed that O'Connell will have the future on his side. For his concept of using the legal and constitutional means to create a better order and redress wrongs is in line with the implications of civilized life. And this is true despite his final failure to restrain Young Ireland, the disorders of the next generation, the limited success of Sinn Fein's revolution, and the crimes and disorders of our own time. The O'Connell prescription is, we hope and believe, the ultimate way.

despised, he led, not always unsuccessfully, in its controversy with
another nation, the strongest perhaps and the proudest in Europe.

I accept the term but would qualify it with the word
magnificent, for even his excesses demand our admiration.
The characteristics which were suggested by the word
demagogue carried no moral stain. The demagogue, as
the Greeks knew him, was a person who used his talents
in behalf of causes which were of vital concern to masses
of people. To the fastidious mind of Lecky, such vulgar
weapons as were sometimes used by O'Connell were re-
pulsive and obscene. But Lecky was writing half a century
after O'Connell's rise to power and his definition of
statesmanship was a restrained and correct affair which
had already failed to win respect for Ireland over the
generations. His regret that O'Connell, with his acknowledged gifts, should not have been a Chesterfield must be
dismissed, for the times and the conditions and the materials with which O'Connell had to shape a nation demanded a certain lowering of the sights. O'Connell's
words, when he heard of the assassination of Prime Minister Perceval, may not have been those of a statesman of
Lecky's preference, but, as O'Faolain comments, "It was
the kind of talk that the country wanted to hear." †
    In commenting on O'Connell's agitation in the years
before 1829, we must keep in mind that repeal of the
Union was always his ultimate objective, although his
concentration at the moment was to remove the civil disabilities which weighed upon the Catholics. To free the
Catholics to enjoy their civil rights was to give them a
powerful weapon to use in the long war for repeal. For a

† When O'Connell heard of the assassination in May 1812, he included in
his remarks a comment about a poor Irish woman whose boy had been killed
in an Orange clash, and added: "Are all your feelings too exhausted by the
great? Have you no pity for the widow who lost her son? Are her feelings to
be despised and trampled on? Is the murder of her boy to go unpunished? Is
there no vengeance for the blood of the widow's son? Yes! The head of the
government which allowed the blood of that boy to flow unrequited may have
vindicated the idea of a divine Providence."

time the Catholic cause was promoted by the Catholic
Board, which included a few Catholic peers, and several
others, including the young barrister O'Connell. But in
1814 Dublin Castle suppressed the Board and the members immediately reorganized as the Catholic Committee.
The major activities of the Board and later the Committee were to hold meetings, listen to speeches, debate, pass
on resolutions, and prepare petitions which Henry Grattan duly presented in the House of Commons. Completely
negative results followed. The Catholic question languished during those years after Pitt's resignation in
1801, but when he returned to office in 1805, there were
high hopes that because of his earlier position he might
respond favorably to a new petition. This was entrusted
to a highly respectable delegation from the Catholic Committee which appeared before Pitt in London. Pitt dashed
their hopes, saying that he must accede to the implacable
opposition of the King. He would neither present the
petition to the House nor support any other such demand.
In fact, he said that he would oppose any relief for the
Catholics of Ireland. The delegation then turned to
Charles James Fox, a far more sympathetic statesman
than Pitt. Fox presented the petition to the House where
it lost by a heavy majority, and the delegation returned to
Ireland empty-handed.

In the following year both Pitt and Fox died.

In 1807 the Committee met and took under consideration, not only the growing distress which had followed the
Union, but the problem of Catholic Emancipation. At
this meeting it was apparent that the Committee itself was
undergoing change. Old John Keogh, who had been the
leader in securing a large measure of Catholic relief in
1793, had retired to his hermitage at St. Jerome and seldom attended meetings of the Committee. Leadership
then drifted into the hands of a group of young Catholic
lawyers which included O'Connell. Quite naturally these
young men were very impatient with the old routine

which got nowhere. They believed that a more aggressive policy was called for. The stage was thus set for the emergence of O'Connell as the real leader of the movement, not only for Emancipation but for Repeal. In a speech in early 1808 which was a bold bid for leadership, O'Connell first reminded the Committee that under the Convention Act any organization which claimed to be *representative* was prohibited, and that if Dublin Castle should place a ban on the Committee, recourse should be had to what were called "aggregate" meetings, which were in no way representative.

O'Connell's remarks from then on were a forerunner of what was to characterize his methods. He turned to a bitter personal attack upon the individuals who were the responsible government, upon Perceval the Prime Minister, and upon Canning and Castlereagh. His strong language swept aside the old humiliating routine of petitioning and assumed the thrust of a demand. Since patience had been exhausted by a long succession of rebuffs, this new tone—and it was tone and emphasis rather than substance—inspired not only the Committee but the reaches of literate understanding all over Ireland. It was clear that a messiah had risen over the gloom of a depressed land.

In the years from 1808 to 1812, it became clear that O'Connell had risen to a position of leadership which had not been held by anyone in the years before. His name and reputation, in part because of his successes in the law courts, were becoming household words all over Ireland. From then on, the Irish people, even including the most depressed illiterates, recognized O'Connell's primacy. His attack upon individuals was exactly what made his appeal so telling, because as long as the discussion was about issues it had little appeal for the semi-literate masses. But they could understand villains and O'Connell was a master in delineating the people's enemies. From there on it was a duel, with the establishment in

Dublin Castle and London on one side, and the people's champion on the other.

The background of conditions in Ireland spoke even more eloquently of the need for change. O'Connell was able to show that the effects of the Union, which he had predicted in 1800 in his first public political speech, had been more than realized. Hunger and want had been rising among the workers in the towns and cities. Such industry as had existed in the years of the Irish Parliament had languished. Trade with England designed to favor the English had been imposed by the government as a matter of policy. Irishmen bitterly complained about the increased burden of being compelled to pay a share of England's expenses.

In those years his emphasis was upon repeal of the Union with secondary stress upon Catholic Emancipation. The meetings of the Committee were repeatedly harassed by Dublin Castle. Some arrests were made but sentences were light, and with O'Connell's astute legal strategy the Committee was kept measurably within the law. At the opening of the year 1812 the Committee put into effect plans to broaden its base by creating committees in many of the cities and towns over the country. Also, since the Convention Act clearly stood as a bar against anything that suggested a representative group, "aggregate" meetings were addressed by O'Connell and others which were designed to keep the issue of Repeal and Catholic Emancipation constantly before the public, and to pour the virus of protest into every peasant cabin and to instill inspiration, courage, and hope into every peasant heart. O'Connell's speeches were designed at all times to strengthen the spirit of the Catholics without in any way attacking the Protestants as such. He was seeking nationality without division and, as we have seen, the tone of his philosophy was religious liberty for all.

At this point in 1812, a new and portentous figure entered the scene. Robert Peel, the son of a rich textile man-

ufacturer in Yorkshire, had been making something of
a reputation in Parliament and was rewarded by appointment as Irish Secretary. He was only 24 at this time,
thirteen years younger than O'Connell, but with the arro-
gance of youth and the cockiness inspired by this early
bestowal of large power and responsibility he seemed
from the outset to be determined to put a stop to the agitation he had been hearing about. From that time on
Peel and O'Connell were to be for many years the bitter
opponents in a battle, on the one hand to impose the
English will upon Ireland, and on the other to create the
frame and sinews of a new nation. Since Peel's antecedents
and his already well-known prejudices forbade any accommodation, O'Connell immediately personalized the
issue by attacks on the new Secretary. He was referred to
as "orange Peel" from the beginning:

> This youth, squeezed out of the workings of I know not what
> factory in England, who began his parliamentary career by ridi-
> culing the gratuitous destruction of our soldiery in the murderous
> expedition to Walcheren, and was sent here before he got over the
> foppery of perfumed handkerchiefs and thin shoes—a lad ready to
> vindicate anything or everything.

The death of Prime Minister Perceval by assassination
was followed by signs in London which encouraged the
Catholics of Ireland, for Perceval was succeeded by Lord
Liverpool, whose cabinet included at least three members
who were favorable to the Catholic cause. One of these
was George Canning who insisted on the introduction of
a Catholic relief bill. It was sufficiently vague to win support and it passed the Commons but was defeated in the
House of Lords. In Ireland the General Election indicated many signs of growing Catholic strength; Grattan
in 1813 presented the usual resolution, and it carried by
forty votes. Later he introduced a bill designed to carry
into law the terms of his resolution, and this was successful
in the Commons. For a moment it seemed that the road

to Catholic Emancipation was quite open. But a new complication destroyed these hopes. The Catholic bishops had agreed in 1795 and 1799 in their negotiations with the government to allow the King (i.e., the government) the right of veto in appointments to vacant bishoprics. The negotiations in both cases had involved a *quid pro quo*: that is, Catholic Emancipation. George III, however, objected to Emancipation and the right of veto was not agreed to.

At a later date, Canning formulated his plan for Emancipation and included a proposal which would provide a commission composed of Catholic landowners who would have the responsibility of approving or vetoing all such Church appointments. O'Connell considered this to be a thinly disguised form of state interference, however, since the landowning members of the commission would be hand-picked by the government. But in London, Grattan, hopeful in the face of Canning's interest and no doubt anxious to crown his long career with an act of Emancipation, had conceded the veto in the proposal which he made. And yet, the storm in Ireland, in which O'Connell was foremost, turned the tide of opinion against Grattan despite his long service to the Catholic cause. With the members from Ireland firmly against the plan, Canning's bill foundered in the House of Commons.

But the controversy flared again over Grattan's bill. During the absence from Rome of the Pope (Pius VII), who was in France as a virtual prisoner of Napoleon, a faceless functionary named Monsignor Quarantotti presumed to issue a rescript saying, in part, that in the absence of the Pope he had brought the matter of the veto before a special congregation of the most learned divines and prelates, and that he had decided that Catholics might, with satisfaction and gratification, accept the Grattan bill. When the news of Quarantotti's action reached Ireland, the bishops there, strongly supported by O'Connell, raised a vigorous protest. In one of O'Connell's most

powerful speeches, he made a plea for the separation of
Church and State, concluding that he would as soon "take
his politics from Constantinople as from Rome." When
the Pope returned to Rome after Waterloo, he received
emissaries from Ireland and he repudiated the action of
Quarantotti. Consequently, the failure of Grattan's bill
ended the controversy over the veto for a long time.

Shortly after Peel arrived in Dublin, the young man,
apparently anxious to exercise his new powers, began his
attack upon the Catholic agitation by prosecuting certain
newspapers which favored the Catholic cause. The instrument used by Peel for this purpose was Saurin, the
Attorney-General. John Magee, proprietor of *The Dublin
Evening Post,* had published an article which, according
to the government, libeled the Duke of Richmond, who
had recently been made Viceroy. Magee retained O'Connell for his defense. The jury was carefully hand-picked
to provide the verdict wanted by the government. With
the outcome thus foreordained, O'Connell decided to use
his role in the defense to make a thundering attack upon
the government and thus revive the lagging spirits of the
Emancipation movement. It was, he believed, too good an
opportunity to be missed, not only to hold up the Castle
to public ridicule and rebuke but to give the young Peel
a sample of what he must encounter in his new office. The
fact that the poor defendant in the case, Magee, must be
thrown to the wolves did not seem to matter. He was just
a casualty in the fight for a good cause, and it was certain
that he would be convicted anyhow. O'Connell spoke for
four hours, bitterly indicting the personal motives of
Saurin and, by implication, the authorities in Dublin
Castle. The jury, too, came under his lash and at times
the Chief Justice himself.

The sudden boldness of O'Connell's attack and the audacity of his strategy were such that only the most feeble
protests came from the bench. Quite clearly, O'Connell's
purpose was to reach out beyond the courtroom and into

the Catholic population. Read in retrospect, the speech must be ranked with the great philippics of history. It was taken down in full by representatives of the press who were, of course, against any government effort to restrict a free press, and it was published. O'Connell also had the chance to include in his speech the entire text of the article which was the cause of the prosecution. This gave it even greater prominence. For this new publication, Saurin instituted another charge against Magee and this brought about another confrontation with O'Connell. In the interest of brevity, I do not include quotations from this great performance. It is quoted almost in full by O'Faolain and in part by Gwynn, but the comment upon it by O'Faolain is pertinent:

> Everybody, indeed, who regards gracious living, nobility in thought and word and behavior, must read this demagogy with a curl of distaste. Only the vulgar fellows down in Kerry laughed with delight, like the vulgar fellows they were, and whooping their hats in the air, and straightening their backs that had been bent with a century of cringing, cried out that he was their Man. And everybody who had since been able to live in grace and luxury bought by the sweat of these peasants has shuddered at them and at him. . . . Heaven knows, they may well do so, for O'Connell did a great deal to kill gentle manners in Ireland, and to vulgarize and cheapen us. One might even forgive them [the genteel critics] *if there had been any alternative*. The trouble with gentle manners is that they become the justification of injustice.

The true measure of a statesman's words cannot be taken against the standards of a world of peace and urbane living. They must be weighed in the scales against cruelty, injustice, and stupidity in high places.

The violence of O'Connell's language in the Magee trial brought him a stiff rebuke from the venerable Hunting Cap who grew more conservative and cautious with the years. "I have therefore most earnestly to request, and will even add to insist, that you will in future conduct yourself with calmness, temperance and moderation . . .

and . . . will not suffer yourself to be hurried by hate
or violence of passions to use any language unbecoming
the calm and intelligent barrister. . . ." The nephew
answered as always to his uncle with soft words, saying
that the intemperance of Saurin's attack had justified the
response. No doubt Hunting Cap communicated his
worry about Daniel to the Colonel, who was living in
Paris again. He wrote more mildly than his brother, but
with the same admonition. Perhaps the comment of a
modern Irish historian will suffice concerning these warn-
ings. "O'Connell would never have been known to history
if he had taken his uncles' advice." *

Magee's sentence was severe. He was fined £500 and
sentenced to two years' imprisonment. In addition, he was
compelled to post sureties in considerable amounts for
good behavior in the future. Considering the price he
paid, he deserves to be placed among the great throng of
patriots who have served the cause of Irish freedom. The
Magee trial and the conduct of O'Connell had a substantial impact upon the Catholic cause and the opposition to
the Union. It repelled the moderate reformers who had
with such puny results supported the cause for years. It
created a regrettable rift between O'Connell and Grattan,
but it put steel into the backs of the young men who were
to be the future fighters for reform. In today's phrase, it
marked off the men from the boys.

Peel, who had witnessed the Magee proceedings from
a seat in the court, was greatly stirred. He well realized
what a formidable antagonist he was destined to cope
with. This was an Irishman who could with impunity vio-
late all of the amenities of the courts and still escape
punishment. This was a figure who must be confronted
with all the administrative and legislative tools which
Peel in his position could fashion.

After the Magee trial and the temporary resolution of

* Pertinent excerpts from these letters are printed in the Appendix.

the veto question, a casual remark in one of O'Connell's speeches plunged him into a wretched and near-tragic affair which he was to regret forever after. He had referred to the "beggarly" corporation of Dublin, and an obscure member of the Board of Aldermen named D'Esterre took offense. In an exchange of letters O'Connell was given the impression that the hurt feelings had been eased, but D'Esterre was not satisfied. He demanded satisfaction and paraded the streets carrying a horsewhip. The matter ended in a duel in which O'Connell, aiming low to avoid fatally injuring his opponent, lodged a bullet in the little man's thigh which caused a fatal hemorrhage. His conscience was deeply hurt. He wrote to D'Esterre's widow, offering "to share his income with her" but she at that time declined to take money. She did, however, agree to an annuity for her small daughter which was paid regularly for thirty years. Somewhat later he was informed that Mrs. D'Esterre was involved in a court suit in Cork. He appeared in her behalf and won a verdict for her.

Beyond provoking some comment about "murder" among O'Connell's enemies, mostly in England, the D'Esterre affair did not impair the massive reputation of the counselor, but ridicule far more dangerous to a public image struck O'Connell a short time later. This, too, involved dueling and the confrontation with Peel. The complicated details of this affair are not relevant to this account. Briefly, O'Connell had heard a grossly garbled account of some comments about him which Peel had made in a speech in the House of Commons. Without getting the facts straight, O'Connell denounced Peel and challenged him to repeat the comment without the immunity he enjoyed in the House. Peel seemed to lose his head in the exchange and a duel was agreed to. But Mrs. O'Connell wanted no more of dueling in her family and saw to it that the sheriff and two deputies came and arrested her husband during his sleep. The next day O'Connell was bound over to keep the peace with the posting of a bond for £10,000. Peel, who was also the object of Mary O'Connell's complaint, escaped arrest by going to a friend's house. By this time the matter had made the newspapers and O'Connell was subjected to a great deal of public ridicule, especially since the author of his embarrassment was his devoted wife. Following this, the action in the case moved to England and to Ostend, where Peel and his representative went to escape the authorities. In O'Connell's efforts to get to France for the meeting with Peel, he was apprehended in England where he was arrested and brought before the Bow Street Court. There the judge bound him and his friend over to keep the peace. And so the whole affair ended. The comic details of the whole case echoed for years, and O'Connell had to bear the taunts that he had made it easy to be apprehended in England. The matter did not seem to affect the career of Peel.

Only O'Connell's colossal reputation and the ignorance of his Irish public could have survived the repercussions following this absurd affair. But it caused severe damage to his image. A public man can shake off calumny, abuse, and defeat, but he suffers most when he is made the object of ridicule. For many years O'Connell suffered malicious references in courts, in public meetings, and in the press. Moreover, it helped to usher in a period of years when the agitation for Emancipation rested in a stagnant pool of apathy.

For many generations the policies of the government had prevented any growth of manufacturing or the rise of a numerous middle class. The maintenance of Ireland as an agricultural society had suited the convenience and limited vision of a landlord class. Those landlords, many of whom were in England, had permitted a considerable number of middlemen to serve their purposes as collectors. Sometimes there were several of these agents between the actual owner of the land and the peasant upon whose labor and productive capacity the whole system rested. The agent exacted his take for what he collected, and therefore the amount received by the actual proprietor was only a fraction of what had been exacted from the tiller of the land. The harshness of these collectors beggars description. In addition to the exactions in what was called rent, there was the tithe system. The rural population, mostly Catholic, was required to contribute in tithes to the support of the Protestant establishment which it neither respected nor subscribed to, and this exaction was in addition to the few pennies which were given to the churches of the peasants' choice. Under these conditions the peasants had long been living in the most abject poverty. Except on the seacoast where fish were available, the diet was substantially reduced to potatoes with water and a little salt. What they called their homes were mud huts, with little that could be called furnishings, where the family ate, lived, and slept along with domestic animals, sheep, goats, and an occasional cow. In 1825, when there was a select parliamentary committee investigating the conditions in Ireland, it was testified that in some provinces the land allowed to be operated by a peasant was limited to half an acre of potatoes which was supposed to maintain his family from year to year.

After the war ended in 1815, two factors greatly aggravated these conditions. The high prices of agricultural products which prevailed under war conditions suddenly fell, and the rural population had, since the Union, greatly increased. Since there was no industrial life to provide employment, the young men grew up in these miserable families and, when there could be no need for their labor, were virtually thrown upon the countryside where all too often they gave their energies to lawless and marauding bands preying, not only upon their own kind, but upon the property of the landlords and sub-landlords. It would be difficult to imagine anything that might further contribute to the general distress and unrest. But nature in 1821 and 1822 loosed upon the land a failure of the potato crop which meant famine and its inevitable partner, pestilence. In 1825 O'Connell described these conditions before a select parliamentary committee. Under these circumstances it was inevitable that in the years from 1815 to 1823 the agitation for either Catholic Emancipation or Repeal should languish. When starvation looms, any suggestion of civil or religious liberty seems irrelevant.

Meanwhile O'Connell kept busy with his still-growing practice in the courts, in the Four Courts in Dublin, and on circuit, diverting himself on occasion for speeches at special occasions and dinners. In 1822, there came a breath of hope with the appointment of Richard Colley Wellesley (Lord Wellesley), elder brother of the Duke of Wellington, as Lord Lieutenant. Wellesley had enjoyed a brilliant career in various public offices, including considerable time as Governor General of India. He was essentially an enlightened and immensely sympathetic friend of the Irish Catholics, and much was expected of his administration. He remained only until the Duke of Wellington became Prime Minister, for he believed that, because of Wellington's opposition to Catholic claims, he could accomplish nothing in Ireland. He returned as Lord Lieutenant in 1833. In 1822 when Wellesley came to Dublin Castle, he discovered that for years the Irish administration had been under the malicious influence of Saurin, the Attorney-General. Wellesley realized that if there was to be any improvement in Catholic relations, he would have to rid the service of Saurin. He offered him an appointment as Lord Chief Justice and, on his refusal, a peerage. Saurin refused both offers. His preference for retirement was eagerly accepted by the Lord Lieutenant.

8

The Association and
the Catholic Rent

IT WAS EARLY IN 1823. O'Connell, at the age of 48, had
been a member of the bar for a quarter of a century and
during all those years had given lavishly of his time,
talents, and substance to the Catholic cause. But that cause
was sinking into a dangerous apathy. There had been
many petitions to the Parliament in London and all had
failed to move the House of Lords and the King. Grattan,
the faithful channel through which these petitions passed,
was dead. Older leaders, Catholic and Protestant, who
were sympathetic with the Catholic cause, either were
dead or had retired, weary and spent. The peasants who
were concerned with the movement, but more vitally concerned with the pursuit of a bare living after a disastrous
famine in 1821 and 1822, were bowed down beneath what
seemed an inexorable fate.

It is true that at that moment in 1823 there were encouraging signs. Lord Wellesley, an avowed friend of
Catholic Emancipation, sat in Dublin Castle as Lord
Lieutenant, and the execrable Saurin was no longer Attorney-General. By a curious chance O'Connell had obtained possession of a Saurin letter indicating that as Attorney-General this old enemy had been guilty of a gross
indiscretion, if not a crime, and O'Connell's exploitation of
this had added disgrace to enforced retirement. It seemed
as if this were a moment for the greatest hope for success. But to achieve the final objective the Irish masses

had to be stirred out of their apathy. O'Connell, the utter realist, realized that something must be found to arouse those millions with a new interest. His mind, fertile and teeming with ideas, suddenly fastened upon a totally new concept to replace the old round of meetings in Dublin. What was needed next was a new plan and also talented people to work with him. To that end he arranged a dinner party to be held at Glencullen, which was close to the Wicklow Mountains. Richard Lalor Sheil, a brilliant barrister somewhat junior to O'Connell, and others were invited. The stated purpose of the meeting was to introduce some of the younger men of promise who might be used in strengthening the agitation. Sheil himself was deeply depressed about conditions in the country, and years later he wrote of his feelings at that time:

> There was a total stagnation of public feeling, and I do not exaggerate when I say that the Catholic question was nearly forgotten. No angry resolutions issued from public bodies; the monster abuses of the Church Establishment, the frightful evils of political monopoly, the hideous anomaly of the whole structure of our civil institutions, the unnatural ascendancy of a handful of men over an immense and powerful population—all these, and the other just and legitimate cause of public exasperation, were gradually dropping out of the national memory. The country was then in a state of comparative repose, but it was a state of degrading and unwholesome tranquility. We sat down like galley slaves in a calm. A general stagnation diffused itself over the national feelings. The public pulse had stopped, the circulation of all generous sentiment had been arrested, and the country was palsied to the heart.

Thus the state of the country at that fateful hour, and this the mood of the most talented lieutenant whom O'Connell was to call to his side in a new and extraordinary adventure. O'Connell demonstrated remarkable judgment in selecting Sheil as his associate in the business he contemplated. He needed a spellbinder whose genius matched his own, for there was a deal of persuading to be done.

In 1823 Sheil's age was 32. He had finished his education at Trinity College and had risen rapidly at the bar.
This had brought him a reserve of capital to sustain him
in a diversion into political agitation. Nature had not been
generous in its endowment of Sheil. Contemporary accounts describe him as small of stature, dark-featured,
with fair hair which was constantly in disorder. His attire
was unkempt. Lecky, who must have known him in his
later years, says that "He was wholly devoid of dignity.
His voice was harsh, shrill, and often rose to a positive
shriek, his action violent, theatrical and ungraceful." His
dress suited his determination to be seen and remembered
as well as heard. His hands were covered with black
gloves. When he came to a climactic moment in his
speech, he would remove the right glove and thrust his
small white hand in a gesture designed to signal a curse
on his country's oppressors. His speeches, many of which
survive, were elegant, flawless in syntax, and replete with
color and imagery. His oratory must have been, in a
phrase applied to Burke's discourse, "half poetry, half
prose." While Sheil, like O'Connell, was prone to exaggeration, he often soared far beyond believable reality for
he knew well that this way with the facts was what the
Irish ear was attuned to. From the most remote parish
priest to the mitered heads of the Church, no short word
would suffice when a longer one was available. I may add
that from my own observation this extravagance prevails
today wherever Irish priests address their countrymen.
The congregation may not know the meaning of the poly-
syllables, but they are proud to be served by men of such
learning.

Mary Frances Cusack writes that Sheil "generally entered the Association meetings while O'Connell was
speaking . . ." and O'Connell, taking note of his presence, would say something like "my eloquent young
friend, whose power and genius are unequaled by the orators of Greece and Rome in the days of their brightest

glory." The Liberator was not to be outdone in his en-
comia.*

When they met at that dinner party, Sheil himself was
astounded at the daring and ingenuity of O'Connell's
plan. The proposal was nothing less than the total organization of the whole population in a vast association, no
longer the proscribed representative body, but a monster
league in which even the lowliest peasant was a constitu-
ent part. The very size and spread of such an aggregate of
human indignation and purpose would create an irresistible force. It would defy the efforts of legislation, for it
was neither representative nor violent in purpose. No law
can indict the totality of a people united. No doubt at this
moment O'Connell's friends propounded the quite natural
questions. How was such an association to be united? Who
were to be the officers and managers of such a mass movement? And where was the money to be found to service
such an organized effort? All these, O'Connell had anticipated. The cement to hold the millions together would be
their common faith, their religion, which was their greatest possession. The priests of that religion would be the
officers, the mobilizing factors to inspire and direct the
immense following. There were also agents who might
supply the intellectual leadership and the source of inspiration which would be needed to carry on the momentum of the masses. These, like Sheil, were already in the
membership of the Irish bar. O'Connell had lost all faith
in the country gentlemen and titled nobility who had
formed the various Catholic boards and committees in the
earlier agitation. The lawyers were, like O'Connell and
Sheil, accustomed and trained in the arts of persuasion in
the courts. Theirs would be the voices of the new demand
for Emancipation.

In the next year, 1824, O'Connell answered the remaining questions about finances for the Association. The

* *The Liberator, His Life and Times.*

membership would support the joint effort by subscriptions. Those who could would contribute a guinea. Every Catholic priest would automatically become an honorary member, and the mass of the people would purchase membership by a very modest contribution of one penny a month—a shilling a year. These dues, called Catholic rent, would be collected by the priests at the church doors of the entire country. The political genius of O'Connell was revealed in his idea of enlisting the priests as the lesser officers who were closest to the rank and file. This concept has been the pattern of political organization which characterizes the operating power of politics wherever it has existed. It is all well and necessary to have the orators and luminaries to provide inspiration and encouragement for the masses, but there must always be the minor leaders who live with the citizenry and who maintain interest in the long periods between elections.

The priest lives with his flock. He is their friend, comforter, and adviser. Perhaps, indeed, O'Connell's concept of organization came from the organization of the Church itself, which for so many centuries had preserved itself despite all the vicissitudes which it had faced, even in the days when there was corruption at the very top of the Church organization. Thus the Church survived, as the old hymn said, "fire and sword" and also despite the sins of its own major leaders. Throughout, there was the dedicated zeal of the little people far down the line. As might be expected of any plan so bold and so unlike earlier patterns of agitation, there were during the first year discouraging signs of doubt. There were some who sneered at O'Connell's visionary plan of redemption by a penny a month. But O'Connell himself was undaunted and simply pressed his efforts with characteristic energy. Moreover, there were powerful reinforcements. Foremost among these new supporters was Dr. "J. K. L." Doyle who, at the age of 32, had been appointed Bishop of Kildare and Leighlin. When O'Connell organized the Catho-

lic Association, Dr. Doyle wrote a letter to the Lord
Lieutenant (who might have known of the prelate because of the help he had given to Lord Wellesley's
brother, the future Duke, in the Peninsular campaign),
vigorously supporting the right of the Irish Catholics to
strive for civil as well as religious liberty. This was regarded as a sensational development, since Doyle became
the first high officer of the Church to take a position in
this agitation. The Doyle stand had a great deal to do with
enlisting the priests in the new Association.

The income from the rent increased to several hundred
pounds a week. In 1825 *The Morning Register* was established by Michael Staunton and it vigorously supported
the Association. O'Connell permitted the Association to
provide a subsidy for this newspaper but, because of the
danger of legal complications, such as libel suits, would
not permit it to become the official organ of the movement. *The Freeman's Journal* and *The Dublin Evening
Post* (both Protestant newspapers) also carried the news
and official releases of the Association to all parts of the
country.

Meanwhile the center of interest in the Association,
the team of O'Connell and Sheil, moved over the country
stirring the embers of interest in Emancipation. The
burden falling on these two orators was heavy, but the
response was enormously stimulating. The movement and
its progress in Ireland excited great concern in the government in London. Peel was now Home Secretary and
the reports he received of the activities of O'Connell,
Sheil, and Doyle were most disquieting. But the unique
nature of the Association presented Peel with a serious
problem. Earlier methods of suppression were some years
old and were aimed at an entirely different type of agitation. The total situation had been undergoing change.
The population was growing (it was near seven million),
and so were new methods of education. A considerable
middle class had appeared, despite the depressed econ-

omy. Peel's own Tory party was showing signs of division about Irish policy. He could be safe in counting on the firm support of only the House of Lords and the King. Wellington before assuming the post of Prime Minister in January 1828 held high military authority, and in his advice to Peel he said that, although the growth of the Association might lead to civil war and was, therefore, a cause of deep concern, any effort to suppress such an aggregate of numbers and excited interest might lead to an even worse situation. Peel, confronted with doubtful support in his own cabinet, was led into a gross blunder. Under Peel's orders to find a way to prosecute O'Connell, the Attorney-General brought a charge based upon a comment by O'Connell that, unless concessions were soon offered, the Irish movement might produce "another Bolivar," the South American patriot and hero. It was a fragile case for, after Bolivar had succeeded, his revolutionary government had been recognized by the government in London. At the preliminary hearings, the reporters who had been present when O'Connell made the reference were stricken with a loss of memory. So the jury threw out the charge and found no indictment.

This futile effort of Peel's ended in even greater popularity for O'Connell's cause. The Association adopted strong resolutions declaring its conformity with the law and complete loyalty to the crown. It was also decided to send a delegation to plead the cause of Emancipation at the bar of the House of Commons. O'Connell and Sheil were the centers of interest in that delegation. This mission, for a time, met greatly encouraging signs. As the two delegates traveled through the country on their way to London, there were joyful greetings from friends of the Catholic cause. Gwynn notes that the theatrical instincts of O'Connell fully rose to the occasion. He "sat on the box of the landau, enveloped in his great cape, making himself deliberately conspicuous everywhere."

In London they were greeted by many of the radicals:

Cobbett, Sir Francis Burdett, Brougham, and Sidney Smith. They visited the House of Commons and, according to the letter O'Connell wrote to his wife, he was not greatly impressed. They were invited to appear and testify before an inquiry into the state of Ireland, conducted by the House of Lords. At this hearing, Bishop Doyle joined them. Two of the lords arranged a public meeting at which the Irish orators evoked great enthusiasm. The English Catholics seemed to have been won over to the Irish cause, and O'Connell's letters home reflected a joyful expectation that Emancipation was all but assured. But several weeks passed and Daniel ultimately found that, though many people seemed to be quite amiable and friendly, these were not the people who were to make the final decisions. The people at the top were still irreconcilable.

But there was sufficient courtesy to keep their hopes alive. At a levee of the Duke of York's, the Irishmen were treated with courtesy and O'Connell's hopes reached new heights. But he failed to anticipate that a month later that same Duke of York, heir to the throne, would say in a sensational appeal to the House of Lords:

> The Roman Catholics will not allow the Crown or Parliament to interfere with their Church. Are they nevertheless to legislate for the Protestant Church of England? I have been brought up in these Protestant principles, and from the time when I began to reason for myself, I have entertained them from conviction; and in whatever situation I may be placed in life, I shall maintain them, so help me God.

When royalty speaks, the Lords listen. And so the bill was thrown out.

O'Connell returned to Dublin, sad and disillusioned. To make matters worse, the concessions he had offered in London raised criticisms among his supporters at home. He faced an altogether unfriendly meeting of the Association. But a new demonstration of his skill won him back the old popularity. In the bill prohibiting all Catholic organizations, he found a means of saving the Association from extinction. Peel had permitted a loophole to be included in the law. It exempted purely charitable organizations to carry on. So O'Connell proposed that the Association's purpose be restated in its name. Henceforth the new Association was specifically dedicated to education and charity "and all purposes not prohibited by law." The money in the Association's treasury was saved and the newly named Association entered upon a fresh and vigorous life. O'Connell, Sheil, and others addressed innumerable meetings, and the enthusiasm for Catholic relief mounted to new heights.

While O'Connell and Sheil were preparing for their mission to London, the news came that Hunting Cap, at the age of 96, had died at Derrynane. Under his will, the punishment inflicted upon Daniel for rejecting his uncle's recommendation of a bride was still in effect, but Daniel was given about a third of his property, including the house and grounds at Derrynane. This, Daniel decided, would be his country home and, by straining his purse to the utmost and borrowing what he could, he added extensively to the old place as an establishment fit to provide him with a place to find recreation and rest and to entertain the people from Ireland, England, and the Continent who, in increasing numbers, were intent upon visiting him.

9

Triumph

THE YEARS FROM 1825, when O'Connell clearly saw that in creating the Association he had loosed an irresistible tide, to the moment of Emancipation in 1829 were the happiest of his life. He and Sheil were getting ever-larger crowds at their meetings, and the peasants who flocked to hear them and the priests who collected the rent seemed to respond to the spirit of the speakers. At those meetings it was felt that the character of the Catholic Association could be made more effective if the leaders wore distinctive regalia. This wearing of uniforms would hint—only hint—at the militancy of the movement. It would, it was thought, meet the eternal human love of pomp and ceremony. The garb was a blue coat with a velvet collar, a yellow waistcoat and white pantaloons. For O'Connell, as a symbol of his leadership, there was a gold button on the shoulder.

The vitality of the movement had one disturbing ancillary effect. It enlarged the numbers of young men who joined secret societies, such as the Whiteboys, Ribbonmen, and the like. Since the violence which these gangs carried on was a constant threat to the legitimate aims of the Association, O'Connell, joined by Bishop Doyle, appealed to Plunket, the new Attorney-General, to increase the means of suppressing this species of outlawry. The growing treasury of the Association made it possible to implement its professed charitable and educational purposes in the new name prudently given the organization. There were established benevolent societies, measures for agricultural improvement, and, above all, subsidies to schools of all kinds and for newspaper publicity. In all this the priests were vigorous agents. The number of members in the late 1820s has been variously estimated by historians. It probably exceeded a million in 1825. Contributions to the rent could reach £2,000 in a single week but only at times of great political excitement. During dull periods the weekly subscriptions fell off. It was now evident, how-ever, that the Association was becoming a government within a government.

O'Faolain speaks of the population, which at that time listened so eagerly to the two inspired missionaries, as sharing in some sort of new hope that Emancipation would directly benefit them: "this army of beggars . . . so defenseless, so without tradition . . . the poor illiter-ate wretches." They could not know that Emancipation would still leave them poor and without the means of a better life, but, since the reform they were hearing about would sweep away most of the dreadful remains of dis-crimination built up over the past, somehow there would be leaders for them. It was inevitable that this vast army of aroused people should turn to political action, and the leaders looked to coming elections as a test of the unity and daring of the people. There were zealous men in many constituencies who were thinking about presenting candidates in opposition to the landlords' members who had mostly served since the Union. Candidates were found in several constituencies, but the most formidable challenge was at Waterford. Curiously, O'Connell had not contemplated a large-scale assault in the general elec-tion of 1826 which followed a dissolution of Parliament. But a friend in Waterford, Thomas Wyse, wrote to him to propose that he stand for election there. Wyse was a young man with a notable family tradition. His wife was the niece of the Emperor Napoleon, the daughter of Lucien Bonaparte. Later Wyse was to become a Lord of the Treasury and, still later, British Minister to Athens.

He was also to write the history of the Catholic Association.

So often in political history, there have appeared families whose economic, social, and political connections and assets have been so powerful as to suggest that to challenge them in their own compound would be regarded as extreme folly. A not inappropriate comparison with the Beresfords of Waterford has occurred frequently in contemporary America. In 1795 Lord Fitzwilliam in Dublin Castle had removed John Beresford from his position as Commissioner of Revenue. Thereupon, the entire tribe of Beresfords rose in such anger as to force Fitzwilliam's recall by London. Thereafter, the Beresford power seemed forever assured. During the twenty years prior to 1826, Lord George Beresford had been returned at every election. The family relations held great estates and as landlords dominated the lives, the livings, and the votes of everyone situated thereon. Beresford's father, the Marquis of Waterford, had always been fairly popular with the tenants, and an ally, the Duke of Devonshire, could be counted upon to throw his voting population into any matter in which the Beresfords were concerned.

O'Connell was so doubtful of the plan that he positively declined the suggestion of Wyse that he be the candidate, so Wyse enlisted a landlord in the area who had shown strong sympathies with the Catholic cause, Villiers Stuart. While O'Connell was not the candidate, his personality dominated the election.

The exercise of power had so far infected the Beresford mentality that its reaction to the challenge was exactly what was needed to ignite desperate, infuriated defiance from the tenants. Lord George's election address attacked the priests, the Association, and "a few itinerant orators" emanating from it. This unwonted defiance might at an earlier time have silenced the clergy, but now the bishop himself came out and defended the Association. Troops were sent to Waterford to keep order but were not activated. Gwynn records a significant incident at the outset of the campaign:

> But at the gates of Lord Waterford's own estate, the villagers of Portlaw joined in the general outburst of popular excitement. The old parish priest had refused to allow the chapel to be used for a meeting in support of Villiers Stuart, lest the tenants might suffer reprisals. But they sent a deputation to the Bishop to order it to be opened and, on their return, crowds rushed down from the surrounding mountains in wild enthusiasm, bonfires were lit on every hill, and the crowd surged round, carrying green branches as a symbol of revolt that had now become a feature of every Catholic meeting in the countryside. The chapel door had already been forced open, and the laborers on Lord Waterford's own demesne ran out from their work to join in the popular demonstration. Fiery speeches were delivered, and the crowds thronged the roads when one of the Beresfords appeared himself among them in a belated effort to canvass his own tenants.

When O'Connell arrived at Waterford as the guest and supporter of Villiers Stuart, he still harbored some doubt that the peasants would defy their landlords, but he soon felt the infection that was spreading over the countryside. This is shown in a letter to his wife, Mary: "We breakfasted at Kilmacthomas, a town belonging to the Beresfords but the people belong to us. They came out to meet us with green boughs and such shouting as you have never heard of." An immense meeting was held at which O'Connell spoke for two hours. He declined the nomination for himself but agreed to serve as Stuart's agent. In this capacity he vigorously attacked the Beresfords and urged the election of Stuart "by the choice of free men." He dominated the campaign which followed. The vote for Stuart was so heavy on the first day of the polling that Beresford demanded that the polls remain open for additional days. But this only strengthened the drift toward Stuart. It enabled the Stuart workers to free many voters who had been detained by the landlords. At the end of the extra days, Beresford withdrew. In American terms, he conceded. But he vowed to have the election annulled because of alleged intimidation by the priests.

A most remarkable feature of this election, aside from the sudden show of independence of the voters, was the sobriety which prevailed among the peasants. The porters of Waterford formed themselves into a patrol to prevent violence and drunkenness. This battle against strong drink was always a problem with the agitation. In the case of this election, the sobriety was the more remarkable because the Beresford retainers had in their desperation tempted the voters with strong drink. During all the excitement, the young Mrs. Wyse, with the blood of the Bonapartes in her veins, paraded the streets with orange ribbons under the soles of her small feet.

This election demonstrated once and for all the release of the tenants from the domination of the landlords. It was too late to stage similar contests in many other constituencies in that general election, but revolts behind Association candidates were staged in Louth, Monaghan, and Westmeath, where they won. Cruel reprisals followed this election. Arrears of rent were called for and some landlords destroyed the peasants' livelihood by turning their acres over to cattle-raising. Forty-shilling freeholders had leases which protected them from eviction if their rent was not in arrears. Since there were many so embarrassed, the Association responded with loans. O'Connell, returning to Dublin, pressed the collection of the Catholic rent and established a new Order of Liberators among lawyers which was dedicated to the legal defense of the more unfortunate peasants. After a short rest at Derrynane, O'Connell resumed his law practice and his work for the Association.

At Westminster a new effort was made in behalf of Emancipation. This was solidly rejected, for the government, despite the ominous warning at Waterford, was as determined as ever to resist the demands of the Catholics. Lord Liverpool, who had been Prime Minister for fif-

teen years, retired because of illness and Canning succeeded him. While Canning was favorable to Catholic
demands, they were not fulfilled because Canning died
in a few months. After a short period of caretaker government, the Irish leaders were confronted with a regime in
which Wellington was Prime Minister, and Peel, in the
House, led the government majority. Lord Wellesley was
succeeded in Dublin Castle by Lord Anglesey. Despite
fears that a Wellington government would initiate new
repressions, the Duke moved warily, and Anglesey, showing some signs of moderation, promoted legislation in
London removing some restrictions upon Protestant dissenters. Meanwhile, in the years after Waterford, the
Association staged aggregate meetings all over the country which were marked by increasing enthusiasm. The
smell of victory seemed to be in the air.

At this point in 1828, Peel, perhaps without realizing
it, opened the way for a climactic show-down with O'Connell in County Clare. He secured the appointment of
his old friend, Vesey FitzGerald, to a high office in the
Tory government. This required FitzGerald to vacate his
seat and seek re-election. This meant a by-election in
Clare, at a moment when the Association was ready for
a decisive test at the polling places. At first, O'Connell felt
no special urge to oppose FitzGerald, who had been a
good landlord and was not ill-favored toward the Catholics. Moreover, O'Connell was not hopeful that an Association candidate would win against so popular a member.

However, the momentum of the Association had grown
so great that several of the Association leaders had decided that the Clare election must be contested. Among
these were three colorful characters: One was a bouncy,
aggressive individual called The O'Gorman Mahan, a
graduate of Trinity College, Dublin, who years later
was to serve as a model for Charles Lever's description

of an Irish duelist. Another was Jack Lawless, once an
Ulster journalist, who had bitterly criticized O'Connell
for his alleged concessions in London in 1825 but who
became a lusty follower. A third character was Richard
Steele, a Protestant, who had earlier joined a quixotic
expedition designed to overthrow the monarchy in Spain.
He was a perfect gentleman, an impractical idealist upon
whom O'Connell in a jocular moment bestowed the title
Chief Pacificator. In the preliminaries and in the canvass
which followed, the histrionic capabilities of these three
characters were put on display. They served to supple-
ment the supreme showmanship of the candidate himself.
Present also, to provide the big words and the beflowered
phrases, was Dick Sheil. As the peasants came trooping
in from the surrounding country with their green boughs
and their shouting and marching, there was put on display
one of the great shows of all time. History was being made
and many seemed to know it, but the underlying solemnity
of the occasion did not deter the participants from having
the time of their lives.

All of the philosophical pondering about democracy
that fills innumerable books and gives employment to a
large aggregation of college professors, preachers, and
politicians, seems to come down to at least one conclusion
—that the idea of people choosing their own masters is
absurd, and that the concept of people making the laws
which they must obey is incomprehensible. This, of
course, is pure democracy. But along with the philosophers there are also the practitioners, who call themselves
statesmen. Their purpose is to make the thing work by
cutting off as much of the power of the people as the people will stand for, and by arranging for constitutions,
representative assemblies, and delegated power. We have
thus been able to live with democracy in a limited form,
but while we do so, we recognize its vast inefficiency. We
rationalize the situation, as Winston Churchill did, by

saying that democracy is full of imperfections but it is better than any other form of government that we have seen.

Be that as you choose to take it.

I have noted that, among all the virtues which the philosophers have attributed to democracy, its immense entertainment value has not been noted. The voters are thrilled by their illusions that, on one day in many, they are monarchs of all they survey. They also relish the sporting exercise of trying to pick winners. The politician–managers enjoy the absorbing game of manipulating the minds and emotions of the masses of people, and a few rational observers enjoy the show as comedy of a more serious sort. If these rational observers are touched by the sentiment of humanitarianism, their hearts are warmed, because the proceedings are providing enough enjoyment to make life livable for so many people who otherwise have a fairly drab existence.

Since I mention that forms of political life are to some degree associated with the business of popular entertainment, I must add that despots from the dawn of history have been concerned with keeping people amused. This induces submissiveness, which makes them easier to manage. Consequently, much of the business of government has consisted of getting up great shows, displays of military might, all with gorgeous uniforms, flags, and other ocular displays. Fascist and communist showmen in our time have put on these displays, which thrill the spectators for the moment who do not realize that they are paying for this with their substance now, and probably with their blood later. Democracy's shows exact no blood from the people who enjoy them, but they pay for it in the incompetent service which emerges from the ministrations of the people who are elected. Moreover, democracy's shows have an added virtue because the people take a small part in the action, such as yelling, arguing, and voting. This has the fancy name of audience participation. And now we have the electronic media so that the shut-ins can at least see and hear the performance.

In their preparation for the Clare election, O'Gorman, Steele, and Lawless tried to persuade a Protestant landlord named McNamara to run against FitzGerald, but he declined. O'Gorman then went to Dublin and while there he heard a suggestion from David Roose, a stockbroker and lottery-office keeper, that O'Connell himself be persuaded to run. Old John Keogh had often suggested that the shortest route to Emancipation was to nominate and elect a Catholic who would, when he presented his credentials at the House of Commons, refuse to take the oath which was derogatory to the Catholic articles of faith. The radical idea of a Catholic candidate at first astounded O'Connell and his friends. But after he heard from O'Gorman that there was an uprising of voters imminent in Clare which needed such a sensational candidate as O'Connell to explode, he agreed to stand and issued an election address which was a stinging attack upon FitzGerald.

Business in the law courts kept O'Connell in Dublin but his "team," Sheil, O'Gorman, Lawless, and Steele made all the preliminary arrangements at Ennis where the polling was to take place. The sensational character of O'Connell's candidacy was well understood over the country. At Dublin when O'Connell concluded his last case in the law courts and was ready to proceed to Ennis, great crowds assembled to "send" him off on his journey. The show was on and the acting began. O'Connell mounted to the seat of his carriage, enveloped, according to contemporary accounts, in his "enormous greatcoat and waving acknowledgements to the crowds." Crowds greeted him at every stop on the long route to Ennis. Experienced political managers know that there are three components necessary to win an election: an attractive candidate, preferably already well and favorably known; a believable issue or issues; and hard work to get the voters to the polls. They had the first two of these, a famous candidate and the issue of issues. The Association, however, had little experience in grass-roots politics, so the workers had to learn from the first. At the Ennis election the workers had to rally voters, some of them far out in the country, organize them into groups, tell them to get leafy boughs to carry as they marched into Ennis. But that was not all. The workers for O'Connell had to see that the voters were housed and fed in Ennis. For this there were set up soup kitchens and billeting facilities for several days of voting. Also there should be vigilant measures to protect the voters from the opposition's efforts to seduce them with strong drink, threats, and persuasion, including bribery, for with their backs to the wall the landlords would refrain from nothing that would preserve their ascendancy. In much of this work the priests were most active. They were indefatigable workers. And for money, the treasury of the Association was drawn upon.

O'Connell's trip from Dublin was marked at every stop by assemblies of enthusiastic people. The priests saw to that. At Limerick, as the summer evening was closing in, there was a procession in which all of the trades of the city were represented, for this election was regarded by all concerned as the climax of years of labor in building up the Association. As dusk fell on the road to Ennis, there were seen the bonfires on every hilltop. It was two hours after midnight when O'Connell reached Ennis but the streets were alive with welcoming crowds. For the Catholic candidate there was no time for sleep, only a few hours' rest in the hotel room before the nominating forms must be filed.

The processions of voters which were coming into the city were not all of O'Connell people. There were landlords other than the FitzGeralds, and they saw the election as a threat to their future interests. There were the O'Briens with Sir Edward O'Brien, who proposed Fitz-

Gerald in a speech saying that, if O'Connell won, the county would be unfit to live in. By a curious turn of circumstances, the member from Ennis at that time, representing the borough constituency, was Smith O'Brien who, as we shall see, figured so prominently in the Repeal movement nearly twenty years later. The hotel where O'Connell was a guest had a platform facing the street, and from this forum there poured forth an almost continuous torrent of oratory. Sheil and O'Gorman vied with O'Connell in invective. Extravagance was the order of the day, and the arts of the demagogue were never more skillfully displayed. FitzGerald, a fairly decent public servant, was compelled to hear the most preposterous accusations against him and his record in Parliament. His misfortune was that he happened to be the sacrifice exposed in the pathway of the fury of a political revolution. O'Connell made the most of the fact that, during Fitz-Gerald's service in the House of Commons, he had successively taken the oath which called certain articles of the Catholic faith idolatrous and profane.

In explanation rather than as a defense of these attacks, it should be said that there are no recognized rules of warfare in a revolution, and this was a revolution, however bloodless. Both sides were, they believed, fighting for incomparable values. In the minds of O'Connell's supporters, they were fighting for freedom from landlord domination. On the side of FitzGerald was the order which they believed promoted peaceful relations and the fostering of the sort of civilized life which they considered best for all concerned. This was a game, however; not of debating points but of the mathematics of majority. Logic had little to do with things in that heated climate. The polling continued over five days and with every count the majority for O'Connell grew and grew. Finally the victory was officially announced and O'Connell, seated on a profusely decorated carriage, traveled the narrow streets of Ennis under a laurel wreath and wearing the ribbon and the medal of the Order of Liberators. Passions having cooled in the more gentle air of victory, O'Connell restrained his language and even apologized for some of the excesses which he had directed toward his opponent. In the long days which preceded the final count, the excitement of religion and national pride had been so great that no other stimulant was needed. Indeed, according to one contemporary account, so effective had been the precautions against strong drink that only one man was palpably drunk. He was O'Connell's English coachman.

The sober conclusion was inescapable: that this election had turned the tide. It proved that nothing now except Emancipation could prevent an explosion which, if unchecked, would wash the country with blood. O'Connell's principle of non-violent constitutional change had so far proved its worth. From then on it was the task of O'Connell to quiet the hurricane which he and the Association had created. To this task he turned his great energies. The alternative which faced the government in London was whether it would aid O'Connell's task of cooling the passions by granting the remedy which the Association proposed.

On the morrow after the outcome of the election at Ennis it seemed, according to O'Faolain's account, that everyone was asking questions. Vesey FitzGerald wandered about the streets of Ennis, asking people, "Where will all this end?" Something like this was puzzling Dublin Castle where certain strange things were happening. Lord Anglesey seemed dazed and somewhat irrational. He wrote a letter to a friend in England, saying that nothing now could stop the complete success of the Catholics. He then gave interviews to O'Connell, accompanied by Lawless, and did nothing to impair O'Gorman's status as a magistrate. He stood helpless while members of his staff consorted freely with members of the Association. Even some of his trusted aides were attending meetings of the Association. Finally when a letter he had written was published, which encouraged the Church primates to continue their agitation, his superiors in London recalled him as unfit to continue.

Peel acted with similar lack of rationality. He gave up his seat and sought re-election in his Oxford University constituency. With bitter irony the University voters rejected him because he had agreed to Emancipation. The future Cardinal, but then an Anglican, John Henry Newman, who as a young man was opposed to Emancipation, helped in the campaign against Peel.

Wellington, who had returned to political life as Prime Minister, faced three choices. He could seek a mandate by resigning with a call for a general election. But he knew that in such an election the Ennis experience might be repeated in nearly every Irish constituency south of Ulster. If he decided to use force to suppress the Association, he knew well the ruthless slaughter which would ensue. In cases like this it was the military leaders who knew best the awful reality of armed conflict. The veteran of the Peninsular war and Waterloo turned from that course and decided to grant Emancipation. Another consideration weighed heavily in the decision made by Wellington–Peel. Half the members of the Commons, the Whigs and the Radicals, were prepared to concede Emancipation; so that, if the government decided to use force, it would be in a very embarrassing position with half of the House in opposition. Furthermore, the return of something like thirty Catholics in the general election, who would then be denied their seats because they would refuse the oath, would make a mockery of proceedings in the House of Commons. Peel, after his defeat at Oxford, found another seat, but his loss of prestige was so great that he met hostile receptions in his new constituency. Inexorable circumstances demanded a further blow to his pride when he returned to his leadership in the House and faced the humiliating business of surrender. We can imagine that Wellington had another strong argument when he told his cabinet of his decision to grant Emancipation. Aside from considerations of avoiding bloodshed, he knew as a military man that he could not be sure of the loyalty of the 25,000 troops stationed in Ireland. The contagion generated by the Association had penetrated the ranks, especially of the soldiers and sailors of Irish birth.

In February 1829 when Parliament met, the King's speech virtually announced Emancipation. In March, Peel introduced the measure, which so many times the devoted Grattan had vainly presented, and after a four-hour speech moved its passage. It carried by a majority of two to one. Only the prestige of the victor at Waterloo forced acquiescence from a sad and sullen House of Lords. The King at first refused his consent but, when Wellington threatened to resign, reluctantly agreed.

There is a story, believed all over Ireland, that the King, after signing the Act, threw his pen on the floor and stamped on it. But another bright legend must yield to the fact: by immemorial custom, the monarch does not sign legislation; his oral consent suffices.

10

The Price Paid for Victory

IT WAS SINGULAR IRONY that the greatest individual price
paid for the victory for Emancipation should fall upon
the man who made it all possible. Here was an act of
government which gave hope and inspiration to millions
and was proclaimed to the world as an act of singular
enlightenment, but carried with it a mean and gratuitous
vengeance upon O'Connell. O'Connell, with most com-
mentators since, always believed it to be the work of his
old enemy, Peel. To say that these were bitter disappoint-
ments and embarrassments to the Liberator would hardly
convey the measure of their importance, for they created
a feeling between the two men which festered in the mind
of O'Connell for all the years of his life.

When he presented himself at the bar of the House of
Commons, the Speaker ruled that the change in the prescribed oath ordered by the Emancipation Act was not
retroactive and that O'Connell would still be confronted
by the old oath which, because it repudiated certain articles of the Catholic faith, he could not take. Therefore,
he was required to return to Clare and stand as a candidate in another election. He would have no opposition
this time but there was considerable time and expense
involved. Also, while the Emancipation Act freed Catholic lawyers to become members of the Inner Bar and
several of O'Connell's juniors were duly admitted, the
honor was specifically withheld from him. Peel apparently let it be known that this direct act of discrimination

was because of the King's objections, but again O'Connell blamed Peel. He was deeply hurt by this. It was a blow to his professional pride. Later the objection was removed but, since he no longer intended to practice law, the honor was an empty one. Edmund Burke had said, many years before these incidents, that magnanimity was the hallmark of the true statesman. In these two petty acts of spite against the man who had defeated them, the Tory party, the King, and undoubtedly Peel himself, lost any moral credit for Emancipation by failing this test. Thus the government admitted that it yielded, not because of considerations of justice, but only because of fear and under coercion. This affront was a national loss which became apparent years later. Since O'Connell always blamed Peel for these acts of discrimination, he was ill-disposed to cooperate with Peel when as Prime Minister in the 1840s Peel was in a position to grant a great many concessions which would have helped Ireland.

O'Connell has been seriously blamed for seeming to agree to the disfranchisement of the forty-shilling freeholders, but he really had no choice. The government had the power to put the disfranchisement bill through, with or without O'Connell's consent. For a while he tried to rally opposition to the bill among the Radicals in England, but he found them indifferent. A meeting in London of the Catholic members (the leaders) of the Catholic Association split on the issue. O'Connell's letters to his wife show that he felt a moral obligation to fight to keep this vote for the freeholders but he also felt that the Catholic Association would be stronger without them. It is true that they had revolted at Waterford and Ennis, but they could scarcely be expected to go on revolting against landlords who had other ways of coercing them. If they retained the vote, they would be liable to eviction for political reasons. One reason given for acquiescence in the disfranchisement was that, so long as the freeholders were subject to coercion by the landlords, they would be a peril to the purposes of O'Connell, for anyone who is subject to coercion is an undependable ally. O'Connell raised the issue in the debate on the Reform bill in 1832 when he asserted in the House of Commons that 190,000 of his followers had been denied the right to vote at the time of the Emancipation. The Whigs, however, were quite indifferent to his appeal. It is true that O'Connell tried to prevent the disfranchisement. This is proved in his correspondence. Probably what he would have liked was the enfranchisement of five-pound freeholders as a compromise between the ten-pound and the forty-shilling freeholders.

Friends of O'Connell, who knew something of the tremendous sacrifices he had made over the years in his fight for Emancipation, were sharply reminded of what the expense of a new election in Ennis would mean in the tangled state of his personal finances. They also realized what his new status as a responsible political leader would mean. As a member of Parliament he would be compelled to maintain another residence in London which, added to the cost of the places in Merrion Square and Derrynane, would be beyond any possible resources which were in sight. So, in 1829 his friends organized a testimonial purse to show the appreciation of his countrymen for what he had done for Ireland. A large sum was collected and given to him. Later, in 1830, it was decided to make this an annual affair. This was called the Tribute, and a devoted friend, P. V. FitzPatrick, agreed to be the collector and manager. The relationship between O'Connell and FitzPatrick during the rest of the Liberator's lifetime is a story of singular love and devotion. O'Connell's letters to FitzPatrick reveal a remarkably moving view of his inner life, his worries, his doubts, and his hopes.*

---

* These letters were published in two volumes in 1888.

The size of the Tribute varied from year to year. At its maximum it amounted to £13,000. Over the years there were contemptuous references to the Tribute by O'Connell's enemies, but its defense rested on the proposition that it served, in the absence of an organized government, to compensate a servant of Ireland for what he was required to do for the nation. Considering what it had to cover, the amount was barely enough for such personal expenses as the maintenance of the households and the entertainment he must provide for the visitors who came to confer with him on official business, and for those attracted by his fame who came from abroad. There was also the expense of maintaining a political organization and paying election expenses for his Irish colleagues in the House of Commons. Members of the House were not paid a salary until Lloyd George's reforms in 1911. In the course of his parliamentary career there was harsh and cruel criticism of the Tribute, but generally he permitted the facts to speak for themselves. However, in 1843 he undertook a complete defense in response to criticism by the English Catholic leader, Lord Shrewsbury:

> My claim is this. For more than twenty years before Emancipation, the burden of the cause was thrown upon me. I had to arrange the meetings, to prepare the resolutions, to furnish replies to the correspondence, to examine the case of each person complaining of practical grievances, to rouse the torpid, to animate the lukewarm, to control the violent and inflammatory, to avoid the shoals and breakers of the law, to guard against multiplied treachery, and at all times to oppose at every peril the powerful and multitudinous enemies of the cause. At a period when my minutes counted by the guinea, when my emoluments were limited only by the extent of my physical and waking powers, when my meals were shortened to the narrowest space, and my sleep restricted to the earliest hours before dawn—at that period and for more than twenty years, there was no day that I did not devote from one to two hours, often much more, to the working out of the Catholic cause, and that without receiving or allowing the offer of any remuneration, even for the personal expenditure incurred in the agitation of the cause itself. For four years I bore the entire ex-

DANIEL O'CONNELL *ca.* 1835
Engraving by R. M. Hodgetts (detail;
reversed)
National Library of Ireland

No. 58 (FORMERLY No. 30) MER-
RION SQUARE, O'CONNELL'S
DUBLIN HOUSE 1809–1847
Commissioners of Public Works in
Ireland

THE REAL POTATO BLIGHT OF IRELAND.

(FROM A SKETCH TAKEN IN CONCILIATION HALL.)

A CONTEMPORARY CARTOON OF O'CONNELL AT THE TIME
OF THE FAMINE

O'CONNELL'S MONUMENT WITH THE DESCENDANTS OF HIS
CONSTITUENTS, DUBLIN, ST. PATRICK'S DAY, 1953

Irish Times

pense of Catholic agitation without receiving the contributions of others to a greater amount than 74 pounds in the whole.

In his memoirs, which were not always kind in mentions of O'Connell, Greville said that O'Connell's dependence on his country's bounty was honorable alike to the contributors and to the recipient. "It was an income nobly given, and nobly earned."

The full measure of FitzPatrick's devotion cannot be appreciated without taking account of the improvident habits of his famous friend. In the light of the record, in the years before 1829, managing the financial affairs of the Liberator promised to be an insuperable task. O'Connell's biographers, even the most friendly ones, mention his worries over money only casually. Perhaps that is because he was always reluctant to have any public notice of his debts, and also because the records of these affairs have until recently been buried in the great mass of his private correspondence. The task of unearthing this information has recently been achieved by Maurice R. O'Connell.* O'Connell's financial troubles began when he was a student in London. His letters to Hunting Cap appealing for funds and promising to be prudent in his expenses are revealing. So are Hunting Cap's letters to him, mostly admonishing economy. Then there was an explosion when Hunting Cap heard that the young counselor, disregarding his uncle's wishes, secretly married one of the daughters of an impecunious physician in Tralee. That, for the moment, resulted in the disinheriting of Daniel.

Real troubles began in 1805 when O'Connell purchased a house in Westland Row, for which borrowing was necessary. Perhaps because of the rapid growth of his family, the great increase in his law practice, and his passion to create an ostentatious image, he moved four years later to

---

* "Daniel O'Connell: Income, Expenditures and Despair," *Irish Historical Studies*, 17, No. 66 (September 1970)

a mansion on prestigious Merrion Square. That the expense of this move was highly improvident is shown by the reaction of his wife, Mary:

> For God's sake, darling love, let me entreat of you to give up this house in the Square if it is in your power, as I see no other way for you to get out of difficulties. If you borrow this money [one thousand guineas] for Ruxton how will you pay it back? . . . I scarce know what I write I am so unhappy about this business.
>
> [O'Connell 259; I 205.]

The agonies of Mary were largely due to her husband's habit of lending money to all sorts and conditions of friends and acquaintances. The rumor spread that the counselor was a soft touch, and with the widening circle of his acquaintances came the widening circle of borrowers. Before long O'Connell's brother James was brought into O'Connell's financial affairs. James was a model of thrift and, while occasionally he made loans to his brother, he constantly admonished him about his loose ways with money. Things reached critical proportions when in 1815 O'Connell came to be involved in the bankruptcy of a Killarney merchant named O'Leary. What made matters worse was that Hunting Cap had warned his nephew about O'Leary and O'Connell went to desperate ends to keep the news of his involvement from the "old man." Somehow, with loans even from the military Uncle Daniel, brother James, and others, the crisis was surmounted, but furious letters from Mary and James indicated the seriousness of the trouble. Mary, while critical of her husband, was not a very good manager herself. There are letters from O'Connell, admonishing her to be more careful with spending.

In 1822 a serious famine in the country and an economic tightness created a crisis in the house in Merrion Square. Mary and her husband were forced to adopt drastic measures of economy. They considered leasing the house but compromised by selling the carriage and horses. Also, for some reason which is not very clear, it was decided that, to save money, Mary and the five younger children should for a time live in France. So, amid much sorrowful leave-taking, she departed with the children. This trip gave plenty of evidence that Mary, despite her advice to Daniel, was a bit of a spender herself. The capricious moving about provoked a warning letter from James to his brother that the sojourn on the Continent was anything but economical. Hence, Daniel wrote to his wife suggesting that she return and find some inexpensive place in the country near Dublin. To this she objected on the ground that living in Dublin was better for her health. She returned and the couple agreed that, if they were to stay in the house on Merrion Square, they would economize—only four domestic servants and no horses and carriage.

Daniel's expectation of a large inheritance from Hunting Cap, according to some of his letters to Mary, accelerated his extravagance. In fact, he inherited something from his father as well as his uncle. Morgan, his father, had been quite prosperous in his store at Carhen. When he died, Daniel received the greater part of the estate. O'Connell had never known what he might expect prior to Hunting Cap's death in 1825, for on occasions when he had displeased his uncle he believed that there would be alterations in Hunting Cap's will. There had no doubt been reconsiderations after mature thought. Finally, when the contents of the will were revealed, there was still some discrimination against the adopted son. After leaving Derrynane and some land to Daniel, he divided the rest of the property into three parts. A third went to Daniel, and the other thirds were left to James and John, Daniel's brothers.

There is an old tradition at Derrynane that Hunting Cap made a division of his property, £52,000 in gold, on the dining-room table. But the records show that this is mythical. The approximately £50,000 worth of his estate, exclusive of land, was in mortgages (money lent to the landlords with whom he did business), rents due but not paid, cattle, sheep, and so forth. The bulk of the landed estate had been made over to Daniel and his brothers in revocable deeds. This meant that, if Hunting Cap changed his mind, he could cancel any or all of these deeds. This was one of the reasons why Daniel had to keep his uncle in the dark about some of his obligations. But Hunting Cap kept control of his estate and its income during his life. He left Daniel all of the *inherited* land (that is, all the land owned by the family since the seventeenth century or earlier), which gave an income of about £1,000 a year. The whole of Hunting Cap's landed estate must have yielded an income of perhaps £7,000 a year. When O'Connell had inherited both his father's and his share of his uncle's landed estates, his income from land alone must have been about £4,000.

It was characteristic of the kindly feelings of the Colonel that, during those years of his distinguished nephew's financial difficulties, he took a keen interest in his affairs. Life in the military service normally provides little in savings, and in the Colonel's case the scanty income was pinched by the revolutionary time in which he lived. But he was still able to make small gifts and loans from time to time. In addition, his letters to his three nephews are full of good advice. With the house at Derrynane available for the entertainment of visitors from near and far, the Liberator's financial troubles mounted. In light of this added drain, the help from the Tribute was a legitimate charge upon the nation.

History tells a great deal of the financial trials of statesmen in those years. Pitt and Fox were constantly hounded by their creditors, who in most cases were compelled to wait until Parliament, as a posthumous gesture, enacted legislation paying off all debts. Burke, another statesman who lived beyond his means, was helped in his final years by a government pension.*

---

* Some intimate light is thrown on O'Connell by a letter from him to Mary in 1822 (O'Connell 953; II 372–3):

"Cork, 8 April 1822

If you had a mind, my darling heart's love, to wring your husband's very soul you could not have done it more effectually than by writing the sweet, gentle, uncomplaining letter I got from you last night. Oh, how could I be so base as to write such a letter as I did to such a woman. May the great God of heaven bless you, is my fervent prayer. I expected that you would have at least reproached me in some degree and vindicated yourself with at any rate some firmness. But I did not know what the complying gentleness of your tender nature is capable of and now to my exquisite satisfaction I find that my own darling thinks she was wrong merely because her husband unjustly accused her. It was this disposition of yours, Mary, that fascinated me in early life and that made me continue your lover for twenty years after I became your husband, and indeed, I love you now more than ever I did and I respect you still more than I love you. I do not ask you any more for forgiveness because it would be doing you an injustice to think that a sentiment of anger could be harboured towards me in such an affectionate mind as yours. I was literally insane when I wrote my letter to you and, darling, I now believe that it is on the whole much for the best that you paid that bill of Hickson's. I perceive by a letter I got last night from James Sugrue that Dr. Wilson's bill lies over unpaid. Let it be so, darling, for a few days longer. You have therefore got from me in half notes between you and James Sugrue £200 and he has got £100 from Roger so that, as you gave him the other £50, you will have only to add £12.10.0 to it. Then, giving your mother £15 . . . you will still have £172.10.0 in hands. Take out of that £42.10.0 for house expenses, it will leave you £130 out of which you will, before this reaches you, pay tomorrow £40—Eyre's bill—and the day you get this, £50 Higgins' bill and you will have £40 towards meeting the bills due on Thursday. I believe my letter of yesterday was erroneous in supposing that Eyre's £40 would not be due until Wednesday. I hope this error will not occasion a protest as in the list I sent I marked down a £40 bill as due the 9th. I will, please God, send you a banker's bill for at least £200. The bills which are to be paid are 9th £40 to Eyre, 10th £50 to Higgins, 11th £58 *with interest* to Mr. Mahon—same day, 11th, £138.10.0 to Dr. Wilson, a *fresh* bill not the one already due, 15th £69.19.0 to Roose, 25th £75 Clongowes Wood payable, I think, to Elliot, 28th £50 to Cooper. All these we must take up. They may not be accurate as to the precise day but they are nearly so. I do not believe any other bill can possibly *call* and there certainly is not one which I should wish to have protested. Believe me, sweetest, to be your more than ever devotedly attached,

DANIEL O'CONNELL

[P.S.] Tell *each* of them how I love them. Tell Dan so twice."

11

Parliamentarian and
Party Builder

WHEN, AFTER THE SECOND ELECTION IN CLARE, O'Connell took the revised oath and entered the House of Commons, he was compelled to adjust himself to an entirely new role. The agitator had become the parliamentarian and statesman. There were those who, without unfriendly eyes, had seen him in action over the years before Emancipation, and who wondered how he would conduct himself in his new environment as a member of the House of Commons, with its venerable traditions, its decorum, its rules and customs, and its discipline. With the remarkable capacity which he had always demonstrated in adjusting to change, and with the magnificent endowment which had made him a master in courtrooms, in the various associations he had dominated, and on the hustings, his adjustment was quick and positive. At 55 he became a parliamentary leader overnight.

He faced a major matter of strategy. What should he do in his new role about Repeal of the Union? For thirty years he had believed that Ireland's single most-important need was a restoration of Ireland's legislative independence. Emancipation was the tool through which Catholics in the government itself might work for the larger end. There was a certain sentiment in Ireland that, now after Emancipation was won, Repeal was just around the corner. However, he was too wise, too farsighted, and too much of a realist to regard Repeal as an immediate possibility. In the fight for Emancipation, the justice of the cause had won the sympathy of many public figures in England. These would not be so sympathetic about Repeal, a question less of right than of political organization. The Tory party would be intensely concerned about yielding. To them the Union was a matter of imperial sovereignty. Whigs and Radicals were also ill-disposed to change.

There was also the question of whether the economic troubles which Ireland had experienced over the past thirty years had all been rooted in the Union. It is true that there had been a decline, but it was chiefly confined to manufacturing rather than to agriculture. And this deficiency had been apparent before the Union. The progress of the industrial revolution in Britain, chiefly fueled by plenty of risk capital and coal, had a great deal to do with the relative poverty of Ireland. The Irish did have some capital, but those who had it preferred investing in land or government securities, rather than risking it in manufacturing. And Ireland had very little good coal. O'Connell may or may not have seen this; if he did, he was not likely to admit it, for he always made the Union the scapegoat for all of Ireland's ills.

O'Connell found after Emancipation that many of his leading allies in the fight before 1830 either were not interested in Repeal or believed that it would be wise not to raise the question for a while. Sheil, who had been so close and helpful earlier, was now a King's Counsel with a growing practice in the courts, and, at least for the present, he wanted a respite from politics. Thomas Moore, poet and man of letters, had been an admirer and friend of O'Connell's in the agitation, but he now told O'Connell that he could no longer support him. When his advice was rejected by O'Connell, he became his enemy and composed a poem, "the dream of those days when I sung thee is over." Also Bishop Doyle opposed Repeal. O'Connell was quite conscious of this loss of support and probably he himself secretly had grave doubts, but he realized that if he dropped all efforts for Repeal it might be very difficult to revive it later. Finally, he had grave doubts about whether the Irish were ready for self-government. His efforts had given them a sense of nationalism but he was quite aware that nationalism alone does not carry with it the practical capacity to govern. Up to now there had been nothing in the Irish cosmos which in the least suggested practice in the use of political institutions. There was no party system, no suggestion of a capacity for lawmaking, and the experience of an Irish Parliament belonged to another generation. In the modern world, since the Second World War, we have seen dozens of new nations spring out of the ruins of colonialism. In only a handful has there been the slightest capacity to create orderly government. Indeed in most of these the people have seemed to copy all of the characteristics of misgovernment without the disposition to regard it important to abide by the rules and customs which have prevailed in the more well-ordered governments of the world.

Since he realized that a frontal attack upon the Union was inadvisable in the early years of his parliamentary career, O'Connell associated himself with many issues of reform which might be achieved under the Union. Abolishing the tithe was one reform which he supported. There was also the necessity of municipal reform, a revision of the poor laws, and a thorough shakeup of the police system. These were all matters of concern to Ireland, but as a member of the imperial Parliament he concerned himself also with many issues which were beyond Ireland. His positions on the many measures debated in England at that time mark him in the forefront of the drift in enlightened thinking which in a few years transformed the Whig party into what later generations came to know as Liberalism. (A change in the name of the

Whig party came with the government of Lord John
Russell in the late 1840s.) His support of the great Reform Bill of 1832 won him many friends in the Whig
party. He expected a reformed franchise not only to help
Ireland but to prove his value to the Whigs. He was disappointed when the details of the Reform gave so little to
Ireland, but his aid in passing it was not forgotten. His
speeches in that memorable debate went far beyond anything contemplated at the time. He argued for real universal suffrage and an elective House of Lords.

He was one of the pioneers in fighting to remove discrimination against the Jews. He spoke at length on
simplifying and codifying the laws in several areas. He
was an early opponent of capital punishment. He supported the abolition of usury laws and agreed with Bentham about the folly of regulating the rate of interest by
law. In one of his speeches he denounced flogging in the
army. Indeed, so prescient were his views that he would
have been quite at home in the American Progressive era
of the twentieth century. We have already noted the
powerful voice which he raised against slavery and the
stir which this raised among the pro-slavery elements in
the United States who were also sympathetic with the
Irish struggle for Repeal. He participated in several of
the debates in the Commons on foreign affairs. He denounced imperial Russia. He spoke vigorously when
Belgium broke loose from Holland. He supported free-
trade measures and joined in the opposition to the Corn
Laws* although they gave preference to Irish producers.

The Whig government which took office in 1830 had
at its head Lord Grey, a moderately conservative Whig.
One of the first acts of the Grey government was to return

* The term Corn Laws was applied to statutes dating back to the reign of
Henry VI which regulated the trade in grain and foodstuffs. Included in such
regulation were restrictions on imports, intended to stimulate and protect domestic agricultural production. Agitation against the restrictions on imports
had for its purpose less expensive and more plentiful food.

Lord Anglesey to Dublin Castle. As already noted, Anglesey's sympathetic attitude toward the Catholics had resulted in his recall by Wellington. That sympathy was soon shown in the Lord Lieutenant's attitude toward O'Connell. The earlier omission of O'Connell from the list of the new King's Counsels was rectified and the promotion was affirmed in London. Anglesey next offered O'Connell the high judicial honor of Master of the Rolls. To accept this honor with the considerable emoluments which came with it would have solved the Liberator's financial difficulties. But it would have withdrawn him from the political arena, so he declined, letting it be known that he chose to continue to serve only one master, the people of Ireland.

In 1830 the resentment felt in Ireland over the injustice of the tithe system broke loose in what came to be called the Tithe War. The institution known as the tithe has a history almost as long as taxation. Tithes were collected in much of the ancient world for the support of religious establishments. In the Roman Church tithes seem to have been a part of ecclesiastical policy as far back as A.D. 796. It was introduced in England before the reign of Henry II. According to Blackstone, tithes were in law "the tenth part of the increase, yearly arising and renewing from the profits of lands, the stock on lands, and the personal industry of the inhabitants." The tax was theoretically on the land. When the landlord took responsibility for paying it, he in turn passed it on to the tenant, collection being made sometimes by the landlord and his agents, and sometimes by the local clergyman, operating through his proctor. To the Catholics this was an unholy, unjust exaction. The resentment against paying for the support of the Established Church was intensified by two circumstances, the ruthlessness of the agents and proctors and the unnecessary enlargement of the (Protestant Episcopal) Church of Ireland. To minister to the spiritual affairs of

the 800,000 members, there were four archbishops, 18
bishops, with many deans and other subordinate clergy
in every diocese, and 1,400 parochial clergymen. This gross
waste was recognized by the Grey government and some
minor reorganization was made in the Church machinery.

As one historian has noted, the Tithe War was a night
conflict. The most horrible atrocities were inflicted upon
the tithe proctors and the landlords' agents and their
property. In one year two hundred murders were reported. O'Connell strongly opposed this lawlessness, because he not only deplored violence of any kind but knew
that these crimes would provide the government with an
excuse for coercion. He was right, because a drastic
coercion bill was passed. With no great hope that anything could be accomplished, he joined Bishop Doyle in
a concentrated attack on the tithe system, which came to
nothing. The tithe issue was part of some legislation between 1833 and 1838, but each year remedial measures
failed of enactment. Each year the Whig legislation provided for some sort of "expropriation," that is, that some
of the proceeds should go to the education of the poor.
Finally, in 1838 a rather unsatisfactory solution was
adopted.

Trouble within the Whig cabinet led to the resignation
of the Prime Minister, Lord Grey, and some of his more
conservative (and anti-O'Connell) colleagues. He was
replaced by Lord Melbourne in a ministry which was
more willing to come to terms with O'Connell. In the general election of December 1834–January 1835 the Whig
majority shrank to fewer than twenty. O'Connell's moment had come. He could now move his band of Irish
M.P.s into a position of power. He offered the Whigs the
support necessary to return to, and stay in, office—for a
price. There was nothing the Melbourne people could do
but agree. From this point substantial gains for Ireland
were realized. Where reasoned arguments had failed and
the claims of justice had been rebuffed, this exercise of

naked power by the Irish members was successful. This was to be the pattern of Irish strategy for the next half-century.*

Despite the disappointment in Ireland when the terms of the Emancipation were made public, there was one solid gain, which was to dominate Irish affairs at Westminster for the rest of the nineteenth century. This was the right of Catholics to enter the House of Commons. This, as O'Connell had perceived for a long time, gave even a small minority of Irish members a considerable influence with any government, unless that government had a secure party majority. And since the balance between the Tories and the Whigs (later the Liberals) was frequently thin, the Irish exploited their advantage very effectively. The Irish Party held the balance from 1835 to 1841, but this was not the only advantage exercised by the Irish Party. In the years before 1830 the Irish representation in the House was divided between Tories and Whigs. And after 1830 there was the same division except for O'Connell's Repeal members. It was O'Connell's objective in creating and strengthening the Irish Party to use it in constituencies where it had no candidate of its own, to swing the election to the Whigs—for a price.

The details of political organization are time-consuming and unexciting. They have little attraction for most first-class minds, for when they are not insufferably boring, they involve a type of scheming which often borders on conspiracy. Perhaps that is why so many rather inferior characters rise so high in a party organization. It is also why more people with character and intellectual

---

* In 1833 the sad news reached O'Connell that his namesake and friend over many years, the Colonel, had died at the ripe age of 88. The end came in Paris, the scene of his early triumphs. In the course of his long life, he had won many honors and many titles. He was called by several of these, Colonel in both the French and the English armies. When he died, he had become a Lieutenant General in the French Army. He was also the oldest Colonel in the English service. He had been a faithful counselor and financial benefactor to his famous nephew throughout the years since the Revolution. At all times his effort was to moderate Hunting Cap's impatience with the extravagant nephew.

ability should be encouraged to enter political organizations. For democracy decrees that our government shall
be no better than the average level of the party organization which elects the people who govern us. It is also true
that, since the detailed work of party organization is so
colorless, not to say boring, people who write about politics avoid writing about it. To a journalist the story of one
petty scandal is worth a hundred accounts of how votes
are cast and how voters are induced to go to the polls.
Readers are not interested in such details. Hence historians and biographers, who are reporters of a sort, are
reluctant to cram their pages with dull stuff. That again
is a condition which lowers the level of government. For
the reading public does not know—or if it knows, it is
likely to forget—the primary fact that in those details is
determined the way in which we are all governed.

To O'Connell, however, the maintenance of a strong
party organization in Ireland was of the utmost importance, not only to the future of Ireland but to what he was
doing at Westminster. Hence he never shirked the tremendous labor of party building. He has, indeed, been
called the historical forerunner of the modern political
boss. While most historians and biographers give us nothing about the building of O'Connell's Irish Party, we
have one exception. Angus MacIntyre, in his book about
O'Connell's years at Westminster, *The Liberator,* has
given enormous labor to the reconstruction of the story
of the creation and development of the Irish Party, and
he supplies this information with almost suffocating detail. The Irish Party responding to O'Connell's dictation
first appeared in the 1832 election. Candidates were found
in a considerable majority of Irish constituencies except
the 22 in Ulster, and they were directed against the traditional members who were either Whig or Tory but were
generally from the landlord class. Under O'Connell's direction, a pledge was devised which all candidates sup-

ported by him were required to take. It was a pledge of allegiance to Repeal without qualification or conditions. It is true that many other issues were involved and supported by candidates, but Repeal was the central and cohesive element which held the party together. Thus in the election of 1832 O'Connell created the two essential factors in Irish politics which were to prevail for all the years of the nineteenth century. First, a distinctive Irish Party sufficiently independent to stand between the Whigs and the Tories and to exact concessions and advantages; second, the creation of the cement which held the party members in line—the single issue of Repeal.

The Irish Party under Parnell and later under Redmond thus built upon foundations created by O'Connell. The term Repeal was replaced by Home Rule, but for practical purposes the two expressions meant the same thing. It was at all times from 1832 forward the result of O'Connell's shrewd judgment that this was the only way to prevent the Irish strength from being divided between the Whigs and the Tories. In short, O'Connell created a weapon which was to serve as a means of advantage to Ireland. The numerical strength of the Irish Party was revealed at the 1832 election: there were 39 Irish Repeal members returned, all substantially under the leadership of O'Connell. In the election of 1834–1835, a little over two years later, the Repeal pledge was not so prominently expressed but it was fairly well understood. This election, and the subsequent Lichfield House Compact, showed O'Connell's political genius. Where he saw that a Repeal candidate could not be elected, he did not enter a Repealer but bargained with the Whig candidate. If the latter was fairly agreeable to a bit of mutual backscratching, O'Connell gave him what help he could without publicly endorsing him, and in many cases that private help was enough to elect him. Thus the actual power which O'Connell was able to build up in Parliament was greater

than what the numerical strength of his party in itself
might have been able to muster.

The maintenance of a healthy party organization in
Ireland threw upon O'Connell an immense addition to
his duties as a member in Westminster, for it was necessary to find money for the election expenses of many of
his party members, make speeches in their behalf, and
keep acquainted with conditions in many constituencies.
He had some help in this work at the local level, but not
much. His personal touch was nearly always demanded
and mostly given. A most vital part of O'Connell's political machine was the Irish press. It is amazing to consider
how many newspapers were supported in so poor a country. In Dublin alone there were ten newspapers, and in
every considerable town over the country there were newspapers and editors to be included in all political calcula-
tions. Of the thirteen provincial newspapers, five or six
were strongly nationalist, which meant mostly pro-O'Connell and Repeal. In Dublin he controlled at least three
including *The Pilot*. Tight rein was kept on newspapers
which were receiving favors from the O'Connell organization. These favors were payments for publishing notices of meetings, party resolutions, political speeches,
anonymous articles, and other material. Occasionally
there was a direct subsidy in money. In this business of
getting and keeping newspaper support O'Connell had
to be autocratic and often, by modern standards, ruthless.
However, his opponents in government had no scruples
at all in their dealings with the press.

During the period of the Whig alliance—1835-1841—
O'Connell's party in the Commons averaged fewer than
25. The exact figure is hard to fix for there were various
degrees of attachment. Some of the members of it were
substantial landlords able to procure election on their own
steam: O'Connell might lead but he could not dominate
them. Close to him and acting on his instructions were

his three sons, two sons-in-law, a brother-in-law, a nephew, and a couple of cousins, though they were not all M.P.s at one time. Bringing so many of his relations into Parliament has given rise to the accusation by some historians that he was trying to elevate his own family. Such was not the case. His purpose was to have as many M.P.s as possible whose votes he could command.

As already described, the reduction of the Whigs' large majority to a mere 15 over the Tories made it necessary for them to seek O'Connell's support and cooperation. Consequently, Lord John Russell and other Whig leaders held two meetings with O'Connell in March and April 1835 at the London home of Lord Lichfield. They were amicable meetings in which good will was born of mutual necessity. The agreement (or agreements) entered into— which came to be known as the Lichfield House Compact —was not committed to paper, for practical politics demands that such "deals" be oral and capable of change or denial if misunderstandings should arise. Melbourne himself, for prudential reasons, was not present, and he was thus left free to deny publicly later that he had made an agreement with O'Connell. The particulars of the compact were never explicitly stated by either of the parties concerned but it is safe to assume that they comprised a commutation of the tithe with the greater part of its yield being applied to the education of the (mostly Catholic) poor; a reform of the municipal corporations; an extension of the parliamentary suffrage; a reform of the police; and the appointment of Catholics and liberal Protestants to government office and the judiciary. O'Connell, as his side of the bargain, agreed to drop the Repeal campaign for the foreseeable future, to cooperate with Dublin Castle, and to support the Whig government in the House of Commons and in elections in Irish constituencies where no O'Connellite candidate happened to be standing. This unwritten arrangement, which Lord John Russell later described as "an alliance on honorable terms of mutual co-operation," was to prevail for six years. Those years were not fruitless, as O'Faolain suggests, but favorable to the Irish cause in many ways short of Repeal.

The creation of the Irish Party and the alliance with the Whigs exposed O'Connell to much more criticism than he had suffered heretofore. He had always been attacked in the English press but the new power he held provoked an intensification of those attacks, some of them descending to the level of scurrility. Leading the attack was the London *Times*. Over many years in that century *The Times* was viciously partisan, and took great liberties with the law of libel. It eagerly seized upon pure gossip and innuendo to smear O'Connell, and published 300 editorials about him, some of them bordering on hysteria. Later in the century it was to charge the Irish leader, Parnell, with complicity in the Phoenix Park murders on the basis of forged letters which it made no effort to investigate, acting on the assumption that any charge leveled against an Irish nationalist leader must be true. In the case of O'Connell *The Times* violated not only taste and truth but the elementary test of good writing. An example of what it printed about O'Connell is this schoolboy doggerel:

> Scum condensed of Irish bog!
> Ruffian, coward, demagogue!
> Boundless liar, base detractor.
> Nurse of murders, treasons factor!
> Of Pope and priest the crouching slave.

and so on for 34 lines.

The Times made the most of a fantastic charge made by a Cork actress named Ellen Courtenay. While in a debtor's prison in London she wrote and circulated a pamphlet accusing O'Connell of being the father of her fourteen-year-old son. The late Professor Denis Gwynn investigated this issue and wrote a monograph on it. He reached the conclusion that Ellen Courtenay's charges were devoid of credibility.*

In the well-known exchange of vituperation between O'Connell and Disraeli, *The Times* was a happy confederate of the future Tory leader. This verbal brawl should not merit much space for it reflects no credit for either statesman, but as an example of what sometimes passed as political dialogue in those years, it serves a purpose. The trouble originated in 1832 when Disraeli was first a candidate at Wycombe. A mutual friend asked O'Connell for a letter endorsing Disraeli. O'Connell complied with what was routine stuff in politics. Fully to understand the quarrel—which, as we consider it in retrospect, seems unreal and preposterous—it should be remembered that in 1832 Disraeli was a young man of 28 years. This was his first attempt to enter politics. He was also, even at that age, struggling to attract attention, sometimes by the most gaudy and shameless means—by bizarre personal adornments and by gossipy and sensational writing. The later attacks on O'Connell, which went far beyond what the argument should require, were to create the image of a giant killer, for O'Connell in 1835, when the real heat of the battle erupted, was sixty years old and an international figure. Also in 1835 when Disraeli was running as a Tory, attacking O'Connell and the Catholic Church was bound to appeal to the Tory establishment and the large landowners who were always the chief supporters of Disraeli.

---

* American experience and contemporary observation prove that with rare exceptions any political figure who rises above a fairly low level of note is the victim of charges of sexual irregularities. The extent to which the great part of such accusations is pure fiction is as well known to the public as the charges themselves. Hence they generally do little harm to the victim and are only in extreme cases answered. A politician of large experience once advised a young politician whom I happened to know to ignore such things, "because your enemies will believe anything, your friends nothing, and 98 per cent of the public will forget it—unless you try to answer it." Since O'Connell was such a towering figure in an age where so little restraint was observed in character assassination, the very fact that no firm evidence against his personal conduct survives is the best possible proof that none existed.

At Wycombe in 1832 Disraeli was running as a Radical. He was defeated at this first trial and again at a second candidacy. Then he had the audacity to change his party colors and run as a Tory. He lost again at Wycombe and again at Taunton. Finally he was elected in another constituency. When campaigning in the Taunton election, he made some remarks about O'Connell which were by mistake attributed as his personal opinion although his reference was to what some Whigs had said about O'Connell. Unfortunately O'Connell did not check the facts but launched a fierce attack on Disraeli. Included in the O'Connell attack were several fighting words like "liar" and "ingrate." In the interchange certain expressions of religious prejudice were exchanged which both men must have regretted later. O'Connell likened Disraeli to the "Impenitent thief on the cross whose name I verily believe was Disraeli." Disraeli responded with an attack upon the Catholic Church: "I know the tactics of your Church. It clamors for toleration and it labors for supremacy." He then taunted O'Connell for receiving the Tribute collected by the priests. "I am not one of those public beggars that we see swarming with their obtrusive boxes in the chapels of your creed, nor am I in possession of a princely revenue, arising from a starving race of fanatical slaves."

Disraeli, instead of ending the wretched brawl, came back to the subject of the Catholic Church later. *The Times,* which delighted in this sort of controversy, gave the freedom of its columns to more of Disraeli's articles which the author signed "Runnymede." In one of these, which Robert Blake, Disraeli's latest and best biographer, calls "Disraeli nearly at his worst . . . , [he] reaches depths of verbose invective. . . . O'Connell is the instrument of the Papacy; he is a more terrible enemy of England than Napoleon." In another passage Disraeli says that he cannot agree with the people who accused O'Connell of hypocrisy in "humbling himself in the mud before a simple priest," since

> There was no hypocrisy in this, no craft. The agent recognized his principal, the slave bowed before his Lord. When he pressed to his lips those robes, reeking with whiskey and incense, I doubt not that his soul was filled at the same time with unaffected awe and devout gratitude.

12

Fruits of the Whig Alliance

AFTER THE 1835 ELECTION, O'Connell was quite able to shrug off the attacks in the Tory press and the assaults of his enemies in the House, for the gains for Ireland as a result of the Lichfield Compact were already coming in. Lord John Russell was Home Secretary in the Melbourne cabinet and his shrewd appraisal of the Irish question told him that a very large part of the problem could be solved by getting more sympathetic administrators in Dublin Castle.*

To carry out his policies of reform in Dublin Castle, Russell chose Lord Mulgrave as Lord Lieutenant, Lord Morpeth as Chief Secretary, and a remarkable man, Thomas Drummond, as Under Secretary. "Neither Mulgrave nor Morpeth was a nonentity, and he [Drummond] could have accomplished very little without their encouragement and support, but it was his enthusiasm, his

---

*Lord John Russell was already well known as a friend and supporter of enlightened measures for civil and religious liberty and for his understanding of Irish affairs. Before Emancipation he had once lost his seat in an English constituency because of his support of Catholic Emancipation. He was rewarded by election in an Irish constituency. He led the attack against the Test Act in 1828. In Lord Grey's government he carried much of the responsibility for managing the Reform bill in the House of Commons. In 1833 he visited Ireland and while there formed the opinion that drastic changes were needed in Dublin Castle. In addition to his position as Home Secretary in the Melbourne government, he was leader for the government in the House of Commons. After the resignation of Peel in 1846, he formed a ministry and remained at the head of affairs for six years. During the American Civil War he exercised a powerful influence in restraining England from taking sides in the conflict in the United States. His literary works cover a wide variety of history, biography, and fiction.

knowledge, above all his unremitting labour, that made possible the rapid transformation of the administrative system," is the comment of J. C. Beckett in his (in many ways, the best) history of modern Ireland.† Beckett has this further comment:

> Drummond was a Scotsman, but his employment on ordnance survey work had made him familiar with the Irish countryside. He had been profoundly impressed by the wretched conditions in which the majority of the peasantry lived, and it was to this wretchedness that he ascribed the prevailing contempt for the law. He fully shared the distaste of English liberal opinion for government by coercion; he saw that the only feasible alternative was to create popular confidence in the impartiality of the administration; and many of his most important measures were directed to this end.

In 1836 Drummond reorganized the police in the capital as the Dublin Metropolitan Police Force. He followed this by establishing the police in the rest of the country as the Irish Constabulary (later to be named the Royal Irish Constabulary or R.I.C.). He recruited Catholics to the new forces at all levels so that, soon, some 25 per cent of the officers were Catholic, an enormous step forward in giving justice to the Catholic population. This reorganization meant bringing the police under direct government control and freeing them permanently from the influence of local landlords and, in Ulster, from that of the Orange Order. Henceforth the police were an impartial body, and the Catholic population was rescued from a major injustice. Drummond buttressed this reform by increasing the number of stipendiary magistrates and by adding many Catholics to their number. Being directly under the control of the government, these local judges were comparatively free from the prejudices and influence of the landlord class. He added considerably to the number of Catholics and liberal Protestants among the unpaid mag-

† *The Making of Modern Ireland, 1603–1923.*

istrates, and had some of the more bigoted champions of Protestant ascendancy removed from the bench.

This Mulgrave–Morpeth–Drummond administration went further to make Emancipation a reality by appointing Catholics to the higher levels of government service and to the judiciary. Michael O'Loughlen was made Attorney-General in 1835 and a chief judge in 1836, the first Catholic to be elevated to high office since the reign of James II. Drummond showed great courage early in his period in office by moving against the Orange Order. He helped to have it made illegal, prohibited all Orange demonstrations, and dismissed magistrates of known Orange sympathies. Since its foundation in 1795 the Order had used its influence with landlords and magistrates and with the police to deny justice to the Catholics in Ulster. With Drummond's reform of the police and his impartial application of the law the power of the Order was broken for more than a generation.

The Lichfield House Compact—that alliance between O'Connell and the Whigs—which was responsible for establishing the Mulgrave–Morpeth–Drummond administration, was belittled by the Young Irelanders a decade later. That they could afford to belittle the Whig alliance was a proof in itself of how effective that alliance had been in giving Catholics security and "a foot inside the door." They claimed that only a small number of prominent Catholics benefited. That was not true. Catholics were appointed at all levels of government service. In 1840 the parish priest of the small town of Mallow, County Cork informed O'Connell that the people of Mallow were ready to "shed their blood" for the Whig administration. The people of Mallow were not likely to "shed their blood" for any administration unless they were getting something out of it.

In a letter to me Professor Maurice O'Connell notes that some of O'Connell's biographers have accused

O'Connell of having secured an excessive number of jobs for his relatives. He says:

> This needs to be straightened out. The jobs obtained were two stipendiary magistracies and the Clerkship of the Hanaper for his three sons-in-law, and the Registry of Deeds for his son Morgan. The total income from the four positions was about £3,200, which was less than half of the income he received from his practice at the bar in the last year before he gave it up. The Mastership of the Rolls, a position he refused, was worth about £4,000 a year.

In 1838 an act was passed which for the time removed the tithe issue from O'Connell's immediate concern. It was not a resolution of this obvious injustice but it removed some of the more obnoxious practices connected with its collection. Under this solution, tithes were to be converted into the fixed rent charge and were to be paid by the landlord instead of the tenant. This eliminated that most detested petty tyrant and swindler, the tithe proctor. O'Connell supported the bill because he realized that the government was too enfeebled to pass anything better. The fundamental injustice of compelling Catholics to contribute to the support of the Established Church remained. The tenant realized that he was still supporting the rival Church, but he was finally resigned to pay this price to be rid of the proctor.

In the long debate on revising the Irish Poor Law, O'Connell found himself in distinguished company. The array of talent which addressed itself to the eternal problems of the distribution of the world's goods, the growth of population, and the relief of the poor would compare favorably with what we have seen in our time. There were Bentham, Malthus, the two Mills, James and John Stuart, and Nassau Senior among the outstanding economists. There were Bishop Doyle and Archbishop Whately, in addition to statesmen such as Peel, Stanley, and Lord John Russell. There were several public, private, and ecclesiastical commissions, of which the most famous one was headed by Archbishop Whately. All these people were contemporaries of O'Connell's. Some, like Bentham, had made a positive impact upon his thinking.

Americans, who are professionally concerned with the problem of poverty, might find it interesting and profitable to examine the enormous literature which appeared in those years. They will find that there is scarcely any phase of the problem which was not debated at that time, and many of the plans for poor relief put forward anticipated in many respects what has been proposed here in the decades beginning with the great depression of 1930–1936.

For example, Bishop Doyle advocated large-scale government-promoted emigration; also a massive (for that time) expenditure of government money on job-producing public works. Nassau William Senior, a close associate of Bentham's in his earlier years and an economist who should rank with some of the more famous names I have mentioned, opposed a general poor law for Ireland. He favored, however, medical treatment for the near-blind and the crippled, the chronically infirm and the "mad," but opposed relief for the able-bodied poor. His opinion was that all poor laws hitherto tried discouraged industry, self-help, and mutual benevolence. A supporter of the Poor Law, Lord Clements, published a very interesting pamphlet which argued for cutting some of the large landed estates into small, privately-owned, one-family farms, presumably by lending government money to compensate landlords, the loans to be repaid by the tiller of the land. This idea was followed by other reformers including John Stuart Mill.* Thus this period was teeming with enlightened and humane ideas, but so far the reform was political. The people whose land was to be divided were securely entrenched in both Houses of Par-

---

* A variation of this plan was carried back to China by the reformer Sun Yat Sen, and has been put into operation by the Chinese who took over Formosa in our time.

liament. There was also a powerful sentiment among
many people, like Bentham, against any interference with
the economy. To a certain degree this was the opinion of
O'Connell.

A landmark in the discussion and debate over the Irish
Poor Law was the appointment of what was known as
the Whately Commission. Richard Whately was the
(Protestant) Archbishop of Dublin. His commission
labored from 1833 to 1836 and produced, not only a plan
for poor relief, but a masterly treatise on the economy of
Ireland. It had, however, taken so long in its fact-gather-
ing that the government, tired of waiting, sent another
investigator to Ireland who disagreed with the Whately
recommendations. The Cabinet then decided not to wait
and adopted a plan modeled after the English Poor Law.
O'Connell's position on the Whately and other plans was
vague and ambiguous. From an examination of the available information on the subject, it seems that he quite
definitely favored some sort of relief for victims of catas-
trophes, for the seriously ill and the helplessly infirm; also
some sort of public works as a stimulant to employment.
To a large extent he followed Bishop Doyle. Finally Parliament adopted a bill which was substantially what the
government had favored in the beginning. No one was
greatly helped and no one was happy about it.

In June 1837 King William IV died and the young
Victoria became Queen. In his public life O'Connell had
lived with three of the Hanover line of sovereigns and
had no reason to respect any of them, for all three were
bitterly anti-Catholic, anti-Irish, and anti-O'Connell. But
at all times he had sworn allegiance to the throne. Now,
however, he could associate his respect for the throne
with a lively admiration and affection for a young and attractive woman. The book which he wrote about Irish
history is dedicated to the Queen, and when the Repeal
Association was formed, he ordered printed on the membership cards "God save the Queen." He said shortly

after her accession that the Queen was angry with the Tories and would not let them come to power again. In this he was not entirely mistaken.*

Despite the solid success of the alliance with the Whigs and the improvement of conditions in Ireland, O'Connell was suffering from periods of deep depression. These dark moods were reflected in his letters to the devoted FitzPatrick. As he moved into his sixties he was beginning to feel the effect on his body and mind of the many years of heavy responsibilities and incessant labor. His depression was deepened in 1836 when Mary died at Derrynane. She was buried amid the ruins of the old abbey which, as O'Connell said in a letter, "rears its mouldering head above the ever dashing billows of the Atlantic." In 1838 he took time for a week's retreat at a Trappist monastery. In his letters he deplored his waning popularity among the Irish, a trend which he could measure in the decline of the contributions to the Tribute.

The practical problems of political leadership were unremitting burdens on his mind, for circumstances required him, on the one hand to pacify the supporters in Ireland who were concerned only with Repeal, and on the other to get what secondary gains were possible because of his relations with the friendly Melbourne government. Under the Union and without pressing too much for repeal, his countrymen had gained, through his efforts and the

---

* In the early years of her reign Victoria was a confirmed Whig, growing into maturity under the fatherly supervision of Lord Melbourne. In 1839 there occurred what is known in history as the "Bedchamber Crisis." In May of that year Melbourne's ministry suffered an adverse vote in the House of Commons and resigned. Accordingly, the Queen asked Peel to form a government. He specified that she must dismiss her Whig ladies of the bedchamber. She refused, claiming the royal prerogative. Thereupon Peel refused office, and Melbourne returned. Whig and Radical meetings were held all over Britain and Ireland applauding the Queen for resisting the demands of a "despotic government." One public meeting praised her for "refusing to let her belles be peeled." One historian sarcastically noted that "the Whigs crept back to power behind the petticoats of the Queen's ladies-in-waiting." This incident saved for another year the benign administration in Dublin Castle of Drummond (he died in 1840). After her marriage Victoria's political sympathies changed, for Albert was a bigoted Protestant.

help of friendly Whigs, more solid benefits than in all the years since he had entered public life thirty-odd years before (with the exception of Emancipation).

Of all the elements of governmental machinery under which the people of Ireland were governed, the worst was to be found in the large towns and cities. Theoretically and legally these aggregations of people were governed by the municipal corporations. But these corporations, sixty of them in 1833, did little governing and were of small service to the people. Many of these places had such small populations that they scarcely merited the title of town or city. Even in the actual cities, the corporation sometimes no longer performed the services needed by the inhabitants. In Belfast, for example, a voluntary society, founded a century before, built and maintained the hospital, cared for the poor, kept a school for poor children, brought water to the people, and operated a burying ground. The members of the corporations, except in one instance, were Protestants. They were in some places elected by a very limited franchise, some were self-perpetuating, some were under the control of a patron, and some were named by Dublin Castle. In 1833 a commission was created to investigate these corporations and suggest reforms. O'Connell was a member. The report of the commission was a scathing denouncement of the municipal corporations. It said that they neither governed nor served their communities, and that their members were politically and socially not representative of the people of the community. The magistrates were neither under the control of the crown nor subject to a vote of the people, the selection of juries was unsatisfactory, and the care of the corporation's property was inefficient.

In the bill created to implement the commission's findings, and which was adopted by Parliament, a majority of the municipal corporations were abolished since they represented no real communities. Of the eleven remaining corporations under the bill, the governing bodies were completely reconstructed with the old members replaced by elective council members. The people eligible to vote for the new members were ten-pound freeholders. The powers given to the new councils were more limited in Ireland than in England. They were to have no control over the police. That remained with Dublin Castle. O'Connell was not happy with the reform. He regretted that so many of the old corporations had been swept away, for he intended to make use of these "ghost" towns in his political organization, just as the Tories had in the past. Under this municipal reform, O'Connell was elected Lord Mayor of Dublin, the first Catholic to hold the office since the time of James II.

With the dawn of 1840 it became obvious to the experienced mind of O'Connell that the long period of Whig government was nearing its end. He had gotten real benefits for Ireland during his association with the Whigs and he felt justified in having quieted the Repeal movement in the interim. The great change in Dublin Castle alone was ample compensation for his support of Melbourne. The final disposition of the three nagging issues of the Whig years, the tithe, a poor law, and municipal reform —the word "settlement" would hardly be accurate—was about all that O'Connell could hope for under the Union. With the Whig ministry considerably weakened by deaths and retirements, it was obvious that another general election would bring back the Tories. Drummond died in 1840 and as Beckett says "the liberal spirit which had informed this authority died with him." But certain of his reforms survived in the personnel of the police, in the stipendiary magistracy, in the honorary magistracy, and in all the government offices filled during his tenure.

O'Connell at this time was haunted by his fear that the return to power of the Tories would mean a violent return of Protestant ascendancy. But Peel gave welcome reassurances. He announced in the House of Commons in 1840 that if returned to power he would rule Ireland in

13

Rough Road to Repeal

IN 1840 AND 1841, when O'Connell had passed his sixty-fifth birthday, all indicators pointed to the necessity of a momentous decision. His physical and mental faculties promised several years of unimpaired activity. He never had much trouble which required a doctor's attention. He had inherited the strong constitution of the Kerry O'Connells.

It was fairly obvious that the Whig government, with which he had enjoyed such excellent relations, was approaching the termination of its ascendancy, and the return of the Tories with Peel as Prime Minister was not a happy turn of affairs. O'Connell, it seemed, had three choices. First, he could retire from politics and, with the high judicial office which the Whigs could still bestow upon him, he could enjoy a more easeful mode of life and be free forever from financial worries. This option, which he could have selected at any time during the past ten years, touched his pride, his interest in a more active life, and his sense of obligation to the people of Ireland. He rejected this course as he had before. Active politics had been his occupation for nearly forty years and he would pursue it to the end. Thus, since politics was to be his choice, there were two courses still confronting him. Organizing and directing the Repeal movement was one. Another was to continue his concentration on Parliament and seek whatever accommodation he might achieve with a more mature Robert Peel. To seek what he could get from a government headed by Peel would not mean necessarily the complete abandonment of Repeal. It could be retained as an ultimate object. But in the interim, he could, as he had done during the Whig alliance, get what he could for Ireland under the Union.

If O'Connell could find it possible to consider an effort to live at least as a friendly enemy of Peel, there were fair prospects of some gains for Ireland before the return of the Whigs. Peel when he took over as Prime Minister in 1841 was, at the age of 54, a considerably matured statesman. He had been a leading figure in public life for more than a quarter of a century and during that time had experienced perhaps as many rebuffs as triumphs. He had, during all the time since he first served in Dublin Castle, been concerned, in considerable part at least, with Irish affairs, and when he came again to the head of the government it may be assumed that he had a genuine desire for a peaceful resolution of the question, or at least some progress toward that end. It is not necessary to believe that he wanted to help Ireland, but he did have a passionate ambition to succeed as Prime Minister. As a means to that end, quiet on the Irish front would be a mighty contribution. We shall consider later what he proposed for Ireland.

It is fair to believe that if there was a disposition for cooperation on the part of O'Connell, Peel might have gone considerably beyond what he did, but at that decisive moment no approach to a reconciliation was possible. O'Connell's hatred and distrust of Peel personally and his fierce hostility toward the Tory party prevailed. This made it certain that the old opposition would continue unchanged. Indeed, an element in O'Connell's lack of any disposition to live with the Peel government may have been the result of a conviction that the Peel regime would be short-lived. For the repeal of the Corn Laws was already a vital issue in England, and it was obvious that if Peel cast his fortunes with those opposing the Corn

Laws, he would shatter the Tory party. Indeed, this is what happened after four years. But as O'Connell, rejecting both retirement and accommodation with Peel, came to a decision to press for Repeal of the Union, he faced obstacles which would have dismayed a less hardy statesman.

As a realist who had lived with conditions surrounding Parliament for ten years, O'Connell must have realized what an enormous task it would be to get the House of Commons to regard Repeal with any sort of favor. He had seen scores of issues related to Ireland come to a vote, one or two of which had some relation to Repeal, and he realized that nothing unified Whigs and Tories so much as defense of the Union. The politicians of both parties, in ministries and in parliamentarian majorities, in taking their stand against Repeal were assured of popular support. Many influential people who were not politically affiliated—literary figures, independent journalists, some Protestant clergymen, radicals, and other independents—had been willing to grant Emancipation as a matter of justice, but when it came to accepting Repeal, quite a different consideration prevailed. The familiar anti-Repeal arguments were attractive to those people: the danger to unity of the Empire, the military peril in the event of a war with a Continental enemy of having either a neutral or a hostile country at the rear. Ireland's many good harbors for hostile ships had been an English obsession ever since the Spanish Armada. Even the English Catholics were united in their opposition to Repeal.

In Ireland, O'Connell faced conditions quite different from those which prevailed in 1829. His old supporters and lieutenants were mostly gone or scattered. The Catholic lawyers, Sheil and others, had been raised to the silk of the Inner Bar and some were in public office. They were unwilling to risk their standing and livelihood in a crusade for Repeal which they were convinced would be unsuccessful. O'Connell, therefore, felt that he would have to accept the help of younger people but he doubted the soundness of their judgment.

There had been a sizable number of Protestant landlords in the 1820s who gave sympathy and support to O'Connell, for their sense of justice and their interest in living at peace with the peasants prompted their sympathy in Emancipation. There were also the Dissenters who were burdened with government-imposed restrictions. All these former allies were denied O'Connell in his new crusade. These negative considerations must have been known to O'Connell when he launched his agitation for Repeal. The question which challenges historians and biographers is why he approached the task with such confidence, and why he constantly promised an early success. As late as February 1844, after his Monster Meetings, and when he was arrested and convicted, he issued a signed proclamation, begging, imploring, and ordering his friends to avoid violence. As a reward, the proclamation promised that in six months or a year they would have a Parliament in College Green.

The making of absurd promises is a common phenomenon in politics. Most people take it for granted, and assume that the politicians who make such promises are consciously lying. This is not true. They really believe what they are saying. Making absurd promises and statements at variance with the facts becomes such a habit in the political mind that no moral stigma can be imposed because of these violations of truth. It is almost routine for a candidate in the midst of a campaign to believe he will win when all the collateral evidence says that he hasn't a chance.

O'Connell's promises and predictions, like his preposterous exaggerations, had always been effective in putting spirit and determination in the minds of his followers. Perhaps he convinced himself that this sort of thing would succeed in the new agitation. He had defied the impossible before. Why should faith not prevail again? But whether O'Connell's liberties with the truth in his Repeal campaign were conscious or not, and even if they were deliberate falsifications, they did serve a tremendously important purpose. He realized that Irish nationalism, which had been his great and noble end from the beginning, was served by the campaign for Repeal. Nationalism, in the average Irishman's mind, was not an abstraction. To give it meaning and content, it must be associated with something immediate, concrete, and understandable. An Irish Parliament in College Green was that something which all could understand. Thus, Repeal was the cement which held the Irish people together. It gave nationalism reality as something to fight for, regardless of the odds.

In 1838 he anticipated the organized drive for Repeal by forming what he called "a Society of Precursers," and in April 1840 he came into the open by calling and presiding over a meeting at the Corn Exchange. Only about a hundred attended and only fifteen applied for membership in the revived organization which was rechristened the Loyal National Repeal Association. He modeled the new Association after the Catholic Association of twenty years before. Members paid one pound in annual dues and those who contributed ten pounds or over were called "volunteers" and could wear a uniform. These people who paid a pound or more annually were to be the nucleus, but since he wanted numbers he invited tenant farmers, agricultural laborers, and urban workers to become associate members at a shilling a year. Repeal wardens were appointed to collect the dues and to send the proceeds to Dublin headquarters. These wardens also encouraged Repeal meetings in their local districts. An important feature of the Association's facilities was a reading room in each town where literature, including O'Connell's messages, was displayed.

Another asset to the Repeal Association was Father Mathew's Temperance Society. Father Mathew was a

Capuchin monk whose home church was in Cork. His Society had chapters all over Ireland, and in every town of importance there was a reading room with tracts and other material favorable to the great cause of temperance. Father Mathew's mission was strictly non-political, so he could not align himself with the Repeal Association, but the contribution he made in keeping the people from strong spirits during the great Repeal meetings was of inestimable value. O'Connell supplemented the Temperance Society's efforts by emphasizing sobriety in his speeches. In the years during and after the Penal Laws, the peasant's poverty and unhappiness had found recourse in the bottle as one way of escape from his troubles, but since the habit itself merely added to the misery, it became a general symptom of the prevailing decay. The cause of temperance was aided by the priests who found that religion was the most effective method of enforcing the pledge of temperance. The great meetings of 1843 were distinguished by the decorum of the countless thousands who were in attendance.

In 1841, after his return to Dublin from the sessions at Westminster, it was quite clear that O'Connell's image needed a bit of refurbishing. He had lost his seat in Dublin and was compelled to find another constituency in Cork. The collections for the Association had been much less than O'Connell had expected. Obviously the time had come for something to put him into the limelight again. The opportunity soon presented itself. Although the new Municipal Reform Act did not say anything about the eligibility of Catholics for the office of mayor (they were already eligible *de jure*), it made it possible for them to be chosen by breaking up the old closed councils and vesting the vote for mayor in genuinely representative councils. So O'Connell presented himself and was easily elected to hold the office of Lord Mayor of Dublin. A bit of clowning by O'Connell added to the good cheer of the occasion when, robed in the gaudy regalia of the office, he presented himself before the crowd outside the Council Chamber. Donning the cocked hat and waving at his cheering friends, he called, "Boys, do you know me now?" In the spring of the next year he headed in full regalia a deputation greeting the new Queen at Buckingham Palace. He had a busy year between his duties in Dublin and attending the sessions of the House of Commons.

In October 1842, when the Repeal Association was well off the ground and prospering, a group of young men founded a weekly newspaper called *The Nation* and went on to create a problem which was to pursue O'Connell for the remaining years of his life. It is important to grasp the fact that Repeal was already enjoying healthy support before the young men behind *The Nation* came into the movement, for much of the later writings of the Young Irelanders make the claim that they rescued O'Connell from the failure of the agitation. The fact is that O'Connell had enjoyed the prominence and acclaim of his office as Lord Mayor of Dublin for nearly a year when *The Nation* was founded, and he was almost ready to begin his series of meetings which reached their climax in the next year. The Young Irelanders had little to do with the early stages of the Repeal movement.

O'Connell heartily welcomed the Young Irelanders to the Repeal Association. The painful disagreements with their policies came later.

14

The Meetings and
the Prosecution

AT THE EXPIRATION OF HIS YEAR AS LORD MAYOR, O'Connell procured the election of George Roe, a wealthy whiskey distiller, as his successor. Roe was a Protestant, and with his election O'Connell deliberately inaugurated a rotation of Catholic and Protestant holders of the office. Since the Catholics were in a permanent majority in the reformed City Council, this rotation ensured the Protestant minority a generous representation. On becoming Lord Mayor, O'Connell had boasted that no man would be able to discern his religion from his official decisions. He kept his word: on his retirement several Protestant members of the Council complimented him on the impartiality of his conduct.

The Young Irelanders participated in promoting and managing the Monster Meetings which extended through the summer and into the autumn of 1843. Whatever their later differences in philosophy and objectives with O'Connell, they recognized that the Irish people regarded him as their leader, that only O'Connell could bring out the crowds, and that with illiteracy so widespread, the Liberator's oratory was the basic medium for propaganda. The differences between O'Connell and the young nationalists did not develop until the following year. In May when the series of meetings had hardly begun, there was a sharp reminder that Peel was watching developments in Ireland with increasing concern. Suddenly a large number of Repealers were dismissed from their positions as (unpaid) magistrates. Among these was O'Connell himself. In reaction, Smith O'Brien and other Protestants threw up their commissions as magistrates. O'Connell's resourcefulness came into play immediately. He organized a great many unofficial tribunals which he called Arbitration Courts to hear and dispose of small private disputes of a civil nature. Many years later this method of setting up an unofficial government was adopted by the Sinn Fein movement.

The Repeal Association counted in its membership a majority of the Catholic bishops. Most of these, fourteen bishops and two archbishops, had followed the lead of Archbishop MacHale. Bishop Higgins, on his return from a visit to France, made impassioned speeches at some of the Monster Meetings. As the Repeal movement gathered strength, its reverberations reached an international audience. In France, where opinion was always ready to turn against the ancient enemy across the Channel, expressions of sympathy with Repeal took a turn to violence. Presumably because the *ancien régime* of the eighteenth century had been destroyed by violent revolution, there was plenty of French talk favoring violence in the Repeal movement in Ireland. This French sentiment O'Connell deplored. Again and again he made clear that he would accept no advice from France, that if the French sought to extend military help to Ireland he would be found on the side of the English, and that he would rather give up Repeal than shed Irish blood.

With American help, the situation was different. The sentiment in the United States was affected by the thousands of Irishmen and their families who had established homes in the United States. A transplanted Irishman is more a violent nationalist in his new home than he was before he left Ireland. There was overwhelming sentiment for Repeal and plenty of newly earned money found its way to the Repeal Association in Ireland. There was also hot talk about the desirability of an uprising in Ireland. This was the old call of the bystander, "Let's you and him fight." O'Connell welcomed the money and good wishes but reproved the people who talked violence. Politicians seeking Irish votes found it expedient to endorse Repeal. William H. Seward, who had been Governor of New York and was to be Senator and Secretary of State, was an active champion of Irish causes. Robert Tyler, son of the President, was a speaker at many Repeal meetings. His father, President John Tyler, gave an unqualified endorsement to the cause of Irish legislative independence.

But O'Connell refused to yield on the issue of slavery and this greatly distressed not only the Irish-Americans in the South and border areas, but also the Irish at home who felt that he should be more discreet. The Repeal Association in Cincinnati wrote to the Dublin headquarters, protesting. O'Connell replied with some heat. After stating what he had said many times before about the moral aspect of slavery, he pointed out that Irish-Americans were regrettably among the enemies of the Negroes. He spoke of their "depraved hearts" and asked them to recognize how their treatment of the Negroes had been responsible for their "inferiority." It is interesting to note that John Mitchel, one of the most violent of O'Connell's critics among the Young Irelanders, settled in America some years after the abortive 1848 revolt and became a strong supporter of slavery.

Meanwhile the big Repeal campaign was gaining momentum. Through the summer of 1843 O'Connell addressed a dozen open-air Monster Meetings. The attendance at each of these ran into the hundreds of thousands. At Tara it numbered more than half a million. Even O'Connell's powerful voice could not reach such multitudes, so relay speakers would repeat his words for the benefit of the more distant sections of the crowd—a pre-electronic public-address system.

With enthusiasm mounting O'Connell resorted to more and more incandescent language. At Kilkenny in June he told an audience estimated at 300,000 that they numbered more than all the soldiers who fought at Waterloo. He admitted that the host before him was not a trained army but "they could be disciplined in an hour." Also, "they could walk as well behind a band as if they had red coats."

At Mallow, before a still larger crowd, he uttered what became famous as the "Mallow defiance." His language hinted (only hinted) at armed resistance. It was the most outspoken statement of defiance he had yet uttered. "The time has come when we must be doing. You may soon have the alternative to live as slaves or to die as free men. I think I perceive a disposition on the part of some of our Saxon traducers to put us to the test. In the midst of peace and tranquility, they are covering our land with troops." O'Connell was too experienced in agitation and too good a lawyer to have succumbed to the traditional habit of orators, which is to become the captive of the passions of an audience. This was not Savonarola moved by his hearers to ever-more-extravagant promises. He was, at Mallow, testing a government which was at that moment considering how it was to meet this phase of the agitation. It is believed by Gwynn, a cautious biographer, that O'Connell was seeking to intimidate the Peel ministry. "And as no preventive steps were taken after Mallow, he was convinced that he had succeeded." But he added no more fuel in his speeches. He never went as far again in suggesting violence. He even moved to the opposite extreme. At succeeding meetings he cautioned against the more extreme statements of other speakers by saying that he was more anxious to live than to die for Ireland, and that one living Repealer was worth a whole churchyard of dead ones.

Meanwhile the series of meetings came to a climax at Tara. There, the site of the ancient throne of the kings, on a gently rolling hillside, preparations were made for the largest assemblage of the whole campaign. The geographical location favored a heavy attendance, for it is near the population center around Dublin. But multitudes came also from considerable distances, marching in the dusty roads, sleeping by the roadside, carrying food and (soft) drink. The Liberator, as at all meetings, made a dramatic entry, with his carriage passing through cheering throngs, waving to his people. Once more he implored his people to be orderly, and once more there were the extravagant promises that Repeal was not only inevitable but imminent. It seemed that nothing could exceed in size and dramatic possibilities the meeting at Tara. But the leaders of the Repeal Association decided on a final meeting which, they were assured, would exceed in size any previous occasion. The site selected was Clontarf where in ancient times the Danes had been defeated and driven out of Ireland. Most elaborate preparations were made for this great meeting. Notices were sent far and wide, even across the water to Manchester and Birmingham. And in the week preceding the Sunday on which the meeting was to be held, the roads to Dublin were crowded with people.

During that entire summer, Peel and his cabinet had been planning two courses of action. First it was decided that the Repeal demonstrations should be stopped. Peel had decided that at an early date he would directly challenge the Association and its leader. Then it was decided to arrest and prosecute O'Connell. Peel's Lord Lieutenant, De Grey, had been kept informed of Peel's determination, and had been constantly advising London about the course of events in Ireland. Apparently after the immense gathering at Tara and as the plans for a still larger meeting at Clontarf were under way, Peel decided to strike. Large contingents of troops and police were moved into strategic positions near Dublin. Artillery was placed where it could command the roads, and warships were moved into the harbors of Cork and Kingstown.

But the notice forbidding the Clontarf meeting was for some reason greatly delayed. The meeting at Clontarf was set for Sunday. The proclamation banning it was not issued until Saturday afternoon.

As soon as O'Connell was certain that the government would issue a proclamation banning the meeting, he called Repeal leaders together in the Corn Exchange to consider a course of action. While this discussion was going on, messengers arrived with copies of the government's proclamation. It was carefully read and then, without further discussion, O'Connell said, "This must be obeyed." Considering the explosive situation in which the firing of a shot by either side might result in wholesale slaughter, prompt action was essential. O'Connell issued a proclamation canceling the meeting, and printed copies were posted wherever the government's proclamation was displayed. The great platform was dismantled that evening and Repeal agents were sent to all the roads with orders to turn back all prospective demonstrators. The government was bitterly criticized for the lateness in posting the ban on the meeting and this was held by the cabinet in London as a black mark against Lord Lieutenant De Grey who resigned a short time later and was replaced by a more moderate selection. In the years after, there was interminable debate over O'Connell's decision to cancel the meeting, but at the moment his authority over the masses of the people was so great that there was no disorder. The impact upon the Repeal movement, however, was extremely discouraging.

There was another subject for concern, even more alarming than the canceled meeting. The government moved to arrest O'Connell and several other leading Repealers on charges of conspiracy to undermine the constitution and to excite disaffection in the army. The Tory team in Dublin Castle, obedient to Peel's determination to thwart the Repeal movement, and to bring some of its leaders to trial, had succeeded in the first of these projects

when the Clontarf meeting was canceled. The next step
was to bring charges against the leaders. Indictments
were issued against O'Connell, his son John, Thomas
Steele, Charles Gavan Duffy, Richard Barrett, Thomas
Ray, two priests, and a doctor. O'Connell had expected
that the trial would be for high treason, but was surprised
when the charge was limited to conspiracy. In the preliminaries it was apparent that Dublin Castle was grimly
determined to win a conviction. An obsolete jury list was
successfully challenged and a delay was gained until
January 1844. Even the new jury list was prepared with
a designed exclusion, and the panel finally selected was
entirely non-Catholic.

No effort by the accused to draw attention to the proceedings was omitted. When the time came to start the
trial, O'Connell was escorted by a great procession. He
rode in state in a carriage with the Lord Mayor. He made
a long speech in his defense, an effort in which he clearly
indicated that his powers were failing.

A verdict of guilty was reached in February. The period which followed until sentence was pronounced in
May, O'Connell used to visit England. There he attended
Parliament where he engaged in a debate on Irish affairs.
Greville mentions in his diary that O'Connell spoke with
quiet moderation and was well received, for it was quite
apparent that there was considerable sentiment in England against what seemed a rigged and unnecessary prosecution by Peel. Some of the Whig leaders in the Commons, including Lord John Russell, strongly condemned
the prosecution. A short tour of English cities indicated
that O'Connell still had a very considerable following.

On May 30 sentence was pronounced. O'Connell's sentence was a year's imprisonment and a fine of £2,000, with
security to keep the peace assured by a larger amount. As
preparations for prison were under way, the greatest
concern of O'Connell's was that there should be no disorder by his supporters. The prisoners were given every

consideration at Richmond prison, except their liberty. The houses of the governor and his deputy were placed at their disposal. Relatives and friends were entertained, presumably at the government's expense. It was a social event of considerable consequence. Meanwhile, an appeal against the sentence was made to the House of Lords.

Three months of the sentence passed without incident. O'Connell had little hope that anything would come of the appeal, but his lawyer friends, including the able Pierce Mahony, were busily at work. In the appeal they alleged that O'Connell had been convicted on many irregular counts and that the jury had been packed. By a majority decision of three to two the Law Lords ordered that the conviction be set aside. Whether by accident or design the decision followed party lines, since the three were Whigs and the two were Tories. One of the former, Lord Denman, stated in his judgment that, if such practices were to continue, trial by jury in Ireland would become "a mockery, a delusion and a snare."

When O'Connell heard the news he could hardly believe it, and exclaimed to his jubilant friends: "The hand of man is not in this." In Dublin the excitement passed all bounds. A huge chariot was rigged up (it still stands in a Dublin museum), and seated on top O'Connell was drawn through the streets in a great procession. The chariot was halted when it reached College Green and O'Connell, always ready to seize the dramatic moment, stood upright and pointed in silence to the Bank of Ireland, until 1800 the seat of the Irish Parliament.

All over Ireland the enthusiasm was tremendous. It was O'Connell's last great triumph.

15

The Generation Gap

ONE OF THE MOST PROMINENT of nature's phenomena is the eternal struggle for continuity. The older specimens of plant life fight to hold their places in the sun and only slowly yield to the thrust of the new growths which they themselves created. But the transition is inexorable and the new finds fertility in the rotting remains of the old. In human affairs something like this process reveals itself. The tyranny of nature fixes the life span with measurable uniformity, and when the end comes near, new hands and voices and brains are there to take over. But there is a space of time when both the old and the new have each a part of the action, and the disparity in outlook which follows has been called the "generation gap."

A new generation of educated young men, most of them trained or training in the law, had drifted into some of the early meetings at the Corn Exchange and had become infected with the idea of Repeal as a means of giving reality to Irish nationalism. Most of them, either in college or later, had mixed their law studies with casual writing for newspapers. Among the most active and talented were Thomas Davis and John Blake Dillon who, in 1841, were 27 years of age. Davis was a Protestant, born in Mallow (County Cork), but removed to Dublin at an early age. His father had been an army surgeon in the Peninsular war. Dillon was a Catholic already admitted to the bar and a native of County Mayo. The two had been born in 1814, and had graduated from Trinity College, but not in the same year. Both had drifted into journalism through various newspapers, and in the course of their adventures had been given joint responsibility for editing *The Morning Register*. One of the men writing for the *Register* while they were there was Charles Gavan Duffy, two years younger. Duffy was a Catholic and a native of Ulster. He had only the education which was available to Ulster Catholics, and since he had to find work at an early age, had not attended college. His education was largely picked up in his years of writing for the newspapers in Ulster and Dublin and in the reading rooms of libraries. Duffy, who seemed to have a more practical mind than Davis and Dillon, propounded to his friends the idea of *The Nation*. Their decision to collaborate in this enterprise was made in late 1841. The weekly made its first appearance a year later.

The deep division between O'Connell and the Young Irelanders did not come into the open until the fall of 1844. But it had been evident to the more perceptive people on both sides that there were very important differences in objectives and strategy which might ultimately shatter the Repeal movement. It was clear from much of what had appeared in *The Nation* that the nationalism of the Young Irelanders was of an extreme nature. No one could draw any other conclusion than that their goal was the complete independence (not necessarily separation) of Ireland. In the prospectus which Duffy, Davis, and Dillon issued a year before the first issue came off the press, stress was laid on the objective by which the editors were guided. It was "the great end of nationality," and *The Nation,* in pursuit of that end, would be "able, Irish and independent." While O'Connell had contributed more than any other Irishman to the awakening of pride in their country, pride in themselves, and unity in the name of Ireland, he had never advocated separation from the crown. It is true that he sought the restoration of an Irish Parliament but, at least by implication, this separate Parliament should have limited powers and the Parliament in London would have the final authority in certain matters vital to the preservation of the Empire. His brief flirtation with the federal idea showed quite clearly that his mind was playing with the constitutional question involved in defining the respective powers of two Parliaments, two nationalities, and one supreme sovereign. While many of the Young Ireland group were lawyers, there is no evidence that they had any interest in constitutional arrangements. O'Connell recognized that geography compelled close relations between the two countries of benefit to both. Indeed he saw that, in an ever-contracting world, the future meant a considerable surrender of national independence through the promotion of international cooperation. With respect to his view of nationality, most of which he could not reveal to his followers, we must in the present stage of the world's evolution recognize in him far more kinship with modern thinking than any of the Young Irelanders ever manifested.

Thus the seeds of conflict between O'Connell and Young Ireland appeared, not only in their differences about the objective of nationalism, but in their concepts of the methods which should be employed in working toward Repeal. O'Connell, as he grew older, became more and more opposed to the idea of violence. The Young Irelanders were not so positive that physical force should not be employed. Their writings did not make clear what form violence should take. Perhaps it did not occur to them to be explicit; perhaps they thought of violence as something which could be improvised when the moment came to act. Certainly the abortive insurrection of 1848 indicates that no one had thought much about the practical problems which would arise. But the carefree way they spoke of violence as a means of winning advantage, and the glorification of the revolt of 1798, and of Wolfe Tone's part in it, greatly alarmed O'Connell.

Another subject of contention was the insistence of

Young Ireland's writers, especially Thomas Davis, that
the Repeal movement be entirely divorced from religion.
Davis, who took it upon himself to reply to Dr. Mac-
Hale's* philippics, became so positive in defending the
Protestants' right to participate in the Repeal movement
that he drifted into discussions of religious doctrine which
could easily be interpreted as anti-Catholic argument.
This was entirely outside Repeal. For sheer brilliance and
versatility, Davis towered above the members of the
Young Ireland group. His poetic output, in view of his
early death, was considerable, and it seemed to have been
composed while he was occupied by writing for *The
Nation* on cultural and political subjects. The erratic nature of his thinking is well shown in his expressions about
the revival of the Gaelic language. In a long essay on the
subject he first asks himself whether the ancient language
can be revived. His first answer is that it is being revived
by the Archaeological Society, and he says that he will
discuss the revival "some other day." Then, carried away
with the idea of a revived national language, he does not
wait for "another day," but indulges in an ecstasy about
how unthinkable it is to speak the language of "the alien,
the invader, the Sassenach tyrant" and to abandon the
language of "our kings and heroes. What! Give up the
tongue of Brian Boru [and a whole list of Irish names],
including the language of O'Connell's childhood, and
speak that of [a list of English bad people]." Then his
mood intensifies with, "No! oh No! The green flag shall
fly on our towers, and the sweet old language be heard
once more in the colleges, the mart and the senate." A bit
later in the essay, he is more cautious and says that a
limited use of Gaelic should be taught, apparently as a
cultural accomplishment like the present learning of
French or Spanish. With such a fleeting, elusive, and

* Archbishop of Tuam.

vague mentality to deal with, it is no wonder that O'Connell, the realist, should be confounded.

Very early Davis seized upon the idea of federalism as a compromise and exploited it at length in his editorials and in his private letters. It was just the sort of concept in which a mind like his could revel. The ideal of an independent Parliament for Irish affairs, with a Parliament in London for the Empire, had been in people's minds long before the name federalist had come into use, but when the reality of a specific plan was reached, the trouble began. Just what powers should be given to an Irish Parliament and what should be retained at Westminster? How should the affairs of the dual sovereignty be managed? All the vital issues lay unanswered when the decision to turn to federalism was broached. But Davis was not concerned about such "details." He wanted the word, regardless of substantive matters. As things developed, a lot of trouble came because of that word. In a letter to a friend in 1842 Davis said that federalism was all that Ireland stood to get out of the present political situation. He wrote: "Things have come to that pass that we must be disgraced or defeated, or we must separate by force or we must have a Federal government."

It seemed to O'Connell that Smith O'Brien was also favorable to a compromise along federal lines. Counting on the support of both Davis and O'Brien, O'Connell addressed a long letter to the Association about future plans. He said in part:

> I do at present feel a preference for the Federative plan, as tending more to the utility of Ireland and the maintenance of the connection with England than the proposal of simple repeal. But I must either deliberately propose, or deliberately adopt from some other person, before I bind myself to the opinion I now entertain.

As is apparent from the qualifications in this statement, O'Connell realized that general acceptance of the idea of federalism was not enough. The whole thing depended upon the details. On this, Davis' mind had not concentrated, and O'Brien characteristically had been most vague. But Davis and O'Brien found themselves immediately undercut by Duffy, who came out strongly against any flirtation with federal compromise. Despite the editorial support in *The Nation* for the idea of federalism, and despite Davis' open support of the idea, Duffy strongly condemned O'Connell's suggestion of a compromise. This revealed not only the inconsistency within *The Nation,* but the willingness of Duffy to use any stick to beat O'Connell. It made the ultimate split inevitable.

The sudden switch of *The Nation* from advocacy of to opposition to federalism bewildered and hurt O'Connell. He had written the letter in support of federalism, believing that it would help cement the rift in the movement by bringing Davis and O'Brien to his side. But now he scarcely knew what to think and hastily withdrew his suggestion. Davis, regardless of all that he had said earlier on the subject, felt obliged to switch back to opposition and back to Duffy in opposition. Two weeks later in *The Nation,* Davis came out for "unbounded nationality." With this, O'Connell said, he "snapped his fingers at Federalism" as something that "had let him down."

The revelation that the Young Irelanders and *The Nation* were undependable allies in the Repeal movement colored the relations which O'Connell had with the group from then on until the fatal clash.

The next difference came with the introduction of Peel's colleges bill. The details of this controversy must be considered later but the enthusiasm of the Young Irelanders for the bill and O'Connell's reservations deepened the division. It was in the debate between Davis and Mac-Hale that a serious clash between O'Connell and Davis took place.

In 1844 when O'Connell and the other leaders were awaiting trial, William Smith O'Brien joined the Repeal

Association. This most important addition to the movement was a member of a powerful Protestant landholding family in County Clare. For hundreds of years the O'Briens had been a principal family in Clare, and since the Union a member of the family had always been elected to Parliament. In fact, Smith O'Brien had held the borough seat in Ennis when in 1828 O'Connell had won one of the two county seats, and had sided with his family in opposing O'Connell in that historic election. Smith O'Brien had no ambition to assume leadership in the Repeal Association. He joined out of a sense of justice and public policy, just as he had some years before joined the fight for Catholic Emancipation. His rather quiet nature was in striking contrast to O'Connell's more dramatic behavior. There would never be congenial companionship between the two men, but when he joined the Repeal Association at a moment when its leaders were all headed for prison, Smith O'Brien was giving evidence of complete dedication to principle. His reason for joining was his admiration for the Young Irelanders rather than a wish to be associated with O'Connell. But when he joined, O'Connell warmly welcomed him and he accepted the older man's leadership without reservation. A very close and affectionate relationship developed between Smith O'Brien and Thomas Davis, for Davis believed that Smith O'Brien had the maturity and experience important to him and to the Repeal Association.

During O'Connell's preoccupation with his trial and later his imprisonment, it was quite reasonable that Smith O'Brien should assume a role of leadership in the Association. This O'Connell welcomed and the letters exchanged between the two men were completely friendly. In the dispute the next year over the colleges bill, Smith O'Brien did what he could to prevent an open break.

Davis and Archbishop MacHale represented extremes in almost every aspect of political affairs, and, because their temperaments were so emotional, they both tended

16

Peel and His Reforms

IN O'CONNELL'S SPEECHES AFTER THE PRISON EXPERIENCE, there was a marked element of restraint, and there was no suggestion of a revival of the Repeal movement. In these late years, his insistence upon peaceful agitation seemed to be almost an obsession. He proudly claimed to be

> the first apostle and founder of that sect of politicians whose cardinal doctrine is this: that the greatest and most desirable of political changes may be achieved by moral means alone, and that no human revolution is worth the effusion of one drop of human blood. Human blood is no cement for the temple of human liberty.

William E. H. Lecky, whose biography of O'Connell appeared in 1862, is the only writer of note whose observations were based upon eyewitness accounts. For this reason his appraisal of O'Connell's condition after his release from prison is pertinent.

> The gigantic physical as well as mental strain of the long series of Monster Meetings; the excitement of the protracted trial; the anxiety which for a time deeply preyed upon him lest his people during his enforced absence should burst into rebellion; the interruption of his usual active habits during the more than three months imprisonment; the violent alternations of despondency and exultation through which he had lately passed were too much for a man who was now verging on seventy. He had suddenly aged. His wonderful voice, overstrained by excessive exertion, had lost its old power. His handwriting had grown tremulous. His step was feeble and uncertain. He retained his old clearness of judgment, something of his old ambition, and all of his old love of power;

but his nerve was shaken, his energy was abated. The consciousness of failure was upon him. He had seldom been averse to compromise, and while a more ardent and violent spirit was rising among the younger and more brilliant of his disciples, his own disposition was growing more pacific.

From the late months of 1844, there can be no dispute concerning the *physical* infirmity of O'Connell. The day-to-day mental energy which in the earlier years distinguished him among his colleagues at the bar and in politics had given way to periods of fatigue. He wrote some letters, made a few speeches, and talked with a great many people, and this routine had to be attenuated. But the real test of the brain is the quality of judgment. How wise were his decisions in those last years? How clear and how wise? As Lecky admits, he still had the "old clearness of judgment." The decline in vigor and the need for more periods of rest as well as the changes in his voice and handwriting were in those days the quite inevitable handicaps of a man at the end of his seventh decade. A man of sixty was rated "old" in the nineteenth century. But these limitations which were noted and respected by his friends were seized upon by Charles Gavan Duffy for his malignant purposes later in the century when he was writing his self-serving account of what had happened in the 1840s. In this we come to a matter in which the historian's judgments stand between us and the reality. Whoever writes about the decisions of an historical character is denied the knowledge of the facts and the weighing of considerations which faced the subject of his comment. This lack of knowledge should restrain him in drawing his conclusions, but only the most judicious writers exercise this restraint. They borrow their verdict from contemporary writers who have personal and prejudiced axes to grind.

My examination of the available facts which governed the judgments of O'Connell on the major issues of these last years convinces me that his judgment of fundamentals was clear and mostly wise. His memory, which was unimpaired, permitted him to follow lines of policy formed early in his career. As a confirmation of my judgment, I submit part of the text of a letter written at the time when, according to his traducers, his judgment was most in question. This, I submit, is the best confirmation of what I say about his mental condition.* It was written in a long letter to Devin Reilly which I quote in full:

> The Repeal Association is a legal body because it disclaims any use of force or violence to achieve the repeal of the Union Statute. Because it disclaims the use of physical force to achieve the repeal of the Union, every member of the Repeal Association is at present perfectly safe from any prosecution.
>
> Would the members be equally safe if it were to admit any admixture of the physical force principle as part of the means of obtaining such Repeal?
>
> I am decidedly of the opinion that the members would not in such case be safe from well-founded prosecution.
>
> I take these propositions to be clear in law: First: That any assembly admitting any species of physical force as part of the means

---

* I am glad to see that Robert Kee in his excellent history, *The Green Flag,* agrees with my judgment on O'Connell's mental capacity in those last years. R. Dudley Edwards, Professor of Modern Irish History in University College, Dublin, has always discounted stories of O'Connell's "serious mental decline." It is with quite understandable hesitation that I add to the opinions of Daunt, Lecky, and, more recently, Kee, something of a very personal nature. This is in support of the fact that such physical deteriorations as were manifested by O'Connell were not accompanied by any impairment in his mentality and judgment.

As I complete the writing of this book, I have reached the age of 87. This is an age some years beyond that attained by all the biographers, historians, and other contemporaries when they wrote of O'Connell in his old age. For some years I have experienced those physical failings so common in old age: illegible handwriting, deficient eyesight, unsteady locomotion, and lessened endurance. That these have little to do with the capacity of my mind, I offer as proof this book, inadequate as it may be for the subject.

But since I have never permitted my mind to rest, except for short periods, my capacity for sustained discourse and, I trust, my judgment are as good as they ever were. Surely there will be differences with some of the opinions I have expressed in this story. But I do not believe they will be more serious than they were with what I wrote 25 or 50 years ago, for I have always been regarded as a rather contentious fellow.

of obtaining a repeal of an Act of Parliament is an unlawful assembly, liable to be dispersed by any ·magistrate, and its members punished by indictment.

Secondly, that any such assembly is not only unlawful, but that any acts done by it on furtherance of its objects constitute a treasonable fact, rendering the members liable to conviction and execution for treason.

This opinion, in point of law, I have at public meetings proclaimed.

On one occasion, in the Association, I brought down the legal authorities and quoted them, chapter and page.

It is observable that, often as I have repeated this legal doctrine, no one has had the hardihood to deny its accuracy.

It follows, if I be right, that the seceders cannot safely be admitted into the Repeal Association unless on the fullest and most explicit disclaimer of resorting to any physical force means to achieve the Repeal of the Union.

In order to be enabled to receive the seceders into the Association again, it should be ascertained whether, beyond a doubt, I am right in point of law or not.

At the former periods in my struggles for advancing the popular cause, my judgment in matters of law has been found eminently useful, and my opinion of the state of the law was trusted with implicit confidence. And I have the comfort to know that such confidence was never regretted, nor shown by any fact to have been misplaced.

Now my most anxious desire is to lay the foundation for perfect conciliation, or, if that be refused, to have the universal people understand who it is to whom the continuance of the dissention is justly attributable.

Speculation about the motives of such a complex character as Sir Robert Peel is a highly hazardous business, but it is a fair guess that after Peel's blunder in seeking the prosecution of O'Connell, he decided to do something constructive in answering the Irish demand for Repeal of the Union. Whatever his motives, he planned three measures and secured their approval by his cabinet. One was land reform, a second was a large grant for the improvement and enlargement of the seminary at Maynooth, and the third was known as the Queen's colleges bill.

In approaching the thorny question of land-tenure reform, he caused the appointment of a commission which became known from the name of its chairman, Lord Devon. Since Peel realized that the interests of the landlord were paramount in both Houses of Parliament, he sought to appease this dominant interest by making sure that the Devon Commission should be composed mostly of landlords themselves. He was willing to give the landlords an opportunity to reform their relations with their tenants by their own free will. O'Connell was contemptuous of this reliance upon the generosity of the landlords. He said, "You might as well consult butchers about keeping Lent, as consult these men about the rights of farmers."

Nevertheless the commission worked assiduously to gather facts on all sides of the question. Its members traveled all over Ireland and interviewed a wide variety of people who were close to the realities. Its report, considering the people of interest who wrote it, was not revolutionary, but it was a fair proposal for improving the relations of landlord and tenant. Lord Devon, after rendering his report, pressed the government to move for its adoption. He found one member of the government most receptive, Lord Stanley, hitherto known as a hard-bitten Tory and designated in earlier years by O'Connell as "scorpion" Stanley. But he, like Peel, had decided that Ireland needed something from Westminster other than coercion acts. Stanley, who had been elevated to the peerage, even during the lifetime of his father, made a long and immensely serious speech favoring the government's bill which contained most of the Devon reforms. However, the proposals in the bill, which by modern standards would be regarded as totally inadequate, were bitterly resisted by the representatives of the landlords in the House of Lords. The result was the abandonment of the bill by Peel and Stanley. Land reform was destined to wait another thirty years. And so Peel fell back upon his legislation for Maynooth and the colleges.

Peel's interest in reforms, in which the Catholic Church

would be the chief beneficiary, was, according to a secret memorandum which he gave to his cabinet ministers, intended to win the bishops and some of the priests away from O'Connell. The first of Peel's measures was a proposal to increase the annual grant to the College of Maynooth. This institution, the purpose of which was the education of Catholic priests, was first established by the Irish Parliament in 1795. It had struggled along since on a very inadequate annual subsidy from Parliament. Peel's proposal met with very considerable opposition but finally it was granted. In addition to increasing the annual grant threefold, the act provided a substantial sum for new buildings. Moreover, the grant was made permanent, continuing from year to year. The measure was warmly greeted in Ireland. It is doubtful if the nationalism of the priests, educated under the improved regime, was in any way abated, but the institution thus improved continued to be a famous seminary for the education of priests, not only in Ireland but throughout the world. Responsibility for administering the grants was given to the bishops.

Peel selected Lord Heytesbury as Lord Lieutenant and instructed him to conduct his office with strict impartiality. It also became the new Lord Lieutenant's intention to ingratiate himself with the bishops and higher clergy—chiefly, of course, to draw them away from the influence of O'Connell. At the same time Peel instituted contacts with the Vatican designed to interest the Pope in stopping the nationalistic activities of some of the more outspoken bishops. When a message from the Pope was received, advising the clergy to refrain from political agitation, a majority of the bishops ignored the directive and some expressed rather strong language about the Pope's political relations with the Peel government.

In the spring of 1845, Peel brought forth his most pretentious, and what was to be his last, proposal for the benefit of Ireland. There had been intimations of this a year before and some discussion pro and con in Ireland.

The new proposal involved the establishment of three colleges in Belfast, Cork, and Galway. These were to be called Queen's Colleges. The details of the proposal were given by Sir James Graham whom Peel had consulted in planning the colleges: he announced that the government had decided to establish the three colleges on the basis of complete religious equality. There would be no interference with the religion of the students. But to make sure that instruction in religion would not be neglected, it was intended to make provision for the endowment of professors of religion by private money. These professors would instruct students in the religion of their forefathers, and for this instruction the government-supported colleges would provide space. The professors in the colleges would at first be appointed by the government but after that by some other authority.

This far-reaching measure immediately received widespread support. Even O'Connell's son Morgan made a speech in the Commons supporting the bill. The High Church opposition, which used the expression "Godless education," objected to the non-denominational character of the institutions. Archbishop MacHale opposed the plan and seems to have had considerable influence in swinging O'Connell against it. The Young Ireland group favored the plan and this precipitated a controversy with O'Connell in the Repeal Association. This controversy went far beyond differences over the colleges bill and will be described later. The legislation establishing the Queen's Colleges in Belfast, Cork, and Galway was passed in the summer of 1845.

Beyond his desire to show his appreciation for Mac-Hale's support of the Repeal Association, there seems to be no clear reason for O'Connell's opposition to the colleges bill. Professor Gwynn, who has most thoroughly studied the controversy, is inclined to believe that O'Connell's speech before the Repealers was merely for the purpose of trying to amend, not defeat, the bill. After it was passed, he spoke in Parliament in favor of making the college plan succeed. It would seem, as we consider it at this distance, that every reasonable step was taken by Peel to protect the religious liberty of the students and at the same time provide ample means for instruction in "the faith of their fathers." Certainly Ireland desperately needed educational facilities for the young men who would be the leaders in the nation's affairs. Trinity College, Dublin admitted Catholic students with certain restrictions, but it was the only institution of higher education. Moreover, for reasons of geography and expense, it was out of reach for a large proportion of Ireland's young men. Scotland, with only one-quarter of the population of Ireland, had five universities at that time.

The opposition of Archbishop MacHale to the colleges bill, which was basically a demand for the inclusion of a specifically Catholic college, had a great deal to do with delaying action. In the debate over the colleges bill, the Catholic bishops, under the influence of MacHale, stated conditions which would have, if adopted, undermined the whole educational plan which Peel proposed. They insisted that Catholic students be denied the privilege of attending lectures on history, logic, metaphysics, moral philosophy, geology, or anatomy. To hear these subjects from non-Catholic sources would place their faith "in imminent danger." The government rejected these proposals and this led MacHale to seek the help of Rome in his opposition. After the bill had been adopted and the colleges established, in 1847 and 1848 papal rescripts called attention to the dangerous character of the colleges. In 1850 a Church synod issued a formal condemnation and warned Catholics to shun the colleges. For more than half a century "the university question" was to remain a standing grievance among Catholics and a problem for British ministries.

Peel's success in establishing the colleges was a partial atonement for the many repressive measures which he and his party had imposed upon Ireland. When this business was finally concluded, his ministry was approaching its end. For with the coming of 1846 Peel had determined, despite the opposition of a large part of his Tory following, to move for the repeal of the Corn Laws. The failure of the Irish potato crop and the approach of the Great Famine in Ireland seemed to Peel more evidence that the time was overripe for an attack upon protection. When he first proposed the repeal, Stanley and other ministers objected, and Peel offered the first of his resignations. Lord John Russell was unable to form a government and Peel returned. In January 1846 he introduced his bill for repeal of the Corn Laws and, despite violent opposition, it was carried. Immediately afterward, however, Disraeli mobilized the protectionist Tories and with the aid of the Whigs overthrew the Peel government. It was strange irony that the measure on which the decisive vote came was a bill for Irish coercion.

Here, on the verge of the crowning tragedy of the Famine and the official end of Peel's tenure of power, may be an appropriate place to consider the measures and the character of the man who for so many years had been foremost among English politicians who dealt with the Irish question, during those years since, as a very young man, he had come to Dublin Castle, the antagonist of O'Connell.* Much more might have been gained for Ireland if some means could have been devised to mitigate the mutual hatred and distrust which characterized the relations between Peel and O'Connell. But a review of Peel's record in his relations with O'Connell and his lifelong behavior in his treatment of Ireland would make it highly unlikely that O'Connell would have been justified in giving him his confidence. For that record until late in Peel's life shows a succession of acts revealing, not only a deplorable insensitivity to the distress of the Irish people,

---

* Peel remained in the House of Commons until his death in 1850. The occasion for his death at the age of 62 was a fall from his horse.

but bitter spite toward the man who more than any other represented the Irish nation.

While it is impossible within the limitations of this essay to tell the long story of Peel's policies in dealing with Ireland, it will suffice to illustrate his motivations and point of view to comment upon his actions in two of the decisive moments of his life. One of these was the surrender over Emancipation and the other was the prosecution of O'Connell and others in 1843–1844. For reasons I have already given, the decision to grant Emancipation was largely made by Wellington. In working out the details of the legislation we see the spiteful hand of Peel. For instead of winning a measure of good will in Ireland by the immense fact of granting political rights to the Catholics, Peel managed to intensify the hatred of Irishmen toward the Tory establishment in London. The disfranchisement of the forty-shilling freeholders Peel intended as a punishment imposed upon those tenants who, in a perfectly legal and orderly manner, refused to do what the landlords told them to do. Instead of winning a measure of gratitude for what the government did for them as Catholics, this exclusion infuriated these people as citizens. The decision to compel O'Connell to return to Clare to win another election was pure, unadulterated spite.

To compound the indignity, O'Connell, undoubtedly the foremost barrister at the Irish bar, was denied the coveted honor of the Inner Bar, while several of the Liberator's professional inferiors were admitted. In bringing about the prosecution of O'Connell and others, after the meeting at Clontarf had been called off by O'Connell, Peel gratuitously took a course which again added to the hatred which the Irish entertained for him, and this was at a moment when, if ever, he might have eased the tension in Ireland. It was something which in statecraft is more blamable than a misdeed—it was a blunder; a blunder which could have happened only because his hatred for O'Connell deranged his judgment. He should have known that before the law he had no case against O'Connell, for the defendants in the prosecution had not really violated any law. This made it necessary to win a conviction by corrupt and unfair methods which were denounced in the House of Commons and by the Law Lord, Denman, whose vote turned the tide against the government.

In a quite remarkable book which appeared in 1887, *Peel and O'Connell,* the author, G. Shaw Lefevre, whose purpose was to summarize parliamentary policy from the Union to the death of Peel, and who had served a considerable time as a member of the House of Commons and as a cabinet minister in at least two of the Gladstone cabinets, makes a number of important observations about Peel and his Irish policies:

> In dealing with the reputation of a statesman of the type of Sir Robert Peel, one who never attempted to lead or to form public opinion, who seldom took the initiative on any great question, but who closely observed and followed opinion and gave effect to it when it could no longer be resisted, it is necessary to judge not merely what he effected but what he neglected to do and what he successfully resisted. Judging of Peel in respect to Ireland, it is difficult to come to any other than an adverse opinion of the general drift of his policy. During the forty years that he influenced or determined the policy of England to that country, he did willingly little to unite the two people. He was the principal actor in one great concession and other smaller concessions; but the great concession was made too late, and under circumstances and attended by other measures which destroyed it as a healing measure. . . . But not the least of Peel's defects as regards Ireland was his want of sympathy for the great mass of its people.

I can agree with this estimate in all respects but one. He was not the "principal actor" in the great concession. Wellington deserves that honor.

A period of about nine months in 1845 and 1846 elapsed between the beginning of the Great Famine and the resignation of Peel's government in June 1846. Within this

period Peel made some moves to relieve the growing distress in Ireland. Some of these were to provide food for
the hungry millions and others were to provide employment.*

---

* In his article in *The Great Famine* (ed. by Edwards and Williams), Thomas
P. O'Neill notes that Peel was fairly effective in dealing with the first year of
the crop failure, 1845–1846. That year saw only a partial failure of the potato
crop. The total failure came with the crop of 1846, when Lord John Russell was
in power.

17

The Famine and the Break

ONE CAN CONCEIVE OF AN IMPATIENT DEITY viewing Ireland in 1845, racked as it was by the squabblings of politicians, deciding to give those people something real to worry about, for in the early autumn of that year came a veritable harvest of horror. Nature struck without discrimination, not at the politicians who suffered no physical pain, but at millions of innocent people. These people, about eight million of them according to the census in 1841, and their ancestors, had been living for a century-and-a-half in the shadow of black despair, brightened only occasionally by bits of hope and partial relief. The bulk of the population was dependent upon agriculture, and a considerable proportion sustained their strength and energy on a diet of potatoes. For the other food products and the livestock raised on the land, the landlords had other plans, and most was exported to England. O'Faolain has words to describe what befell that stricken land and those people in the late summer of 1845:

> That summer of 1845, cold and wet, the tips of the potato stalks began to wither, and they dropped off their rotting stems until the stench from the rotting tubers underneath seeped like a gas into their hovels, a forewarning of the stench of death that was later to come out of them. . . . Famine took the land by the throat. Slowly the foul smelling breath of plague rose over their little patches of fields, preparing to exterminate people by the million. The cabins became dens of death.

It seems quite irrelevant to turn from these scenes of despair to the political questions which dominated the scene in Dublin and centered in Conciliation Hall. The participants there who played out the final acts of the Repeal movement, with the exception of the Liberator, seemed unaware that, from the moment when the first potato plant sickened and died, the cause of Repeal, too, was already a matter not subject to debate but food for the historians. O'Connell saw the true significance of the blight and turned to measures of relief.

But earlier in the year the debate, which had been almost continuous for over a year, turned from the issue of the colleges, to splitting hairs over religion, and to the question of his commitment to non-violent agitation. The differences over Peel's colleges bill had provoked an argument between Thomas Davis and Archbishop MacHale and, during a discussion before the Association, a Catholic named Conway made some remarks which caused Davis to rise and reply. O'Connell, growing more and more restive because of the Young Irelanders, interrupted, saying: "It is no crime to be a Catholic, I hope."

Davis hastily replied that, on the contrary, some of his best friends were Catholic. His tone of voice rather than the substance of his words suddenly enraged O'Connell. Without listening to Davis' disavowal, he unburdened himself about his past differences with the Young Ireland group:

> There is no such party as that styled "Young Ireland." There may be a few individuals who take that denomination on themselves. I am for Old Ireland. 'Tis time that this delusion should be put an end to. Young Ireland may play what pranks they please. I do not envy them the name they rejoice in. I stand by Old Ireland, and I have some slight notion that Old Ireland will stand by me.

He had scarcely finished with this burst of unpremeditated rancor when he rose again to withdraw the nickname he had given to his young critics. But the consternation occasioned by this outburst of long-suppressed anger greatly moved Davis who, as soon as he arose, dissolved in a flood of tears. At this the old agitator was himself assailed by regrets for his outburst and he embraced Davis, saying, "I love you, Davis." This episode, trifling in its origin and almost absurd in its outcome, was nevertheless a significant indication of the inevitability of a break in the Repeal movement which, even had there been no Famine, would have crippled the movement. Another tragedy came soon after. In September Davis died after a short illness.

In the summer of 1845, O'Connell, despite his seventy years still fired by the hope of Repeal, staged a new campaign of great open-air meetings. There were a score of vast gatherings, some of them in the hundreds of thousands, at Dundalk, Navan, Tara again, Dublin, Cork, Wexford, Galway, and many in between. There were the same extravagant promises, the old friendly tributes to the Irish character, the familiar exaggerations, and the same friendly responses from the crowds, for he was still first in the peasants' hearts. Then, wearied by the effort, he retired to Derrynane to rest. In the recent American idiom, it had been his "last hurrah." At Derrynane he came face to face with the dreadful reality of the blight and the rot.

If there is needed beyond anything else a refutation of the distortions about O'Connell's mentality by Duffy and the other exiled Young Irelanders, and O'Faolain's disgraceful ending of his otherwise eloquent book, it is a record of what O'Connell did when the full significance of the Famine burst upon him. Professor Kevin B. Nowlan of University College, Dublin, in his essay in the significant book *The Great Famine,* says:

> The early reports of the potato blight produced few striking indications of alarm in Ireland. It was only slowly, almost imperceptibly, that what proved to be the Great Famine came to occupy anything like a central place in Irish politics. Except for the half-hearted espousal of the anti-Corn Law cause, very largely

a gesture to English reformist opinion, and the demand for a closing of the ports, the remedies put forward by nationalists were simply the economic medicines that had long been prescribed for the
ills of the country.

O'Connell's grasp of the situation and his firm belief
that the Whigs were due to return to power occupied his
mind that autumn when he vigorously moved to do something about the consequences of the crop failure. In October O'Connell returned to Dublin and caused the Dublin
Corporation to set up a special committee to inquire into
the cause and effects of the potato blight. O'Connell was
the guiding force in the committee which was expanded
to include many influential elements of the city. He then
had the committee send a delegation to the Lord Lieutenant, Heytesbury, to urge restrictions upon the use of
grains for brewing and the export of foodstuffs. The con-
ference with Heytesbury was unsatisfactory because the
Lord Lieutenant was unsure of his authority and hesitated
to give any promises. O'Connell, with his sure judgment
of political conditions in London, realized that the Tory
party was divided and that the Peel government was destined to fall. But the food crisis was so immediate that
relief for Ireland could not wait.

Fortunately, Peel, despite his insecure tenure, decided to move toward relief. He was not indifferent, as
O'Faolain and others have charged. He had formulated
plans to submit to the cabinet as early as December 1845.
By this time he had decided to move for the repeal of the
Corn Laws despite the strength of protectionism in the
Commons and especially in the Lords. He hoped that
this would measurably help Ireland by opening its ports
and, by making British consumers less dependent upon
food from Ireland, allow that stricken country to retain
what it produced. But Peel went beyond this in his plans
for relief. He secured a large appropriation to bring
Indian corn from America and a relief commission was
created to establish depots of help in various places in

Ireland. He proposed and secured the passage of three
public-works bills to provide employment. In the new
year the pestilence of fever appeared and the government
established fever hospitals to treat the victims. Peel's efforts to relieve distress had to end in June 1846 when his
government fell, and on July 1, Lord John Russell headed
a new Whig administration.

After the death of Davis the policy of *The Nation* became, not only more critical of O'Connell's leadership,
but more outspoken in speaking of violence as an instrument of agitation. This was signalized when Duffy
brought into *The Nation* as a substitute for Davis a pug-
nacious young Protestant solicitor named John Mitchel.
His duties included the writing of editorials. Shortly
after his arrival, he wrote an article that was really an
exposition of the sort of sabotage which might be practiced in case of a conflict with the English government:

> As the Dutch dealt with the French by laying land under water,
> ruining their fertile plains of waving corn—so Ireland's railways
> though most valuable to her, were better dispensed with for a while
> than to be allowed to be a means of transport for invading armies.
> Every railway within five miles of Dublin could in one night be
> totally cut off from the interior of the country. To lift a rail, fill
> a perch or two of any cutting or tunnel, to break away a piece of
> embankment seems obvious and easy enough.

This sort of romancing seems like the boasting of a mis-
chievous teenager. But Mitchel was a qualified lawyer,
and *The Nation* was the most widely read journal in
Ireland. Such romancing could not be treated lightly.
O'Connell, greatly disturbed, went directly to *The Nation's* office and demanded that Duffy in another issue
disclaim any connection between *The Nation* and the
Repeal Association. He added that he had much preferred *The Nation* when Davis was determining editorial
policy than what it advocated since.

As the spring of 1846 came and peasants were digging

in their fields preparatory to planting, the foul remains
of the last year's potato crop was revealed. This reality
provided fuel to the unrest which was always near the
surface. There were more depredations by the Whiteboys
and others, and the peasants, reaching the edge of despair, became less interested in Repeal and more in the
stark question of survival. Reliable historical accounts
prove that at this terribly critical moment the Young Irelanders, instead of seeking unity with the O'Connellites
in the task of relief, were engaged in silly activities designed to show their detachment from the Repeal Association and their determination to declare their detachment from O'Connell's leadership. The most recent of
Irish historians, Robert Kee,* describes their conduct this
way:

> Young Ireland, meanwhile, tended to consolidate its position of
> detachment, meeting as a group from time to time in the gold and
> green uniforms of the '82 Club, often with Smith O'Brien in the
> chair while O'Connell, the titular president, was away in London.
> Gavan Duffy, John Mitchel, M. J. Barry, and Michael Doheny
> were joined by other bright young men, mainly Catholics, often
> dandified in their dress and speech, and drawn with the others from
> the middle class but making up for their lack of contact with the
> Irish people by the zeal with which they held the principle of na-
> tionality in trust for them.

Prominent among the newcomers were Thomas Meagher
and Richard O'Gorman, both sons of wealthy merchants.
Speaking with an accent acquired from his education at
Stonyhurst in England, Meagher made a strong "no compromise" speech to the Association in February 1846.
O'Gorman in the same month made oblique references to
"others choosing the sword" but himself at present pre-
ferring "the might of mind." It should be noted that
Meagher and O'Gorman were in their early twenties.

No one can read the meticulous account of politics in

* *The Green Flag.*

that fatal 1846 in the Kee book but be struck by the apparent indifference of the Young Ireland group to the great calamity of the Famine. They were busy with their writings and speeches over Repeal methodology while O'Connell was giving every ounce of his failing strength to convince the Commons and the government of the need for more relief. Perhaps at that time in 1846 when the new crop was being planted, it was assumed that the failure of the potato crop was a one-year phenomenon and that the harvest of 1846 would bring plenty of food. Meanwhile *The Nation* was nagging the Association about not publishing its accounts. Mitchel continued his half-veiled attacks on O'Connell's leadership. And Smith O'Brien, who was attending Parliament, was taking more and more pains to ally himself with Young Ireland. There was also considerable militancy in what was written in *The Nation*; for example, in speaking of Poland: "Better a little blood letting to show that there is blood, than a patient dragging of chains and pining. . . ."

The actions of the Young Ireland party brought matters to a head in the summer of 1846. The true story of what happened before the withdrawal of the Young Irelanders and Smith O'Brien from the Repeal Association was never clearly told in the century after the trouble. This was because of the influence of the hatchet operation on O'Connell's reputation in the writings of Mitchel, Doheny, and Duffy—especially Duffy. Therefore, it seems necessary to clarify that position.*

On July 13, 1846, at the weekly meeting of the Repeal Association, O'Connell demanded that the Young Irelanders give their assent to his Peace Resolutions. These expressed the principle that "all political amelioration . . . ought to be sought for, and can be sought for successfully, only by peaceable, legal, and constitutional means, to the utter exclusion of any other." In proposing these

* The following account of the split between O'Connell and Young Ireland in July 1846 is based on a paper written by Professor Maurice O'Connell.

resolutions to the Repeal Association he insisted that they must be accepted "in theory and in practice." The resolutions admitted that this principle did not prohibit "necessary defence against unjust aggression on the part of a domestic government or a foreign enemy." This qualification related only to the use of physical force for a *genuinely* defensive purpose. It is something entirely different from the belief in modern Ireland that violence is noble and may justifiably be used, in a positive way, to remedy serious injustice and to gain great objectives.

Nearly all modern historians have stated that O'Connell presented the Peace Resolutions merely for the purpose of driving the Young Irelanders out of the Repeal Association. This consensus is based on three considerations. The first is that the young men had no intention of taking to physical force in the foreseeable future. The introduction of the Resolutions was therefore unnecessary if intended for the purpose of protecting the Association from adopting that method. The second consideration arises from the belief that O'Connell feared the attacks which the Young Irelanders were making on his renewal of the Whig alliance, and that he cast about for a means of getting rid of them. The third, though unexpressed, consideration is that O'Connell was never fully committed to an ideal, not even to the moral-force principle: hence his use of the Peace Resolutions as an expedient for expelling the young men.

The first consideration—that there was no need to save the Association from the advocates of physical force since the Young Irelanders had no intention of taking up arms —does not stand up to examination. Even though they had no intention of using violence in the foreseeable future, they were constantly praising it in their speeches in the Repeal Association, and that praise was winning enthusiastic applause. For years *The Nation,* their newspaper, had been lauding "the sword" as a means of attaining freedom (usually for countries other than Ireland) in editorials and in the poetry it published. In a land in which violence was endemic such praise was likely in the long run to have practical consequences. The second consideration—that O'Connell feared the Young Irelanders' attacks on his renewal of the Whig alliance—can also be questioned. What has been overlooked is the adroit way O'Connell dealt with those attacks. He did so by placing before the Repeal Association on July 6, 1846, a list of eleven bills and procuring their adoption so that he could seek to have them enacted by the new Whig government of Lord John Russell. These bills comprised security of tenure for farmers (a subject O'Connell had been stressing over the previous six months), a tax on absentee rents, an extension of the parliamentary and municipal franchises, and a curbing of the power of landlords in county administration. It was obvious that there could be no hope of having these measures enacted unless the Repeal Party were to make some commitment to the new government: in effect, to renew the Whig alliance. If the Young Irelanders were to continue to attack its renewal they would leave themselves open to the charge of being indifferent to the welfare of the people. In the hands of the politically astute O'Connell this charge could be a powerful weapon. The renewal of the Whig alliance had therefore ceased to be a danger to him *before* he introduced the Peace Resolutions. The third consideration—that O'Connell was never fully committed to the principle of moral force —is the result ultimately of credence in the hostile and prejudiced writings of the Young Irelanders to which I have already referred. There is nothing so frequently expressed throughout O'Connell's life as his hatred of violence and his belief in moral force. This attitude is seen in the diary he kept as a law student, in his letters, private as well as public, in his speeches, and in his conduct for a period of fifty years. It is poor psychology on the part of historians to believe that on moral force he was not really genuine, that in 1846 he would use that principle as a mere expedient.

The Repeal Association was founded in 1840 on the principle of moral force as part of its constitution; and its allegiance to that principle was reaffirmed in 1841, 1843, 1844, and in January 1846. In May 1846 the Young Irelander Michael Doheny made a fiery speech at a Repeal meeting of Irish workers in Liverpool. O'Connell reacted by having the Repeal Association pledge its allegiance once again to moral force on June 1. During the succeeding four weeks *The Nation* in an editorial and the three Young Irelanders Meagher, O'Gorman, and Smith O'Brien made it clear in speeches to the Association that moral force was a *policy* but not a *principle* of the organization. Coming so soon after the reaffirmation of moral force on June 1 these statements left O'Connell no choice but to act vigorously or to reconcile himself to the fact that moral force was no longer part of the constitution of the Association. Since his efforts in having the principle reaffirmed on June 1 had now been negatived he was compelled to have it affirmed once again but this time with such forcefulness as to rule out all further opposition and dissimulation. The Young Irelanders must either accept moral force as a fundamental principle of the Repeal Association or get out. Historians have treated the Peace Resolutions as if they were something O'Connell pulled out of a hat, as something unique, thereby ignoring the fact that they were merely an unusually forceful repetition of declarations which the Repeal Association had made at its inception and had renewed repeatedly through the years. All the evidence points to the simple conclusion that the Young Irelanders tried to change the nature of the Association, but O'Connell refused to let them.

Two weeks later, on July 27, the issue came up in debate again. O'Connell had returned to London, and his

son John had taken his place at the Association's weekly
meeting. Again, Mitchel and Meagher seemed to be the
spokesmen for the opposition to the moral-force principle. In the course of a bitter, snarling brawl (it deserves
no better characterization), Meagher delivered his so-
called "sword speech":

> Then, my Lord Mayor, I do not disclaim the use of arms as
> immoral nor do I believe it is the truth to say that the God of
> Heaven withholds his sanction from the use of arms. . . . Be it
> for the defense or be it for the nation's liberty. I look upon the
> sword as a sacred weapon. And if, my lord, it has sometimes red-
> dened the shroud of the oppressor, like the anointed rod of the high
> priest, it has at other times blossomed into flowers to deck the free-
> man's brow. . . . Abhor the sword and stigmatize the sword? No,
> my lord, for at its blow a giant nation sprang up from the waters of
> the Atlantic, and by its redeeming magic, the fettered colony be-
> came a free republic. . . .

Such frothy stuff and nonsense may well make an American deplore his own Revolution. That at a critical moment
this sophomoric upstart would win a place in history,
seems incredible. But silly stuff as it was, it precipitated
the issue in the Association. For John O'Connell, with
other O'Connellites, incensed at Meagher's speech, declared that the speaker must leave the Association. Smith
O'Brien, by virtue of his age, experience, and foremost
stature in the Association, should have demanded that the
meeting come to order, but he apparently behaved with
characteristic indecision. Swept by the emotional fever
which dominated the occasion, Smith O'Brien marched
out of the hall followed by Meagher, Mitchel, Duffy, and
other Young Irelanders. The seceders gathered outside,
confused for the moment about what to do next. The damage had been done. The split became permanent, and the
united Repeal movement ended.

And well it might, for the tragedy of the Famine was
sweeping ruthlessly over Ireland. The evidence was ap-
pearing in the wretched fields in August that the second

year's blight was under way. This time the entire potato crop was involved.

In the weeks after the Repeal movement was split and when angry recriminations filled the air, there appeared one clear evaluation of the issue, which seems to have been passed over by historians. This was an editorial by Frederick Lucas in *The Tablet* of August 8, 1846. An English Catholic review, *The Tablet* was founded by Lucas who was born a Quaker but became a Catholic about 1838. He was now in 1846 that almost-unique phenomenon in England, an enthusiastic supporter of Repeal. He was thoroughly aware of the issues between O'Connell and the Young Irelanders since he was well acquainted with several of the writers in *The Nation*.

In the editorial, part of which follows, he does not take their side in the controversy but places the case for O'Connell, his convictions, and his services to the Irish nation, in clear perspective. The remarkable thing about this editorial is that, in the midst of the controversy and under the shadow of the Famine, he reaches conclusions which are now coming to be the considered appraisal of O'Connell and his place in history:

> . . . Those who have paid any attention to Mr. O'Connell's speeches for a course of years, must know . . . that the prospects of Ireland after his death, the fate of the machinery of peaceful agitation which he organized has occupied a great deal of his thoughts. . . .
>
> When he entered on the political stage, he found the people habituated to ideas of war and insurrection as the means of gaining political improvements and enforcing the restoration of political rights. During his whole life he has taught them a different lesson. He has instructed them, both by example and precept, in the value of peaceful agitation. . . .
>
> But is there not a danger that they may regard the successes which he has achieved as due principally to his own great genius? That they may look on peaceful agitation as a weapon mighty in his hand but powerless in the hands of more vulgar politicians?

. . . And after his death may be apt to fall back upon the old notions, and put faith once more in war? . . . It was impossible that O'Connell could help watching with the most anxious suspicion every symptom from which he could learn how to act so as to make his system of tactics not a personal possession merely, but a legacy to be transmitted in its full value to distant generations. A nobler, and at the same time, a more necessary thought could hardly enter into the mind of a great popular statesman.

. . . Men who live on the verge of famine, whom penury and oppression keep in a state of ill-disguised hostility, to those who should guide and protect them, and whom past wrong maddens with a thirst for vengeance as the only readily available means of repressing wrongs to come—men so situated are by their very position the raw materials of rebellion, and are exposed to habitual and deadly temptations to breaches of the law. Proneness of physical force is unhappily their disease. The great mission of O'Connell's life has not merely been to gain Emancipation or to secure Repeal, but to drill, instruct, guide, habituate and organize the people so that the instinct of physical force may be rooted out; so that they may be thoroughly masters of the art of peaceful warfare: . . . so that they may never dream of the insanity of shouldering arms to attain whatever results the nation thinks just and reasonable and vehemently desires for itself.

If Mr. O'Connell had never carried Emancipation, had never gained the victories that now salute him . . . and had only taught the people the one lesson we have described, he would have accomplished a greater and nobler feat than all the Emancipations that ever were wrung from the grasp of disappointed bigots. . . .

Dwelling upon these anxious thoughts what does he see? As his sun is hastening towards the western horizon, he beholds growing up under his wing a school of poets, prosemen, patriots and Repealers who profess to join his march, to follow his lead, to help on his purposes; and who, by their connection with the agitation which he has created, have in a marvellously short time gained a comparatively great hold on the public mind of Ireland. . . .

This school possessed an organ—a weekly journal of great merit, *The Nation,* and earning by its merit great influence. And how did this journal bear itself towards that principle which was the great purpose of O'Connell's life? Did it labour to promote that purpose or to thwart it? On Repeal it was his ally. But on a greater question than Repeal; on the question of questions: on the *rationale* of the means by which Repeals are to be gained; on this it was his constant and able antagonist; from the very first trying to undo

18

Unfinished Journey

HAD O'CONNELL RETIRED FROM PUBLIC LIFE or had he accepted the sanctuary of a judgeship when he was in his fifties, he would have been for ages to come revered as the Emancipator of his people. Instead he chose a quite different and vastly more perilous course. He served ten years of his parliamentary career seeking, through the vicissitudes of politics, to win benefits for his country, and then directed his torrential energy to winning Repeal against insuperable odds. In the course of that task, a group of young allies joined him. When he sought to restrain their unwise and dangerous dispositions, they turned against him and, since they had what was almost a monopoly of the literary arts, they made it their task in later years to belittle his services to Ireland and besmirch his reputation.

O'Connell's efforts in the months after the secession were turned toward reuniting the Association. He used several methods of reaching Smith O'Brien with his entreaties. One was to send his friend and favorite spiritual adviser, Father Miley, to see Smith O'Brien at his home in Cahirmoyle. Smith O'Brien received him with considerable mistrust and offered little encouragement except to leave the door open to further negotiations. Smith O'Brien was also receiving appeals from his young friends at *The Nation*. Their advice varied. Some, like Dillon, seemed to believe in O'Connell's sincerity and to see a possible reconciliation as necessary. Others were irreconcilable and anxious to get on with a separate Repeal movement. Others proposed that Smith O'Brien state a series of conditions before returning to the Association. O'Connell at one time asked that the seceders return without any conditions, but in most appeals he asked that the people who returned not only abjure advocating physical force but refrain from any language suggesting it. Finally in December he addressed a letter to Smith O'Brien which in the clarity of his thought and the rational nature of his argument should forever refute the suggestion that his mind as well as his body was failing. The letter said:

> Pardon me when I say that I deem it a sacred duty solemnly to caution you against making light of the physical force question. It involves your personal safety, which I am free to admit is not a paramount consideration in your mind, but it also involves the safety of others. . . . I should vote for readmission into the Association of very many of the seceders if they would disavow the physical force principle; or if without that disavowal the Association would still be a legal assembly. I say emphatically—it would not—and to ascertain this point and this alone, I propose this legal conference as a preliminary step to a complete conciliation.
>
> Forgive me for pressing this topic upon your mind. I do it in the spirit of respect and courtesy, whilst I bitterly deplore that you should not be a party to an amicable ascertainment, of the effects in point of law of any admixture of the physical force principle with the principles and proceedings of the Association.

It would seem that all O'Connell was asking as a condition of the reunification of the Association was the omission from responsible statements by the leaders of any mention of the threat of physical force. And since at that time neither Smith O'Brien nor Duffy, nor any of the other major leaders, really was planning an uprising, O'Connell's legal point was well taken. The omission of any mention of physical violence in fact would have been wise even if an insurrection was in the minds of some members, for surprise is an essential element of success. O'Connell was simply proposing a means of continuing the agitation without provoking action by the government.

The basis of his apprehension about playing with the threat of physical force was his appraisal (confirmed in 1848) of the mentality of the younger members of the group—Mitchel, Meagher, Doheny, and others—who were in fact at that time intent upon turning the agitation into an action force. It is no tribute to Smith O'Brien's judgment that he himself failed to see this. Smith O'Brien's failure is more positively revealed. He was receiving communications from the extremists strongly arguing against any reconciliation. A quotation from one letter from Mitchel is suggestive of their attitude:

> I am heartily glad, as I think most of us are, that the "Reconciliation" is all over. I never for one moment believed the proposal to be bona fide (nor conceived it possible even if it were bona fide) to make a sound safe Association out of the present one. There are certainly other surer and wider spheres of activity preparing for us and better elements gathering around us.

On the side of O'Connell there was his son John who was just as determined that there should be no reconciliation.

The physical failure of O'Connell at that time is told in a memorable quotation from O'Neill Daunt's recollections. He is describing his impressions when he saw O'Connell in November of that year: "At that meeting I was greatly struck with the physical decay of O'Connell. I had not seen him in public for many months and the change was painfully manifest. His intellect was as strong as ever, but his voice was extremely weak." This is another confirmation of the testimony which we find in all the records: a clear mind but a failing body.

With the end of the sad year of 1846 there vanished all hope of uniting the Repeal movement. Thus another cloud was added to the two which darkened the Liberator's last months on earth. The Famine and plague, perhaps the

most catastrophic visited upon any country in modern
times, had reached a new plateau of devastation. Finally
the old warrior himself realized that his days were numbered and *in extremis* he turned to FitzPatrick to put his
house in such order as was possible. He was still in Dublin with the coming of the new year and in January he
spent considerable time with Lord Bessborough, the Lord
Lieutenant, discussing methods of relief. Early in February he went to London for the opening of Parliament. His
despair was deepened when he realized that there was no
comprehension in London of conditions in Ireland. He
said in a letter to T. M. Ray who still presided over the
Association's inactive offices: "The obstacles in the House
of Commons are manifold, and there seems to be an ignorance of the state of horror in which Ireland is
plunged."

When a few days later he appeared in the House, members were shocked at the change in the great figure they
knew in earlier years. His old enemy Disraeli commented
on this appearance:

> His appearance was of great debility and the tones of his voice
> were very still. . . . [I]t was a strange and touching spectacle to
> those who remembered the form of colossal energy and the clear
> and thrilling tones that had once startled, disturbed and controlled
> senates. . . . [T]o the House generally it was the performance of
> a dumb show, a feeble old man muttering before a table; but
> respect for the great parliamentary personage kept all as orderly
> as if the fortunes of a party hung on his rhetoric.

O'Connell's voice was so weak that the press gallery heard
and recorded only a sentence or two: "Ireland is in your
hands . . . she cannot save herself . . . one fourth of
her population will perish unless you come to her aid."
There was little he could do in the House, but he was
able to have an interview with the Prime Minister, Lord
John Russell. He asked that some suitable position be
provided for P. V. FitzPatrick in recognition for his de-

votion to O'Connell's affairs over the years. Russell responded by making FitzPatrick Assistant Register of
Deeds in Dublin. FitzPatrick, knowing of O'Connell's
weakened condition, arranged with Archbishop Murray
of Dublin to send Father Miley to accompany O'Connell
on the trip abroad which had been ordered by the doctors.
In the time which remained many visitors called at
O'Connell's quarters to pay their respects. On March 22
he and Father Miley sailed from Folkstone to Boulogne.

In his letters and recollections, Father Miley left us a
vivid account of the unfinished journey. At several places
in France there were stopovers and the fame of the invalid
brought many admirers to speak with him and pay him
tribute. His complete resignation to the imminence of
death was accompanied by almost continuous prayer. In
Lyons his condition was so grave that Father Miley summoned a physician. A week later Father Miley wrote to
FitzPatrick complaining that, despite their expectation
that some relief might come with a warmer climate, snow
and cold still persisted. Finally, with the coming of May
and their arrival in Italy, there was sunshine and relief
from the cold. But in Genoa the sick man stubbornly refused to continue the journey to Rome. His illness took a
turn for the worse and he was unable to take food or medi-
cine. With the end imminent, the high officials of the
Church were summoned. They came, with the Cardinal-
Archbishop of Genoa in the lead. After the last rites, the
end came rather soon, on May 17, 1847.

His wish that his heart should be buried in Rome was
carried out, and Father Miley and son Daniel were received by Pope Pius IX. The heart was placed in the Irish
College in Rome. His body was taken to Dublin.

The funeral services which had been delayed until
August were preceded by an immense reception as the
funeral ship moved through the shipping on the Liffey.
Tradition has it that, as the ship came in sight, an emi-
grant ship, the *Birmingham,* loaded with Irish families

not until December 1846 that the government woke up to the appalling nature of the disaster and put in motion the radical measures which were so desperately needed.

In January 1847 the Young Irelanders set up the Irish Confederation which they hoped would supplant the Repeal Association. Among the founders was John Mitchel who, in his editorials in *The Nation,* had moved toward more and more extreme political and economic proposals. His intellectual associate in formulating these proposals was James Fintan Lalor. Lalor came from a family which had been active in repeal politics but he had no interest in Repeal, considering it only a half-measure. He was a bitter enemy of the existing order and, in what he wrote while associated with Mitchel, advocated the breakup of landlordism by expropriation of the land. This antagonized Smith O'Brien. Since Duffy agreed with Smith O'Brien, Mitchel was compelled to leave the new Confederation and resign from *The Nation.* Most of the people who had joined the Confederation went along with Smith O'Brien and Duffy in an effort to create a parliamentary party designed to follow traditional methods toward Repeal. Mitchel, after leaving *The Nation,* founded a short-lived rival journal called the *United Irishman.* His radicalism now had full play. His concept of nationalizing the land was supplemented by a call to refuse to pay rents and poor-rates. To back up this economic program, he also advocated preparation for a revolution by gathering weapons and practicing their use.

After the revolution in France in February 1848, the Young Irelanders were led to believe that a similar upset might be engineered in Ireland. Duffy and Smith O'Brien were beguiled by this argument, not realizing that, with hundreds of thousands dying and others crowding the ships to escape the Famine, there was small interest in political change. Encouraged by this change in Duffy and Smith O'Brien, Mitchel rejoined the Confederation and *The Nation.* At the same time, Smith O'Brien headed a delegation which visited the new governors of France. Following the fateful pattern of Wolfe Tone half a century before, these emissaries discussed help from France. Also the Confederation ordered its local clubs to gather arms and prepare for a revolution in Ireland.

This was, of course, known to the government, and Smith O'Brien, Meagher, and Mitchel were arrested and charged with sedition. Smith O'Brien and Meagher were released, but Mitchel was convicted and sentenced to 14 years' imprisonment. He was transported to Bermuda and later to Tasmania. He escaped in 1853 and settled in New York and, later, in Tennessee. He became a vigorous upholder of slavery and a strong advocate of the Confederate cause in the Civil War.

An account of what happened during the fiasco of a revolt that July is almost unbelievable. The promoters of the "uprising" were intelligent, educated men, presumably in full possession of their mental faculties—Smith O'Brien, Dillon, Meagher, and others. They had made no real preparations beyond issuing a great deal of printed material imploring the people to prepare for an uprising. Unlike most revolutions, the center of action was not in an urban center, where facilities for communication could be seized and controlled. What action took place was in a stretch of countryside from Wexford near the southeast coast to Limerick in the southwest-central part of the island. Apparently the leaders believed that, with the sounding of a horn or the explosion of a musket or the loud cry of someone, the population would spring to what arms it possessed and by sheer numbers overwhelm the police and the army.

What happened is not easy to describe in simple terms, although there is a great deal of written material describing the actions of various participants. Never was a revolution so fully reported with so little shooting and such meager results. Every participant, after it was over, rushed pen to paper with his own version of the happen-

ings in his section of the excitement. Indeed, Smith
O'Brien wrote a long account which was for use at his
prospective trial for treason, a narrative which included
much of his public life.

The three who were assumed to be leaders—Smith
O'Brien, Dillon, and Meagher—decided that Kilkenny
should be the center of operations. This city was selected
because it was somewhat beyond easy reach of the warships which were uncomfortably numerous along the
southeast coast. The narratives of the three, especially
Meagher's, then tell of a leisurely journey west from Kilkenny. Wherever they stopped at a town there were excited people to greet them, and they made speeches calling
on the population to be ready for the insurrection. They
made no secret of their intentions. When they got to Car-
rick the enthusiasm was so great that Meagher wanted to
start the uprising there, but the others dissuaded him. And
so they went from town to town until they reached Ballingarry, County Tipperary. There are various versions
of what happened in and around Ballingarry but it appears that Smith O'Brien and his friends managed to
gather a force of about 600 peasants of whom about 50
had muskets and 150 had pikes and pitchforks. Smith
O'Brien and Dillon drilled this strange army.

When news came that forces of police and military
were on their way it was apparently decided not to sound
the call but for the leaders to scatter to neighboring towns
to get reinforcements. Several left but Smith O'Brien remained with some of the original group, and they were
joined by about 100 miners from a nearby colliery. This
small number, anticipating the arrival of government
forces, threw up a rude barricade. A troop of armed
police, alarmed by what appeared to be a large force,
took refuge in a house up the hill belonging to a widow
named McCormick. Mrs. McCormick was away and on
her return was told that her house was occupied by police.
She accordingly confronted Smith O'Brien and berated

him. Then someone threw a stone which shattered a kitchen window, whereupon the police fired and killed two or three of the insurgents.

Terence Bellew McManus, who had remained with Smith O'Brien and who wrote an account of this last day, says that he was determined to set fire to the house but was restrained by Smith O'Brien because of the danger to the McCormick children who were still in the house. Smith O'Brien now called off the insurrection, and he and his companions went into hiding. There were no informers but within a few days Smith O'Brien and several of the other leaders were rounded up, and quiet was restored. Thus ended the Young Irelanders' attempt at revolution.

There remains to tell only the story of what became of the participants. For this fiasco terminated the Young Irelanders as a group, the Confederation, and the Repeal movement. Smith O'Brien, Meagher, and McManus were tried for high treason, found guilty, and sentenced to death. Not wishing to create martyrs the government commuted the sentences to transportation, and the prisoners were shipped as convicts to Tasmania. Smith O'Brien was liberated in 1854 but was not allowed to return to Ireland until 1856. He took no further part in public life except to advise that further nationalist endeavors be limited strictly to constitutional methods. Meagher escaped and found his way to the United States where he became a general in the Union Army during the Civil War. Afterward he was sent as Secretary to the Territory of Montana. Dillon escaped to the United States disguised as a priest. He practiced law there for a while, and on his return to Ireland served for a year as a member of Parliament. Duffy was tried but escaped conviction. He revived *The Nation* and returned to political activity, being elected to Parliament in 1852. In 1855 he emigrated to Australia where he eventually became the Prime Minister of Victoria.

Thomas D'Arcy McGee was another of the insurgents.

Disguised as a priest he reached the United States where he had some success in the newspaper business. Later he moved to Canada where he took a prominent part in politics and became a cabinet minister. Michael Doheny's experiences after the insurrection are told in his book *The Felon's Track,* which was first published in 1849. In the course of his wanderings he met James Stephens and they later found themselves in the United States. There, with John O'Mahony, they founded the Fenian Brotherhood. Richard O'Gorman, a close friend of Smith O'Brien's, remained in hiding in County Limerick and then escaped to New York. He practiced law and ultimately became a judge. There were several other refugees, not mentioned in the foregoing account, who became American citizens. Their history after leaving Ireland, and their writings, show that the Young Irelanders had great talent, and a considerable part of the misunderstanding and derogation of O'Connell in the United States has been caused by the influential writing and contacts of these refugees.

The image of Smith O'Brien, as he participated in the events of those years, is that of a generous, highminded Irish patriot. He had the courage to break from the Protestant aristocracy into which he was born and to give his support to the Catholic population. His considerable experience in Parliament gives the impression of a sober, conscientious member who was independent of any strong party ties. He was not a brilliant man and, as a speaker, he was quiet, factual, friendly, and wholly unexciting. From his first contacts with Thomas Davis, he was immensely impressed by the younger man's brilliance and also measurably flattered by Davis' reliance upon his superior age and experience. Finally, after the secession, his grasp of the realities seemed to desert him. His normal caution was overwhelmed by his emotional attachment to the younger men, and without circumspection he permitted himself to drift along with the hotheads, accepting violence as an inevitable but foolish choice. He

rejected O'Connell's sincere effort to bring about a reconciliation within the Repeal movement. After O'Connell's
death, he might have given strong leadership to the Repeal movement, but at that critical moment, instead of
restraining the younger men, he followed them into an
insurrection which a boy of ten might have told him
would be a fiasco.

20

The Evolution
of a Reputation

THE GHOST OF THE GREAT LIBERATOR was not allowed the
quiet it deserved in the shadow of the round tower over
the crypt in Glasnevin Cemetery. For the storm of controversy which saddened those final years broke afresh
after the hapless revolt of 1848. It continued until practically all of his contemporaries followed O'Connell to
their graves. The reputation of the man whose name
meant so much in the years after Emancipation was the
subject of prejudicial and ill-conceived attacks. O'Connell's most hostile critics, mostly survivors of the Young
Ireland group, were passionately concerned not only with
justifying their own ideas and course of action but with
discrediting the man who had in his life sought to restrain
them. Ill betides the public man whose critics are young
enough to survive him and are able to have their way with
him. And this ill fortune is multiplied many times when
those critics are armed with the talents of professional
writers. Duffy, Mitchel, Doheny, and several others produced books which portrayed the story of their country's
fight for liberation. Noteworthy among these were two
written by John Mitchel; one was entitled *The Last Con-
quest of Ireland,* which appeared in 1860, and the other,
The Jail Journal, was published in 1854. Michael
Doheny's *The Felon's Track* was published first in New
York in 1849. But the most effective hatchet job was from
the hand of Charles Gavan Duffy. In 1880 he produced

*Young Ireland: A Fragment of Irish History, 1840–
1845,* and in 1883 another book, called *Four Years of
Irish History, 1845–1849,* both published in London. In
1898 he summed up his whole life in two volumes, *My
Life in Two Hemispheres.* The Duffy output was enormous. Understanding, as a journalist, the effectiveness of
reiteration, he repeated much of his story in the various
books he produced. Recent scholarship has convicted
Duffy of exaggeration, misinterpretation, gross prejudice,
and subtle falsification. But the "big lie," boldly and repeatedly asserted, does not wither and die: it seeps into
unwary minds and remains. Moreover, since violence was
so widely accepted in the years after Duffy's books were
published, there were hundreds of thousands quite willing to accept prejudiced testimony against O'Connell, the
man of moral force.

The damage to O'Connell's reputation caused by those
books was compounded by what the refugees who settled
in the United States did with their prejudiced stories. A
large contingent of the lesser figures in the Young Ireland group, as well as more prominent ones like Meagher,
either by word of mouth or in scribblings in the press,
effectively indoctrinated the Irish-American population.
The result, even now, is a widespread lack of knowledge
about O'Connell and his significance in Irish history.
Even Irish-Americans who have visited Dublin reveal
little understanding of the reason for an O'Connell Street
or an O'Connell Bridge, or what the huge monument in
the street means.

Professor Oliver MacDonough says that a friend of
O'Connell's told the Liberator after his victory in the
Clare election in 1829, "Othello's occupation's gone."
This was intended to suggest that in achieving Emancipation for the Catholics, O'Connell "worked himself out
of a job." The termination of Protestant ascendancy was
finally and completely achieved only after the enactment
of the various land reforms from 1881 to 1903. With the

coming of complete equality, the memory of years when the Catholics were subject to legal discrimination was so faded into the past that the memory of the man who fought against that discrimination measurably faded too. Also, with the popularization of violence in the twentieth century, another of O'Connell's great ideals, moral force, lost much of its appeal.

Nothing succeeds like success. The hard fact that Irish self-government came in the twentieth century, after a bloody revolution, seemed to justify violence by the proof of cause and effect. When the war erupted in 1914, a constitutional crisis was interrupted and the Nationalist and Unionist leaders, Redmond and Carson, agreed to support the war effort under the terms of a compromise proposed by the Asquith government. This provided for the enactment of Home Rule legislation, with the proviso that the plan would become operative at the end of the war. This peaceful settlement was never to be consummated. Irreconcilable elements in Ireland, rejecting Home Rule, were determined upon separation by violent means.

The insurrection of Easter Week 1916 made Home Rule difficult if not impossible. A leading historian of Sinn Fein has said that the 1916 insurrection made Partition inevitable. It was likely to come anyway, given the Northern Protestants' determination to oppose Home Rule, but the outbreak of nationalist violence played into the hands of the Orangemen. The 1918 general election and the declaration of the Republic by the 1919 Dáil ruled out Home Rule since the Sinn Fein movement would no longer accept a moderate settlement. In November and December 1913 the leaders of the Tory party in Britain had decided to allow Home Rule to be granted to the 26 Counties provided the Six (northern) Counties were excluded from the Home Rule bill. Henceforth, the real issue was the fate of the Six. Thus the Sinn Fein revolution, using violence, achieved independence only for that portion of Ireland to which Home Rule would have been granted had constitutional methods been pursued. The fact that independence for the 26 Counties was achieved with the aid of violence convinced a whole generation of Irishmen and Irish-Americans that moral force, constitutionalism, and non-violence were an insubstantial vision.

After O'Connell's death and for thirty years or more a great deal was written about him. There were several biographies and countless articles. Unfortunately, most of these publications were so partisan and uncritical and so badly written that they ill-served the reputation of the man. There were several exceptions, however. In 1848 O'Neill Daunt produced his personal recollections of O'Connell in two interesting volumes; and in 1888 William J. FitzPatrick published a limited edition of O'Connell correspondence.

The first good historical study was by the distinguished historian William E. H. Lecky, in his *Leaders of Public Opinion in Ireland*. This book appeared in 1861 when the author was only 23. Considering that O'Connell had been dead only fourteen years and that much of the relevant source material was not yet available, the young historian produced a remarkably fine and objective work. However, Lecky's objection to Repeal, his sympathy with the landlord class, and his belief that O'Connell was wrong in bringing the priests into the Emancipation movement, twisted his final judgment. This opinion must have been deeply rooted, for it survived in revisions of the book. Here is his conclusion in the edition of 1903:

> The more I dwell upon the subject the more I am convinced of the splendour and originality of the genius and of the reality of the patriotism of O'Connell, in spite of the animosities that surround his memory and the many and grievous faults that obscured his life. But when to the great services he rendered to his country we oppose the sectarian and class warfare that resulted from his policy, the fearful elements of discord and turbulence he evoked,

and which he alone could in some degree control, it may be questioned whether his life was a blessing or a curse to Ireland.

In some ways the most important evaluation of O'Connell came not from an historian but from a statesman, William Ewart Gladstone. His article (it was a review of an edition of O'Connell's correspondence) appeared in 1889 in *Nineteenth Century,* a periodical, 42 years after the Liberator's death. It is true that the great Liberal's disposition was highly favorable to Irish claims in the year in which he wrote. Four years before, as Prime Minister, he had introduced his first Home Rule bill and in 1893 he was to make his second attempt to establish an Irish Parliament. But these manifestations of sympathy for Ireland were not based solely upon personal preferences. They were the settled policies of the Liberal Party and the greatly altered state of English opinion. Gladstone's estimate places O'Connell as the greatest Irishman who had ever lived, greater than Grattan and Swift and comparable only with Burke. Among European nationalist leaders of the nineteenth century, such as Kossuth and Mazzini, he was most closely comparable with Cavour. But with Cavour and Burke the comparison is difficult, according to Gladstone, for their reputation rests upon parliamentary activity and political theory, while O'Connell's greatness was as a popular leader. "Almost from the opening of my Parliamentary life I felt that he was the greatest popular leader whom the world had ever seen." He continued:

> It would not be easy to name a man who has attained to equal aggregate excellence with O'Connell in the threefold oratory of the bar, the platform, and the senate. As a parliamentary speaker, no one, in matching him with his contemporaries of the House of Commons, would have relegated him to the second class; but it might be difficult to find his exact place in the first. He was greatest when answering to the call of the moment in extempory bursts, and least great when charging himself with extended and complex exposition. As an advocate, it may, I apprehend, be asked, without

creating surprise, whether the entire century has produced any one more eminent. . . . It is here that Brougham, greatly his superior in Parliamentary eloquence and in general attainments, falls so far behind him. As orator of the platform, he may challenge all the world; for who ever in the same degree as O'Connell trained and disciplined, stirred and soothed, a people?

The perceptiveness of this estimate of O'Connell's power as a speaker comes with the authority of a statesman who himself ranks as an orator among the immortals.

Gladstone, who created and led the Liberal Party, speaks of O'Connell's service to that party: "having adopted the political creed of Liberalism, he was as thorough an English Liberal, as if he had had no Ireland to think of. He had energies to spare for Law Reform . . . , for Postal Reform . . . , for secret voting, for Corn Law Repeal, in short for whatever tended, within the political sphere, to advance human happiness and freedom." Finally, Gladstone praises the consistency of O'Connell. "He never for a moment changed his end; he never hesitated to change his means. His end was the restoration of the public life of Ireland. . . ." Here Gladstone's opinion takes issue with many of O'Connell's critics who have accused him of being addicted to expediency in his relations with the Whigs.

> Early in 1835 came the epoch of what was termed the Lichfield House compact. "Compact there was none," says Earl [Lord John] Russell . . . , "but an alliance." Nothing could be more honourable, nothing more wise. O'Connell was ready, like a man of sense, to try out fairly and fully the experiment of government from London, and on the condition of justice to Ireland, if attainable, to waive, even to abandon, the policy of Repeal.

Gladstone quotes with approval the estimate of the great diarist, Greville, whom he calls "most dispassionate of judges," who said of O'Connell's position in British politics: "there never was before, and there never will be again, anything at all resembling it. [He was] the most important and the most conspicuous man of his time and country."

With the turn of the century and the end of the Victorian age, a process of political change swept over English politics which to a degree was favorable to Ireland and to Irishmen. It was inevitable with the resurgence of liberal ideas and the Liberal Party that a more rational and sympathetic hearing be given to the perennial Irish question. And in the course of this change it was inevitable that the name and reputation of O'Connell should be rescued from neglect and obloquy. In 1900 a little-known and rather undistinguished biography was published in the United States. It was *Daniel O'Connell and the Revival of National Life in Ireland* by Robert Dunlop. In 1903 the first edition of Michael MacDonagh's fine biography appeared in Ireland. This work, greatly enlarged and rewritten, came out during the centenary of Emancipation. A most impressive volume appeared in 1906 by Arthur Houston, K.C. It is entitled *Daniel O'Connell: His Early Life and Journal, 1795–1802.*

In the series of events which ended with the establishment of the Irish Free State, O'Connell's name suffered a great deal from the bitterness of Arthur Griffith and others who had rejected non-violence in the years of the revolution. But after the new government had taken office, and with reasonable quiet restored, the centenary of 1829 was marked by the appearance, not only of MacDonagh's revised biography, but the first edition of Denis Gwynn's biography. This appeared in revised form in the centenary of O'Connell's death.

In 1964 Dr. Angus Macintyre published a detailed account of O'Connell and the Repeal Party in his *The Liberator.* And in the United States the University of Kentucky published in 1966 and 1968 two books by Professor Lawrence J. McCaffrey, one on O'Connell in 1843 and the other a history of Ireland under the Union. In 1966 a history appeared which did much to set the O'Connell record straight, and with much precision, clarity, and objectivity. It is *The Making of Modern Ireland, 1603–1923,* by Professor James C. Beckett of Queen's University, Belfast. Professor Beckett's estimate of O'Connell is noteworthy as an indication of how far the Liberator's reputation has been restored:

> He remains a man of transcendent genius, which he devoted to the service of his native land; no other single person has left such an unmistakable mark on the history of Ireland. The character of the revolutionary tradition, which he detested, and the political development of the Protestants, whom he attempted in vain to win over to Repeal, were both affected profoundly, though in different ways, by the career and achievement of O'Connell.

21

The Durable O'Connell

I HAVE BECOME CONVINCED, in composing this essay, that the slate is sufficiently clean, and the passions of the nineteenth century sufficiently stilled, to take the measure of this man, soberly and clearly. For a reconsideration of the lineaments of his mind, the content of his message, and the political methods he invented and used, should provide for Americans of all national origins and creeds a better understanding of the political world in which we live. Moreover, what is called the science of politics, which is not a science but an art occasionally trying to be scientific, may well profit by a consideration of this master who for decades held the allegiance of millions of his countrymen.

In appraising any consequential political figure, we consider first the purpose or mission which dominated his actions and after that the methods he employed to achieve his ends. To determine this is not always easy, for the reality is not always found in what a politician says. Politics involves much that is pure make-believe. It is part of the rules for a politician seeking power to claim an objective which is frequently so vague and contrived that in reality it must be regarded as a mask to conceal the selfish pursuit of position or power. To get at the reality we must test the claimed objective in the light of the subject's behavior.

With O'Connell the test is easy to make, for even his hostile critics have not denied the consistency with which he pursued his mission. This mission was, according to

Gladstone, "the restoration of the public life" of his country. We can doubt whether the word "restoration" is appropriate, for it is to be doubted whether, at least in the two centuries before O'Connell, there was such a thing as national consciousness in Ireland. His great contribution to modern Ireland was in calling into being something like mass opinion which encompassed not only the great Catholic population but all Protestants who were willing to claim an interest in Irish nationality. The nationality he evoked was never merely chauvinistic or sectarian. He knew his history too well to exaggerate what some called the glories of the past. He knew well that the tales and the songs of the bards were not concerned with the real heart of the Irish race. What glory they celebrated was concerned with the great families and landlords who lived off the labor of the poor. O'Faolain says in alluding to the poets that they were concerned only with "the nobles, friars, clerics, learned folk, poets, heroes, seers, and bards," never with the peasant.* By contrast, O'Connell, with copious doses of that flattery which became habitual as the years passed, gratified the peasant's heart by extravagant references to the virtues of the poor, and, in the process of awakening the most abject creatures' hearts, he drew a certain advantage from the oppression inflicted by the English, for whatever the Irish lacked in achievement, in initiative, and in industry could be blamed on the oppressors. Along with this lifting of the hopes and aspirations of his people, his oratory warmed their hearts with happy pictures of a possible future on earth.

O'Connell realized, when he began his agitation shortly after the imposition of the Act of Union, that his first task was to awaken the people of Ireland, the millions who

---

* O'Connell's one contribution to historiography was his volume, *An Historical Memoir on Ireland and the Irish*. This was dedicated to the young Queen Victoria. It consisted of a documented account of the English depredations from 1172 to 1660. A promised second volume never appeared.

tilled the soil, populated the towns, and filled the
churches, and make them want what he was trying to get
for them. He must make them understand that the wretchedness which was part of their lives was imposed not
solely by nature like the weather and bodily ills, but by
something called government in Dublin Castle and London. And that to get relief they must believe in themselves,
have pride in being Irish, and, by all means short of violence, fight for their rights. To accomplish this was a
massive task, for more than a century of oppression had
reduced these people to an inert, sodden mass of serfdom.
It meant that something of his courage, pride, and force
must be absorbed by the millions who heard his message.
That he succeeded in this was proved by the support of
the Catholic Association and also by the elections in
Waterford and Clare when the peasants defied their landlords. It must be written always that the crowning glory of
O'Connell was that he inspired pride in the Irish people
—pride in themselves and in their country.

Sheil put this into words in a speech in the House of
Commons:

If we were seven millions of mere dull, uneducated, degraded
serfs, a mere mass of helotism, to our seven millions little regard
should be paid. Once, indeed, we were sunk by the Penal Code.
But a marvellous change has taken place. . . . Not only has the
plough climbed to the top of the mountain and cultivation pierced
the morass, but the mind of Ireland has been reclaimed.

You educate our people, and with the education of our people,
the continuance of unjust and unnatural institutions is incompati-
ble. But if education has done much, agitation has done more. Public opinion, which before did not exist, has been created in Ireland.
The minds of men of all classes have been inlaid with the principles
on which the rights of the majority depend. This salutary influence has ascended to the higher classes, spread among the middle
and descended among the lower. The humblest peasant has been
nobly affected by it.

Even in the most abject destitution he has begun to acquire
self respect. I remember the time when, if you struck an Irish
peasant, he cowered beneath the blow. Strike him now and the

spirit of offended manhood starts up in a breast covered with rags. No sir, we are not what we were. We have caught the intonation of your rhymes. Englishmen, we are too like you to give you leave to keep us down. . . . We are an undecaying and imperishable people.

A hundred years later, no doubt inspired by Sheil, whom he quotes, O'Faolain is compelled to admit:

> He taught simple men to have pride. . . . He gave them the elements of life, cleverness and the seed of a civilization. . . . He gave them discipline and a great tolerance, and between them he moulded many divergent elements into something approaching unity.

O'Faolain merely mentions "discipline" in passing, but this is something so important in appraising O'Connell that it has been in my mind throughout the writing of this essay. An immensely important matter in seeking to interpret the Irish race is that never, at least in the three centuries before O'Connell, did the Irish have what in a modern nation can be called discipline. Discipline, in the sense in which I use the term here, is applied to people living together and with an ingrained response to some sort of authority. This may be a king, a legislative body, a council of elders, a court, or an elected chief of state. Whatever it is, it elicits a measurable response and obedience. It is the cement which holds societies together. There are all sorts of responses to this authority. It wields its governance by consent of the governed. Without it, a society or nation dissolves in chaos. Since before Elizabeth, Ireland had known authority as an alien force, centered far away, unseen except through its inimical instruments, something to be hated but endured. There could be no feeling of kinship between masters and subjects, no understanding or acquiescence—only submission, sullen, grudging submission, always secreting a determination to disobey when the opportunity offered.

Law, in a modern free state, is something which facilitates transactions and relations among individuals, singly or collectively, or with the state. It is regarded either as beneficial or as an annoying but necessary factor in life; however, in those centuries it was almost wholly negative, surrounding the individual on all sides, commanding, forbidding, and specifying the compulsions under which someone, usually the landlord, was authorized to make his exactions. It is true that there was the discipline of religion operating through the priest and the bishop, but this almost exclusively related to the compulsions of the Church's rituals and to matters of faith and morals. In the vast area of secular affairs, discipline was a negative matter to be endured or evaded. With the coming of O'Connell the great masses of the Irish people who heard, or heard of, him felt something in their drab lives which they had never known before. Here was a compelling force, visible, articulate, speaking what they conceived to be their thoughts, and putting into patterns of words the privations, the exploitation, and the injustices which they felt. They conceived of him as one of their own kind, embodying in his massive personality their affections, tribulations, and prejudices. The language he used in addressing them was the Gaelic–English patois which was the currency of their daily lives, mixed with passages of "high falutin'" rhetoric, the meaning of which was beyond them. But the rhythm pleased the ear, and withal the beautiful voice quickened the currents of their emotions.

Generations of these people who had long since lost the energy and knowledge to do for themselves had developed a great hunger for leadership. True, they had a number of illustrious men who were speaking for them, Grattan and Keogh, for example; but the appeals of these statesmen were directed to parliaments and committees which were far from the lives of the subjects of their discourse. O'Connell was near and vital and understandable. As they gave him their love and devotion, so they gave him

their obedience, and from this tie, which grew stronger
with the years, they felt the discipline which made for
unity, and Irishmen could hear in their mind's ear the
gate of a new life creaking open.

While O'Connell the agitator came to be renowned
over the Western world as the embodiment of the revival
of Irish nationalism, the mind of O'Connell the statesman
ranged far beyond nationalism in the world of the future.
In this respect he ranks high as a prophet. He was quite
aware that nature had imposed bounds to Ireland's independence. A glance at the map told him a great deal.
England enjoyed all the advantages and dangerous responsibilities of her nearness to the Continent. The
Thames estuary was the gateway to the Continent and the
world. It was the pathway of Empire. Ireland by comparison was remote. To the west was the broad ocean, and
to the east dependence upon England was decreed by
nature. The climate, the soil, the location of the rivers
decreed that Ireland should be heavily agricultural. Its
location did not favor wide commercial relations. When
the industrial revolution came, England's primacy was
assured, for there was coal to feed the new steam monsters
and iron could be imported by the great merchant marine.
Ireland had no iron and virtually no coal. With amicable
and logical relations, without the impediments of politics
and religion, it would have been quite in the course of
things for Ireland to provide food and manpower to the
neighbor to the east.

The industrial revolution was in progress during
O'Connell's lifetime. He recognized that one result of
this development in England was a tremendous formation of capital. Ireland could not create capital.* Its chief
outlet for export was to the east and its materials for ex-

---

*Perhaps I should qualify this by saying that it had practically no risk or
mobile capital. Money saved was invested mostly in land or government securities. Even so, the amount of this sort of non-risk capital was minute compared
with what prevailed in England.

port came from its fruitful land. All these natural in-
centives for close commercial relations were frustrated by
political and religious factors. Consequently, as O'Connell
saw it, the destiny of Ireland called for the removal of
those frustrations, and, in free trade and mutually advantageous economic arrangements, he could see a bright
future for Ireland. These projections, however, were far
beyond the comprehension of the masses. They were im-
parted to his intimates or kept to himself.

The course of events since O'Connell's death has seen
a series of developments which reveal the soundness of
his views as a prophet. He was never a republican. He
realized that complete independence would not serve the
best interests of either country. However, the experience
of Ireland under the Union pointed to the absolute necessity of legislative autonomy under some sort of Home
Rule. The idea of governing a restive nation through an
alien Parliament, even though representatives of the subject nation are elected, is preposterous. Such a governing
plan violates every political principle evolved since the
dawn of history. It is worse than a protectorate, in which
a proconsul or viceroy is sent by a master government to
rule over a colony, because such a governor must, if he is
to maintain order, have some sort of advisory help from
the native population. Under the Union the people sent
over to dwell in Dublin Castle were, in the climate which
prevailed for many years, except during the Drummond
period, sealed off from the nation they were supposed to
govern. Their contacts with the common people of Ireland were through an aggregation of mostly ignorant, corrupt middlemen and police who served little purpose
except to plunder and irritate the governed. It was clear
to O'Connell that this could not prevail. His effort to
"make the Union work" under the Whigs failed. Home
Rule was bound to come, he reasoned, and therefore it
should come peacefully and by constitutional means.

We shall never know how long O'Connell nourished

the idea of federation. It seems wholly likely that he had secretly entertained it long before he proposed it in his letter to the Repeal Association. But when he proposed such a compromise with Repeal, he had entered that physical decline which precluded an explanation of the subject which would have offered a chance for a fair consideration. What happened was a heated claim that O'Connell was "selling out Repeal," a protest in which the Young Irelanders were vociferous. He could not endure the prospect of what would have been bitter controversy on the subject, and so he withdrew the suggestion. He could not know, however, that in suggesting federation he was pointing with true prophetic foresight toward the future. For what is the Commonwealth system but a form of federalism on a world-wide scale?

The political strategy to which O'Connell adhered throughout his career centered on his conviction that his agitation must persuade, not force, the government of England to grant what he conceived to be the rights of Ireland. Although on one occasion, the "Mallow Defiance," there was the threat of violence, his opposition to violence as a means of attaining political ends was emphasized in every speech and public paper. In his final years, disturbed and annoyed by the Young Irelanders' belligerent nationalism, non-violence became almost an obsession. To give maximum effect to his agitation, he relied upon two supports. One was the mobilization of a unified public opinion in Ireland, rich and poor, tenant and landlord, in short a nationwide constituency; and also the moral support of the more liberal-minded people of England, including as many of the new industrial workers as he could influence.

When O'Connell entered Parliament, opposition to the Tory ascendancy was passing through its historic transformation from traditional Whiggism to what Lord John Russell later officially called Liberalism. As Gladstone noted, O'Connell embraced the principles of this new

Liberalism. Foremost among these evidences of political change was the Reform Act of 1832. O'Connell's strong support of this measure won him friends among the Whigs, but as a party, the Whigs included little in the legislation which benefited Ireland.

Critics of O'Connell have complained that the ten years which followed his election to the House of Commons were largely misspent. If so, this is to be doubly deplored because they were the very heart of his productive career. So far as these criticisms were voiced by the Young Irelanders, they may be dismissed because of the prejudice of the authors, but even O'Faolain who is measurably sympathetic speaks of the "barren" labor of those years.

It has been noted that most leaders in the political life of Britain made their way to the top (of what Disraeli called the "greasy pole") by getting into the House of Commons early in life and making a career of parliamentary activity. This means mastering the infinitely complex and technical habits, procedures, rules, and standards of value which make up life in the House of Commons. It should be noted that O'Connell entered the House when he had attained the age of 54. His whole public life had been spent on the hustings in Ireland, in the law courts, and in committees and the meetings of associations. When he finally took the oath as an elected member, it still was to be shown whether a man, however renowned, but a novice in parliamentary affairs, would acquit himself in the new climate. Professor Oliver MacDonough has this estimate of how O'Connell performed as a parliamentarian:

> O'Connell became one of the handful of men who came late to Parliament with a large reputation, and retained it undiminished. When one adds to his name those of Cobden, Joseph Chamberlain and Ernest Bevin, one has practically exhausted the category. With his marvellous plasticity, he caught the tone of the House at once. From the moment of his first speech in the House until three months before his death, O'Connell was a major Parliamen-

tary figure, one of the significant contributors to the heroic element in the British Parliamentary tradition.

One answer to the charge that his parliamentary labors were barren is to point out that, since the Act of Union, which was the law in the two countries, it had seemed advisable to O'Connell that he work with the people who could change that law and restore a separate Parliament in Ireland. Within the party system the Whigs offered far more hope than the Tories. They were the loyal opposition to the Tory government when O'Connell appeared and took his seat at Westminster. His decision was to work with them in the hope that his services might purchase concessions for Ireland. Gladstone expresses this policy of O'Connell's as a desire to see if, with cooperation from Ireland, Union could be made to "work." This is not quite true, for the evidence is overwhelming that O'Connell firmly believed at all times that Ireland must have its own Parliament.

Since O'Connell proposed, when he entered Parliament, to work with the Whigs, let us see what he had to offer which was advantageous to them. First, he had his vote and that of a small group of O'Connellites which came to be called his "tail." This group had seldom more than 25 members, of whom several were not wholly dependable. He never had the large and well-organized Irish Party which later recognized the leadership of Parnell.* He also had the solid support of the millions in Ireland who recognized O'Connell as their leader and master. He could speak with the moral sanction of those millions and, despite their limited power to throw their weight in the electoral balance since the forty-shilling freeholders had lost their vote in the Emancipation Act, they were a force to be reckoned with. Finally, there was

---

* The open ballot and the limited franchise prevented O'Connell from having as large a following as Parnell. By 1880 there was a secret ballot, and perhaps 25 per cent of all tenant farmers and a majority of town workers had the vote.

what may be called the O'Connell machine. In any general election, the Whigs were compelled to contest about from thirty to fifty seats in Irish elections. O'Connell's wide connections in Ireland and the great worth of his name made it possible to throw his influence behind Whig candidates in constituencies where he himself had no candidate. This was an asset of incomparable value to the party which must match itself against an almost equal number of Tories. And, finally, his "tail," small as it was, could be the vital margin in organizing the House and in maintaining a government—although, throughout most of the ten years, his cooperation with the Whig party was an effective arrangement which was to the advantage of Ireland. The real masters of the Whig party, the men whose skill in the political art held it together, like Lord John Russell, recognized O'Connell as a brother in a common trade, and also that he was an innovator and master. For he was not merely another parliamentary operator of great capacity, but the dominating figure in a great constituency. Above all, he scrupulously adhered to the true politician's code. He kept his word. He was faithful in fulfilling his promises. He could be depended on. In part of this story I have described the methods employed by O'Connell in building the political power which made his support worth so much to the Whigs.

O'Connell's relations with the Grey government were not pleasant. Grey obviously disliked the Irishman. It was only because O'Connell, in the debates on the Reform bill, was useful that he was recognized at all, and when the Reform measure was passed, there was nothing of substance for Ireland in it. Melbourne was vastly more favorably disposed toward O'Connell than was Grey, and Lord John Russell was exceedingly friendly. The Lichfield House Compact sealed an arrangement which served very well for years. Of the three fruits of the alliance with the Whigs, the new spirit in Dublin Castle was of supreme importance. The administration of Lord Mulgrave as

Lord Lieutenant, Lord Morpeth as Chief Secretary, and Thomas Drummond as Under Secretary, was extraordinarily happy. Drummond, always with the backing of his nominal superiors, was not only a miracle of efficiency but altogether sympathetic to the Catholic majority. During the regime of these three, O'Connell enjoyed a most intimate relationship with the Castle and, with his cooperation, they substantially reorganized the internal machinery of Ireland.

As I have indicated earlier, the reorganization of the police by Drummond was of enormous importance. Under the Drummond reform, the police became a permanently impartial force, especially in Ulster where Drummond suppressed the Orange Order and made the individual Orangemen obey the law. He also enlarged the scope of the authority of the stipendiary magistrates. Under this regime, a considerable number of Catholics were given commissions in the police and in the higher ranges of the civil service. O'Connell feared that, when the Tories returned to power, much of Drummond's reformed establishment would be undone. But Peel had learned a great deal since he first came to Dublin Castle, and during his period of power in the 1840s he effectively kept the Protestant extremists under control and prevented any effort to dismiss the Catholics who had come to office in the Drummond era.

It may be that O'Connell shared the overly optimistic views of some Irishmen that surely Repeal would quickly follow Emancipation; but if he did, he was soon disillusioned. It was quite apparent that there was beyond O'Connell's Irish members virtually no one in the House of Commons who favored Repeal, and no ministry, Whig or Tory, would even consider giving Ireland its own legislature. Moreover, opinion in Ireland was shaky on the subject. When O'Connell realized that working for Repeal in those years would be wasted effort and time, he

decided to take the practical course of trying to improve
Irish relations by cooperation with the Whigs and by
winning sympathy for Ireland among the workers in industrial England.

However, during those years a substantial part of
O'Connell's time was spent in Ireland: speaking at all
sorts of meetings, writing public letters, and exposing
himself to the people. Thus the business of popular education was carried on as it had been in the years before
Emancipation. His true mission in life, the contribution
for which he will always be celebrated, was not neglected
in those years. The measure of any great popular leader is
not how many laws he succeeds in getting enacted or the
diplomatic victories he achieves or the elections he wins.
It is the degree to which he uses his capacity to educate
his people. In the United States, presidents like Jefferson,
Theodore Roosevelt, and Wilson will be remembered
mostly for the moral leadership they exercised rather than
for the measures they succeeded in enacting into law.
O'Connell's greatest contribution was what he taught the
Irish people.

Critics of O'Connell have repeatedly charged that, although he was at all times profoundly concerned with the
hard life of the poor, his position on government-supported
poor-relief ranged from opposition to indifference. The
part which he took in the debate over the 1838 bill to extend
the English Poor Law to Ireland is offered as an example
of his lack of humane instincts. In the first place the English Poor Law was a wretched affair, unfair to the recipi-
ents as well as the taxpayers. One has only to read Dickens
to know what a travesty it was. O'Connell opposed government poor-relief on grounds which were spelled out by
Bentham. He believed that when government assumed
much responsibility for the poor it would dry up private
charity. In the particular bill before Parliament in 1838
he objected to the aid it provided for the able-bodied, and

he preferred a system of aid for emigration and public works; also for the imposition of a tax on absentee landlords. In the end he voted against the bill.

O'Connell was also greatly concerned with the abuses imposed upon the non-union worker by the labor unions of his time. The fact is that, though he denounced the methods which some of the primitive unions of his time used, he was not an opponent of labor organized to secure better working conditions and more compensation. But unlike many Liberals and Radicals at the time he always defended the right of workers to organize in unions.

The conclusion which I reach is that O'Connell's preoccupation was with creating in Ireland a political system through which these matters of government-supported welfare and government regulation of working conditions could be solved by representatives of the people concerned. And, considering that in both England and the United States the problem of abolishing poverty is still unsolved, we are entitled to reserve judgment. Perhaps this comment of O'Faolain's is appropriate:

> In other words, he was not a humanitarian; he was a brutal realist occupied with the present conditions in his own country. His vision of Irish democracy was limited by those conditions, as we have little reason to ask him to vision that democracy as a kind of Worker's Republic, seeing that no Irish politician of our own day so visions it [1937]. He saw his people as a free people in the sense that they would have their own parliament, a popular franchise, popular education, security of tenure on the land, freedom of speech, and freedom of worship, and it was his aim that they would be able with these institutions to choose their own mode of life. . . . In brief he was a political revolutionist first and foremost. He was a social revolutionist only in that he would first provide something to revolutionize.

In this summation of the historical fact of Daniel O'Connell, his ideas, his actions, and his impact upon his people, his country, and the Western world, we come face to face with the need to explain the phenomenon of his leadership. What is it in some extraordinary men which gives them power over their fellows? What is the explanation of leadership?

As a student of politics, I have been intrigued for years by the quite obvious fact that the vast majority of human beings know very little of the society in which they live. Beyond the exercise of their primitive instincts, they have very little capacity to know what to believe, what to say, what to do, and where to go and why. The individual is thus caught in the great flow of circumstance, wholly dependent upon his friends and neighbors, who, in turn, respond to some leader. This is true not only in matters of a political nature but in most everything in life. And I might add, without venturing to probe into the mysteries of scientific psychology and biology, that most animal life shows this pattern of the many directed by the few or the one. In politics, which concerns us here, the incapacity of individuals to think or act upon their own initiative always produces someone to supply direction, usually someone from the ranks whose native gifts set him apart from his fellows. His first concern is to win attention, then interest, then confidence. Finally, he serves as their agent, their spokesman, and almost always their master.

Nature had been lavish in endowing O'Connell with physical characteristics which set him apart from most men.

I have noted earlier from the Journal he kept in his student days that in his frequent visits to the theater he was apparently absorbed in studying the manner in which the actors used their voices. His voice, with the powerful intelligence behind it, was to be the instrument which captured not only the devotion of his nation but the interest and attention of people wherever English was spoken. There are many citations in the O'Connell literature which echo Gladstone's estimate of O'Connell's parliamentary oratory. There is ample evidence in the prints of his time of how O'Connell exploited his physical characteristics and his dress to dominate the stage which he occupied at any specific time or occasion; his great cloak is repeatedly mentioned and his distinctive headgear still strikes us in the old cartoons and the statuary erected in his honor.

The perfection of the image is one of the many factors involved in establishing the association of the leader-politician with his followers, which in recent years has been called a personality cult. We know in O'Connell's case how his personality came to impress itself upon the Irish people, and how those people came to see in him the promise of the good which they themselves could scarcely define but which would bring relief from the burdens of their present life.

He realized when he began his agitation that he must bring those people understanding and, through understanding, unity of purpose. His instinct told him that he could best achieve that end, first by identifying the purpose he sought with his personality, and then by merging his personality with the people. Everyone who has thoughtfully studied his career has commented upon the manner in which O'Connell identified himself, first with the cause of the people, and then with the people themselves. O'Faolain says:

> In whatever way we may try to define the ideal life of the Irish people, his image is likely to rise before the mind—always remembering that he came at the beginning and was only following his instinct in a groping use of the materials at his hand. Lecky said that he studied men, not books; in studying men he found himself, and in finding himself he presented to the people the mirror of their reality.

In countless ways he gratified their feelings, inspiring, amusing, flattering them. In his appearances he swaggered, postured, suited the actions to the words. His language ranged from the Gaelic of his native Kerry, to the half-English spoken by the less-educated even today, to the hightoned diction of the court and the senate. Words, which hearers cannot define, flatter because they carry the assumption that those who hear them deserve the best. There is, even among the most friendly of written comments about O'Connell, repeated assertions that on occasions his language went well beyond the limits of propriety, even in the age in which he lived. Violent, vulgar, and graceless are some of the adjectives used to describe these lapses into billingsgate. Gladstone mentions this habit as "O'Connell's greatest fault" and cites as an example what O'Connell wrote in an attack on Lord Althorp, incidentally a fine man:

> I promise to demonstrate that he has been guilty of the most gross and shameless violation of a public pledge that ever disgraced any British minister since Parliament was first instituted. I do expect to demonstrate that no honest man can vote for Lord Althorp in any county or borough without being content to share his guilt and disgrace.

In his comment on this excessive abuse, Gladstone said that by such excesses O'Connell not only injured himself in the minds of reasonable people but unnecessarily added to the "cruel and inveterate prejudice" which characterized public opinion against Ireland. It is hard to deny this charge and, in the light of the evidence, I do not. But it should be said that some excuse is provided for some of the language in the House for which O'Connell was censured by the Speaker, by the behavior of the Tory benches. According to the record in *Hansard,* whenever O'Connell rose to speak, he was interrupted by discordant outcries and abusive epithets.

In some of his intemperate speeches in Ireland, such as the long tirade in the Magee trial, he was aiming his remarks at his followers all over Ireland. In that particular instance what he said was printed and distributed throughout the country. The semi-literate, uneducated Irish peasants needed to be reached by language they could understand. Their talk was as rough as the life they lived. Their Dan could do no wrong. He said what was in their hearts. It must be remembered that O'Connell's purpose was not merely to explain and inform; it was to excite his friends and provoke his enemies.

Lecky explains that O'Connell was quite aware that the violence of his language was subject to criticism. He said, according to Lecky,

> that he had found his co-religionists as broken in spirit as they were in fortune; that they had adopted the tone of the weakest mendicants; that they seemed ever fearful of offending the dominant caste by their importunity, and that they were utterly unmindful of their powers and of their rights. His most difficult task was to persuade them of their strength, and to teach them to regard themselves as the equals of their fellow countrymen. The easiest way of breaking the spell was to adopt a defiant and overbearing tone. The spectacle of a Roman Catholic fearlessly assailing the highest in the land with the fiercest invective and the most unceremonious ridicule, was eminently calculated to invigorate a cowering people.

His habit of gross exaggeration is easier to explain and forgive. In the first place, exaggeration is an Irish habit, and O'Connell, beneath his education and refinement, was Irish to the marrow of his bones. Perhaps his excesses of flattery were intended to gladden the hearts and awaken the pride of his people. Perhaps his preposterous promises, like his prediction of Repeal "within six months," were to lift up flagging expectations. Perhaps they were to cheer himself. Certainly it harmed no one to be told that the Irish mountains were the "highest in the world."

In all the years of my life, years which have been not without political excitement, the shadow of the Liberator has hovered in the back of my mind. I ask myself now, with such political wisdom as I may have accumulated from my life's experience, what it is about O'Connell which makes him seem so much a contemporary figure, whose ideas and personality have so much that is pertinent to the world today.

Among other reasons why he has been so comfortable to live with, there is the fact that he was never doctrinaire. All manner of damage has been inflicted upon this world by leaders so wedded to dogma and ideology that, in the name of a conviction, they have been willing to wade through turmoil and blood to impose upon the millions who have been foolish enough to accept them as leaders: Stalin, Hitler, Cromwell. O'Connell, in taking positions on public questions, always made sure that there was room for readjustment when conditions changed. He also had that redeeming virtue so rare among reformers—indeed in all political leaders—a sense of humor. Dogma and humor make uneasy partners.

Consider nationalism. O'Connell has rightly been given credit for reviving the spirit of Irish nationality after the long, hideous night of the eighteenth century. But his vision for Ireland went far beyond nationalism. He saw his country's destiny as a prosperous member of a world of interdependent nations. He never favored severing the ties with England. And his suggestion of federalism, rather than Repeal, has had fulfillment in the Commonwealth system. He observed the vast chasm which divided reform from revolution. He distrusted Young Ireland because these brilliant young men were making nationalism into a religion. This, he believed, opened the road to violence or the threat of violence. Even the advocacy of violence was slamming the door against reason and common sense. He regarded democracy with reservations. He accepted reform of the suffrage as an act of justice. Michael Tierney lends the support of his name to the proposition that, except for O'Connell's support, the Whigs would never have been able to pass the Reform Act of

1832. But perhaps with the memory of his boyhood brush with the French Revolution, he believed that to associate liberty with equality was to fly in the face of the obvious.

He loved the stories about his valiant ancestors but his common sense told him that there was ugliness as well as beauty in the past. The veneration of the Irish past by the Young Irelanders he regarded as a useless diversion from more constructive efforts to improve the condition of the people. The revival of the ancient language, he believed, contributed nothing for the future.

A devoted follower of Adam Smith and Bentham, he strongly opposed the projection of the State into the life of the people. His fear and dislike of the State were no simple abstraction born of his reading in his student days. It was a conviction based upon the realities of the government which Westminster provided for Ireland before and after the Union. Religion, economic affairs, and humanitarian measures were best served when divorced from the rules, restrictions, and agents of government.

I venture to suggest that a majority of my contemporaries will conclude that O'Connell's foreboding that the State was a false god must be taken in the context of conditions as they existed in his time, when the State was benighted, oppressive, and corrupt. Great majorities since have decided that the very necessities of the people have compelled State intervention.

But despite changes in conditions and in public opinion, certain basic facts remain. The State is human beings vested with power: power is a narcotic which creates a passion for more power; and as the power of the State expands, the borders of individual liberty are progressively constricted.

I count myself with those who see solemn prophecy in the Liberator's warning.

APPENDIX

Selections from O'Connell Letters

As INDICATED BY Hunting Cap's letter, the occasion was the arrival of news at Derrynane of O'Connell's attack on Saurin at the Magee trial. The immediate reply by the nephew was characteristic of the tender concern he always had for the feelings of his testy uncle, from the time the correspondence started when he was a schoolboy. His first letter defending himself was followed by another of reassurance that his conduct had been well received by people on the scene. And apparently Hunting Cap's feeling about his nephew's conduct had been communicated to the Colonel who, six months later, writing from France where he was living in retirement, more gently admonished the nephew to be more restrained.

FROM HUNTING CAP TO 30 MERRION SQUARE

Derrynane, 14 December 1813

Dear Dan,

The [*Dublin*] *Evening Post* of Thursday the 2nd of this inst. brought me the speech of the Attorney General in aggravation of punishment on Mr. John Magee and your reply to it, and though he denied alluding to you in that speech, yet I think every person who was present must have entertained a different opinion. But though some of them were rather sharp and indecorous yet I must say I do not think they merited or justified the intemperate and vehement reply you set out with and continued to pursue till prevented by the interposition of the court. However averse and hostile the Attorney-General may be to the Catholics and to their constitutional pursuits to obtain Emancipation, the high situation he enjoys as first law officer of the Crown demands a degree of respect and consideration from the bar which should not be lightly forgot or neglected. In some cases, perhaps, the prejudice and animosity of an Attorney-General may carry him beyond the limits of temperance, discretion and decency, but the rank which his situation gives him and the consideration in which he is held by the court should restrain the bar from treating him with the harshness and severity which his conduct and language may perhaps otherwise demand, and to this may justly be added the risk the advocate runs of being committed by the court for using intemperate or irritating language towards him in their presence, as they may construe it into a disrespect and insult to the Bench.

I have therefore most earnestly to request, and will even add to insist, that you will in future conduct yourself with calmness, temperance and moderation towards him, and that you will not suffer yourself to be hurried by hate or violence of passions to use any language unbecoming the calm and intelligent barrister or the judicious and well-bred gentleman, or that may tend to expose you to the reprehension, if not to the resentment, of the court. The trial of Mr. Magee next month for publishing the Kilkenny resolutions will, of course, bring on discussions between the Attorney-General and you. I have not only to entreat, but decidedly to insist, that on your part they will be carried on with calmness, discretion and decency, and that you will not in any degree glance at anything that has passed between you on former occasions or animadvert with severity or strained conclusions on what may fall from him. The flattering power of popular applause has often subdued reason and laid people to acts for which they severely suffered, but believe me, my dear friend, it has ever proved a very perishable commodity. No man of solid sense will ever be anxious to look for or obtain it. The part you take at the Catholic Board is the more laudable because it is the result of an honest, firm, unalterable desire to bring about the Emancipation of the Catholics, but ever in the pursuit of that very desirable object, moderation, prudence and deliberate reflection should never be lost sight of. This I strongly recommend to your serious consideration. . . .

(O'Connell 449; I 346–7.)

TO HUNTING CAP

Merrion Square, 28 December 1813

My dearest Uncle,

The very kind and affectionate tone of your last letter, a letter in which I easily recognize the parental cordiality of the best of parents and friends, consoles me entirely for the species of reproach which that letter contained. I am also consoled by being able to assure you that, had you been present and seen the situation in which I was placed, you would be far, very far from thinking that there was an excess of violence in my language which was not called for by the attack made upon me. I stood in the novel situation of a barrister put upon his trial, with the grossest language used towards him by the Attorney-General who had arranged his plan with the Bench beforehand and introduced, an hour before the court sat, as many of the placemen of the Bar as he could collect in order to support and cheer him. He had arranged with the Bench to condemn me if I retaliated upon him and, thinking himself thus secure, he addressed the entire of his discourse *at me*. The report in the newspaper can give you but an insignificant idea of the tenor of his language, and of his insulting manner it can give you no idea whatsoever.

Under those circumstances, believe me, my dearest Uncle, there was but one course to be pursued. If you were present you would advise but one course, the fixing *on him* a decided insult at all risks. There was no chance of lying by and sending him a message for he would then indeed file an information and I should have to remain two years in Newgate. There were many enemies of mine and of our cause present. There were also several friends, and both enemies and friends agree that it was impossible for any man to get out of such a situation better than I did, and they all attribute my success to the manner in which I put *the quarrel* on the Attorney-General. George Lidwell was in town and attended in court to be my friend if the attorney-general should make a friend necessary. Lidwell highly approved of my conduct and published at all the clubs here that the Attorney-General had disgraced himself for ever, first in attacking a gentleman of the Bar virulently and then in shrinking from the retort in a cowardly manner. In short this is the universal opinion, and I mention it to you only to show you that there were circumstances connected with this which cannot be present to your mind, and which if they were, would fully vindicate my violence. I entreat of you to bestow that in thus seeking to justify myself I do not argue from any vanity or self-sufficiency, but it is a duty which I owe you as well as myself to state to you those facts from whence you will be able to draw the conclusion which the public have done, that unless I replied in the manner I did I should have been put down fully, even personally and in profession. And as to the interference of the judges I am safe in telling you the fact that partiality so gross was perhaps never before exhibited.

With respect to the ensuing trial I will, of course, punctually comply with your directions, and indeed those directions besides the implicit obedience which I owe them are recommended to me by every consideration. Even as a point of honour there would be no merit in trampling on a fallen man. I could not say anything so unbearable by a gentleman as what I have already said to him, and it is my duty as well as my inclination now to abstain from anything harsh and degrading. But should he rally, should he attack me again, should he use disrespectful and contemptuous language to me, surely in that case you do not direct me not to retort in similar terms. What am I to do in that case? I pledge myself to you not to begin, I pledge myself to you not to travel out of the strictest line of moderation in tone, manner and language unless I am first attacked. But if I am assailed with foul and intemperate language you would not, I know well, have me put up with it or allow any man to tarnish my character or honour with impunity. And it is in this sense that I understand your direction. . . .

(O'Connell 452; I 349-50.)

TO HUNTING CAP

Merrion Square, 6 January 1814

My dearest Uncle,

Since I wrote to you last I am in possession of a second letter from you directing me to pay 10 guineas as your contribution to the vote of the Catholic Board to me. I am very proud of this mark of your approval, and entirely agree with you that my immediate relations ought not to take any part in the collection of this money. Nor is it indeed at all necessary that they should, for I never could believe there existed so strong a sentiment of kindness towards an individual as I am told has been evinced on this occasion. Several Protestants have contributed, one gentleman of that persuasion sent yesterday ten guineas, and I am told—for, of course, I do not take any part in the business—that the list of subscribers is filling up very fast. The articles have been nearly arranged, and there seems not the least doubt of the complete execution of this vote. I own I am not a little vain of this mark of kindness from my countrymen as it seems to prove to me that the disinterested purity with which I have endeavoured to advocate the liberty and religion of Ireland has not only been appreciated but *very, very* much indeed overrated.

My last letter has given you, I trust, complete satisfaction with respect to the line of conduct which I mean to pursue towards the Attorney-General. Rely on it that your affectionate commands shall be most scrupulously obeyed. I will not say or do anything that can be constructed into offence but, if I am attacked, I will repel the assault with interest. I do not at all imagine he will recommence; on the contrary, I am told there does not exist a more miserable man than he has been since his last attempt. I have heard this from excellent authority. The attempt to which Finlay alluded in his speech related in truth to a case before the Chief Baron at Limerick where I got a verdict from a jury in a cause in which he imagined I had made a personal allusion to him and in which he certainly took a strong part against my client. The report of that transaction reached town in a very exaggerated shape, and the Attorney-General's partisans endeavoured to call a meeting of the benchers to have a censure voted in general terms which, without directly naming me, might be understood to mean me. The Master of the Rolls was sounded by the Chancellor on the subject. His reply was, "I tell you, my Lord, I will give any man who gives me an opportunity of speaking of Mr. O'Connell's conduct at a meeting of the Benchers £500. I never was so grateful to any man as I should be to the person who gave me such an opportunity." This fact I have from the *very* best authority. But this determination of Curran and, indeed, the opinion of the chief baron himself concurred in having all notion of a meeting of the Benchers on the subject abandoned. This it was that Finlay obscurely hinted at, for with respect to stripping me of my gown the benchers could no more do it (unless for some *scandalous crime* which I presume they do not reckon upon) than they could strip you of your estate. They have no authority to do it and the entire Bar would, for their *own* sakes, revolt at any attempt of the kind. Set your mind at rest on that subject. Believe me, you never will hear of any effort being made with that view. . . .

Believe me, my dearest Uncle, that your kindness is not thrown away upon cold ingratitude. Never was there a man more beloved and reverenced by his relatives than you are, and never did any man deserve affectionate veneration so much.

(O'Connell 453; I 350–2.)

FROM COUNT O'CONNELL TO MERRION SQUARE

Paris, 6 June 1814

My dear nephew,

In vain would I attempt to give you a true idea of the pleasure and emotion with which I perused your very kind and affectionate letter. . . .

I was long since well informed and not a little flattered at your success in your profession and am rejoiced to find you daily rising in the public estimation. I fondly indulge the hope that, whenever

Index

Heytesbury, Lord, 174, 184
Higgins, Bishop, 154
Home Rule, 127, 211–13, 223
Houston, Arthur, 32n, 49
Howitt, William, 59–60
"Hunting Cap" (see O'Connell, Maurice [uncle])

Inner Bar, 41, 52–53, 109, 120, 123, 147, 178
Irish Confederation, 202–03, 205

Kee, Robert, 171n, 186–87
Keogh, John, 14, 73, 103, 221
King's Counsel (see Inner Bar)

Lalor, James Fintan, 202
Lawless, Jack, 101, 103, 106
Lawyers' Corps of Artillery, 42–43
Lecky, W. E. H., 9, 60–61, 72, 87, 169–70, 171n, 212, 234
Lichfield House Compact, 127, 129, 135, 137, 214, 227
Lichfield, Lord, 129
Limerick, Treaty of, 7
Liverpool, Lord, 76, 99
Lloyd George, David, 112
Lucas, Frederick, 192

MacDonough, Oliver, 225
MacHale, Archbishop, 154, 164, 166–68, 175–76, 182
MacIntyre, Angus, 126
Magee, John, 78–80, 233
Mahoney, Pierce, 60n, 160
Maire-ni-Dhuiv (see O'Donoghue, Mary [grandmother])
Malthus, Thomas, 138
Mathew, Father, 149–50
McGee, Thomas D'Arcy, 205
McManus, Terence Bellew, 205
Meagher, Thomas, 186, 190–91, 197, 203–05, 210
Melbourne, Lord, 124, 129, 135, 141, 141n, 143, 227
Miley, Father, 195, 199
Mill, James, 138
Mill, John Stuart, 138–39
Mitchel, John, 65, 155, 185–87, 191, 197, 201n, 202–03, 209
Monster Meetings, 69, 148, 153–55, 169
Morning Register, 90, 162
Moore, Thomas, 120
Morpeth, Lord, 135, 137, 228

Mulgrave, Lord, 135, 137, 227
Municipal Reforms, 142–43, 150
Murray, Archbishop, 199

Napper Tandy, 15, 15n
Nation, The, 151, 162, 164, 166, 185, 187–88, 190, 192–93, 195, 202, 205
Newman, John Henry Cardinal, 107
Nordbury, Lord (Judge Toler), 47
North, Lord, 13–14
Nowlan, Kevin B., 183

O'Brien, Sir Edward, 104
O'Brien, William Smith, 105, 154, 165–67, 186–87, 190–91, 195–97, 202–06
O'Connell, Catherine (O'Mullane; mother), 22, 31
O'Connell, Daniel: ancestors, 18ff.; childhood, 17, 21–22; education, 9, 22–29, 31–39; student life in London, 27ff., 31ff.; authors and books read, 33ff., 38–39; journal, 32ff., 43, 49, 66n, 231; physical and mental attributes, 48–50, 71; financial affairs and inheritance, 26–28, 44–46, 53–54, 93, 111ff., 115–16; political convictions, 55ff., 63ff.; religious attitudes, 34–35, 51, 55ff., 66–67; beginning of public career, 44ff.; early legal practice, 41–48, 51–54; Inner Bar, 41, 52–53, 109, 123, 178; Magee trial, 78–80, 223; duels, 81–82; Lord Mayor of Dublin, 143, 150–53; "Mallow Defiance," 156; trial and imprisonment, 158–60; first election (Waterford), 96–99; first Ennis election, 100–06, 219; second Ennis election, 109–11, 119, 219; physical and mental decline and death, 169ff., 197–200
O'Connell, Dan (son), 117, 199
O'Connell, Daniel Charles (uncle; the "Colonel"), 19–20, 23–28, 45, 80, 114, 116, 125n
O'Connell, Daniel (grandfather; Donal Mor), 18–19
O'Connell, Daniel (great-great-grandfather), 18
O'Connell, James (brother), 114–15
O'Connell, John (son), 159, 191, 197
O'Connell, John (brother), 115
O'Connell, John (great-grandfather), 18
O'Connell, Mary (wife), 35, 45–46,